WOMANSPIRIT

RISING

WOMANSPIRIT

RISING

A Feminist Reader in Religion

Edited by CAROL P. CHRIST
and JUDITH PLASKOW

Harper & Row, Publishers, San Francisco
New York, Grand Rapids, Philadelphia, St. Louis
London, Singapore, Sydney, Tokyo, Toronto

*This book is dedicated
in sisterhood to each other*

Designed by Jim Mennick

Library of Congress Cataloging in Publication Data

Main entry under title:
WOMANSPIRIT RISING.

(A Harper forum book)
1. Woman (Theology)—Addresses, essays, lectures.
I. Christ, Carol P.   II. Plaskow, Judith.
BL458.W66 1979   261.8′34′12   78-3363
ISBN 0-06-061385-8

89 90   20 19 18 17 16

Contents

Preface

Our friendship and collaboration on feminist theology began in the fall of 1969. Retiring to a local hangout after the first meeting of the Yale Women's Alliance (the first feminist group at Yale), we discovered that we shared many of the same frustrations with Yale's graduate program in theology. We were both interested in Jewish thought and felt there was something wrong with a university religious studies program that focused exclusively on Christian theology. We both thought theology ought to speak to important political and moral issues such as starvation in Biafra and the war in Vietnam. And we both felt that the male faculty and students saw us primarily as women, not as theologians.

Over the next two years, our friendship grew as we found ourselves constantly calling each other to verify our sanity and intelligence and to seek support in specific situations. "I said so and so about Tillich in a seminar today," one of us would say, "and everyone ignored me. Was I wrong, or am I stupid?" "No. You aren't stupid. That's an important point," the other would reply. "They didn't hear you because you're a woman." We remember the day we proposed to a professor that we might take one of our comprehensives on the history of Christian attitudes towards women. Although we were armed with seven or eight pages of sources on the subject, we had no sooner mentioned the topic when he slammed his fist on the table and shouted, "Not for me, you're not!" We also remember Carol's turning in a seminar paper on Barth's view of women to a professor who glanced at the title and remarked that he had never considered *that* a very important topic. He then went on to discuss the papers presented by the males in the class. It is little wonder that, given repeated incidents like this, we might neither of us have finished graduate school at all without the support, encouragement, and intellectual comradeship we gave each other.

But the attitudes toward women we found at Yale were mixed blessings. We learned to trust our own judgment and intelligence earlier than many graduate students do. Yale forced us to become feminists, for which we are grateful, and Yale made us confront the male bias of theology in which the sexist attitudes of our colleagues were rooted.

It was our gradual awakening to the fact that theology is very much rooted in experience—generally, male experience—that made us decide to pursue dissertation topics that took experience seriously. Here again, when no one else supported us, we supported each other. Judith encouraged Carol to write her thesis on Elie Wiesel and the holocaust even after the man who had been Carol's advisor dismissed the subject with "Why would you want to write about a depressing topic like that?" Carol encouraged Judith to stick with her thesis on theology and women's experience when the director of graduate studies told Judith she had a good subject if only she would drop the references to women! (We must mention that Julian Hartt, who became our advisor, encouraged us to pursue our own interests, keeping us on as his students even after he left Yale for the University of Virginia.)

Because our own experience convinced us that we would never survive in the field of religion without the intellectual and emotional support of other women, we began to organize others, both for mutual assistance and to encourage scholarship on women and religion. We brought the women in religious studies at Yale together for the first time, and our "social evening" led to a sit-in to liberate the only bathroom (for men, of course) in the stacks of the Yale Divinity School Library. Later, we joined together in the more serious project of demanding that women be hired in religious studies at Yale. We became involved in establishing the nationwide Women's Caucus— Religious Studies and in building the section on women and religion in the American Academy of Religion. When we moved to different cities to begin teaching, our personal relationship and discussions of theology continued in long letters.

Our commitment to research and teaching in the area of women and religion grew out of our friendship. In 1972 and 1973, we began to teach courses on women and religion. Those early years were a struggle because there were so few sources. Eventually Rosemary Ruether's *Religion and Sexism* (1974) and *Women and Religion* by Elizabeth Clark and Herbert Richardson (1977) were published. These two works brought together the essential sources for studying the history of sexism in Western religion. But we and our students were frustrated by the overwhelmingly negative picture of religion that emerged from these two volumes. While we agreed with the critiques of Judaism and Christianity presented, we wanted also to show our students that religion could be reconstructed or recreated to speak to the experiences of women. *Womanspirit Rising* brings together the positive and constructive articles on women and religion that our students have been reading in the library over the past several years. We have found that the historical, theological, and ritual pieces collected here provide a clear overview of constructive feminist writing in religion and stimulate exciting class discussion. Sometimes we have used selections in this volume to stimulate students' own creative work. For example, we have asked students to write their own myths using Judith's "The Coming of Lilith" as a model or to use some of the rituals as a basis for creating their own rituals that express women's religious experiences. Students have loved these assignments and have displayed amazing creativity in doing them.

Our teaching and our conversations have continued to stimulate our work on women and religion. We have been able to move in different directions in our current thinking, while maintaining respect for each other's interests. This made it easy for us to work together on this book. We outlined the introductions together, divided up the writing, and then revised each other's work. Our collaboration has been a joy, and it is for this reason that we dedicate this book, in sisterhood, to each other.

CAROL P. CHRIST   JUDITH PLASKOW
San Jose State University   *Wichita State University*

Introduction:
Womanspirit
Rising

Feminists have charged that Judaism and Christianity are sexist religions with a male God and traditions of male leadership that legitimate the superiority of men in family and society.[1] This new challenge to traditional faiths just confirms the view of some feminists that society has outgrown its need for religion. They agree with Freud and Marx that religions keep people dependent on authority and thwart their desire to improve their material situations. Other feminists, however, are convinced that religion is profoundly important. For them, the discovery that religions teach the inferiority of women is experienced as a betrayal of deeply felt spiritual and ritual experience. They believe the history of sexism in religions shows how deeply sexism has permeated the human psyche but does not invalidate human need for ritual, symbol, and myth. While differing on many issues, the contributors to this volume agree that religion is deeply meaningful in human life *and* that the traditional religions of the West have betrayed women. They are convinced that religion must be reformed or reconstructed to support the full human dignity of women.

RELIGION, SYMBOL, AND MEANING

Those who abandoned religion in childhood or adolescence may find the juxtaposition of feminism and religion bizarre and misguided. For them, religion is identified with the Judaism and Christianity taught in Sunday schools; *symbol* means the crucifix or Star of David; *ritual* is nothing but going to church or synagogue; *tradition* is the Bible or the teachings of popes and rabbis; and *myth* refers to the unscientific beliefs of primitive people. Even a cursory examination of the function of religion in all cultures would reveal the limitation of such a view. Religion is a constant in human life. Even so-called modern secularists have developed symbols, rituals, and traditions that function strikingly like religions.

Theologian Paul Tillich defines religion more inclusively as the expression of humanity's ultimate concern—the articulation of longings for a center of meaning and value, for connection with the power of being.[2] Ultimate concern centers life and enables people to choose among competing values. According to Tillich, Marxism and existentialism—and, if he were living today, he might add feminism—are secular equivalents for religion because they function to give meaning and direction to human existence.

Likewise, depth psychologist Carl Jung, although critical of institutional religions, was convinced of the meaning of myth and symbol in human life.[3] While Jung's views of women and the feminine principle are problematic,[4] his theories of the function of myth and symbol in the unconscious and in dream life remain important. Like Freud, Jung believed that consciousness is but a small part of life. People's deepest feelings and attitudes, he felt, are produced by symbols that rise from the unconscious and are expressed in myth, dream, and fantasy. The modern embrace of scientific rationality has produced an illness of the soul, a lack of meaning that, according to Jung, can only be cured by a return to myth and symbol. Jung encouraged those who found the symbols of traditional religion lifeless to turn to their own dreams as sources of meaning.

Anthropologist Clifford Geertz adds an important social dimension to the theories of Tillich and Jung. "Religion," Geertz writes, "is a system of symbols which acts to produce powerful, pervasive, and long-lasting moods and motivations" in groups of people.[5] Religious symbols are both models *of* divine existence and models *for* human behavior. Christians do not flee martyrdom, because the central symbol of their religion is the crucifixion of Christ, which is both a model *of* divine suffering and a model *for* acceptance of human suffering. Similarly, Orthodox Jews rest on the Sabbath because God rested on the seventh day of creation. Geertz' understanding of the function of religion is particularly useful for feminists because it provides a way of understanding the interaction between sex roles and religious symbols. God in "his" heaven is both a model *of* divine existence and a model *for* women's subordination to men.

Tillich, Jung, and Geertz challenge the naive view that religion and myth have outlived their usefulness. But these men's theories by no means vindicate traditional religions in the eyes of feminists. On the contrary, it is only when the crucial importance of religion, myth, and symbol in human life are understood that feminists can begin to understand how deeply traditional religions have betrayed women. If religion, myth, and symbol have outlived their usefulness, then one should be no more than irritated at the quaint archaism of traditional religious sexism. But, once one recognizes the importance of religion, then an enormous sense of injustice must follow the discovery that religions are sexist and that they continue to exert a powerful influence on society.

FEMINIST CRITICISM OF RELIGION

It is precisely this sense of injustice that lies at the heart of the first feminist criticisms of religion. Most of these criticisms originated in an often inarticulate sense of exclusion from traditional religious practice or theology. Women who felt called to be rabbis, priests, and ministers frequently found themselves barred from these vocations. Orthodox Jewish women who wanted to participate fully in worship were excluded from the praying community and seated behind a screen. Catholic and Protestant women who wanted to serve communion were asked, instead, to serve church suppers. Women in every congregation heard phrases such as "God of our Fathers," "men of God," and the "brotherhood of man" preached from the pulpit. Everywhere they turned, women found signs reading "For Men Only."

The women's movement enabled women to turn private pain into a systematic feminist critique of religion. Women began to examine traditional arguments for their subordination and to reject teachings that denied their personhood. And, like scholars in other fields, feminist scholars in the field of religion learned to ask new questions, such as "Does religion enforce and perpetuate sex-role stereotypes and the power of men over women?" While sociologists, psychologists, and literary critics examined social attitudes and behaviors, scholars of religion examined teachings and pronouncements that purported to reflect the nature of reality. The stakes in religious studies were higher, or at least they seemed to be.

Feminist criticism of religion began with the obvious. Explicit statements of female inferiority or subordination, exclusion of women from the ministry, and teachings on marriage and family were scrutinized and deplored. Jewish women examined the traditional view that women are unclean during menstruation and seven days thereafter, and they also asked whether the traditional centering of Jewish women's religious lives in the home was sufficient. Christian women questioned Paul's teaching that the wife must be subordinate to her husband as the church is to Christ, and they rejected the passage traditionally read at weddings that asked the wife to *obey* her husband but simply asked the husband to *love* his wife. Sexism in scripture and tradition was made a subject of widespread scholarly study for the first time in history.

The image of God as male was at once the most obvious and most subtle sexist influence in religion. Women who were bold enough to address this issue directly found that nothing aroused the ire of male theologians and churchmen so much as the charge that traditional language about God is sexist. The question seemed to challenge the fundamental core of biblical revelation. Women were told that God transcends sexuality and were advised not to bother with trivial questions of language. Many feminists also failed to recognize the crucial importance of God language. Mary Daly made the image of God central in the feminist critique of religion in "After the Death of God the Father," published in 1971 and reprinted here. Recent resurgence of interest in Goddesses has brought the issue of sexual imagery in God language to the forefront of feminist thinking in religion.

As the feminist critique of biblical religion developed, scholars began to recognize that the issues of God language, exclusion of women in leadership and ritual, and teachings on marriage and family were systematically related to the theological world view of the biblical faith. This was most obvious in Christian theology, which is more systematic than Jewish thought. According to a theory developed by Rosemary Ruether, stated in her essay in this book, and elaborated by other feminist theologians, the sexism of Christian tradition is integrally related to the dualistic and hierarchal mentality that Christianity inherited from the classical world.[6] This dualistic mentality opposes soul, spirit, rationality, and transcendence to body, flesh, matter, nature, and immanence. God is identified with the positive sides of the dualism, and "the world" with the negative sides. In this view, human beings stand between God and the world, spirit and nature, and must learn to subdue the irrational desires of the flesh. This is a model for domination, because reality is divided into two levels, one superior, one inferior. In this way of thinking, even the doctrine of the incarnation, which is intended to symbolize God's relation to the world, must be understood as a paradox, or as Kierkegaard was later to say, as an absurdity. The distinctive dualism of Western thought can be understood by contrasting it to some American Indian world views in which divinity is seen as (naturally, not paradoxically) resident in stones, animals, and members of the tribe. Scholars have noted that the dualistic world view contains the seeds of ecological crisis; for, if the world and nature are seen as mere matter, then they are subject to human control and exploitation. Classical dualism also became the model for the oppression of women when the culture-creating males identified the positive sides of the dualism with themselves and identified the negative sides with the women over whom they claimed the right to rule. Ruether has noted further that this dualistic pattern has been adapted to the oppression of other groups, including Jews and blacks, who, like women, are seen as more carnal and irrational than the dominant men. When this dualistic pattern of thinking is combined with a symbolic tradition in which God is addressed and conceptualized in predominantly male language and imagery, the sexism of religious thinkers appears logical and consistent. No longer can sexist statements of theologians be excused as trivial and peripheral slips of men whose thought is otherwise free of sexism.

EXPERIENCE AS A NEW NORM

Articulating a coherent critique of tradition was only the first task of feminist scholars in religion. Like their colleagues in related fields, women in religion felt the need to move beyond criticism. Believing that Western religion has failed to acknowledge and incorporate their presence and experience, feminists have begun to search the history of religion for positive and constructive alternatives to sexist theology.

Where in the history of religion have women's voices and experience contributed to the molding of tradition? What would it mean for women's experience to shape theology and religion in the future? The word *experience* becomes a key term, a significant norm for feminists reconstructing tradition and creating new religious forms.

For feminists, *experience* refers simply to the fabric of life as it is lived. The image feminists have in mind when they say *experience* is the consciousness-raising group, which was developed to enable women to "get in touch with their own experience." Because women have often shaped and understood their lives according to norms or preferences for female behavior expressed by men, there is a sense in which women have not shaped or even known their own experience. What they *have* known is the false consciousness created by male ideology. Men are therefore excluded from consciousness-raising groups so that women will not hide their true feelings or experiences in fear of men's disapproval. In consciousness-raising groups, every woman's experience is heard, and judgment is not immediately made as to whether certain feelings are good or bad, appropriate or inappropriate. Women are encouraged to speak what has not previously been spoken. Often this speaking leads to the discovery of shared experiences. The woman who tearfully admits that she sometimes hates her children finds that other women feel the same way too; their experiences of motherhood are similar. The woman who timidly ventures that she often doesn't enjoy sex hears others say, "me, too." She is not alone. The graduate student who tells how her contributions to seminar discussion are ignored by male colleagues discovers that this, too, is a common experience. Even the smartest woman has had it many times.

Naming experience and recognizing that it is shared is liberating and energizing. Many women experience a kind of rebirth through consciousness-raising and feel that feminism has allowed them to live fully and authentically for the first time in their lives. The feeling of release that comes from casting off men's definitions of women within a community with other women is the source of the early feminist slogan, "Sisterhood is powerful!"

This feeling of release that leads to jubilation also has a critical side. Sharing their experiences, women begin to realize how fully the world has been defined by men. As they begin to question woman's place in man's world, they also begin to question the world that men have constructed. As they recognize that the institutions of culture were constructed by men without regard for the experiences of women, feminists begin to question even those institutions that seem most sacrosanct. If marriage has always included the notion of female subordination, then perhaps marriage is not the only or the best way to organize sexuality and the rearing of children. If the great works of Western literary and philosophical tradition view women as less than fully human, then perhaps those great works do not reflect the highest human values. And, if the Bible and religious tradition teach sexism, then perhaps those traditions are not inspired by God in the ways their adherents have claimed. While feminists do not reject all cultural institutions, they recognize that feminism has placed a question mark beside all of them. No institution is viewed as inevitable or necessary. All are examined and challenged.

Consciousness-raising thus leads to a critique of culture and to the tasks of transforming or recreating it. Feminists have called their task a "new naming" of self and world. It is through naming that humans progress from childhood to adulthood and learn to understand and shape the world about them. Under patriarchy, men have reserved to themselves the right to name, keeping women in a state of intellectual and spiritual dependency. Mary Daly suggests that the Genesis creation story, in which Adam names the animals and woman, is the paradigm of false naming in Western culture.[7] If the world has been named by Adam without Eve's consultation, then the world has been named from the male point of view. As women begin to name the world for themselves, they will upset the order that has been taken for granted throughout history. They will call themselves and the world into new being. Naming women's experience thus becomes the model not only for personal liberation and growth, but for a feminist transformation of culture and religion. "What would happen if one woman told the truth about her life?" asks poet Muriel Rukeyser. "The world would split open."[8]

TWO VIEWS OF WOMEN'S EXPERIENCE

While feminists believe that women's experience may become the basis for a transformation of religion and culture, they recognize that women's experience is difficult to define. Although it can be distinguished from roles or attitudes prescribed for women by men and male culture, women's experience is always shaped to a greater or lesser extent by the male-centered cultures in which women live. Feminists concerned with experience thus disagree about which of women's experiences are authentic and which alienated, about which can become the basis for cultural transformation and which must be repudiated because they have been created by sexism. Two poles emerge within the feminist understanding of experience. These poles may be called (1) women's *feminist* experience and (2) women's *traditional* experience, which includes, but is not limited to, women's body experience. These experiences are not incompatible, and, indeed, many women have experiences in both categories. But the categories reflect different understandings of what is valuable and potentially transformative in women's experiences. It is important for the reader to decide which meaning of experience is primary in a given work.

According to the first model, what is valuable in women's experience is the experience of liberation itself—recognizing oppression, confronting sexist culture and institutions, and moving into freedom. This model of women's experience is limited in that it does not speak to women who do not consciously view themselves as part of an oppressed group seeking liberation. But, on the positive side, it often enables women to affirm solidarity with other oppressed groups. Many of the articles in the first two sections of this volume use women's feminist experience as a norm. Rosemary Ruether, Elisabeth Fiorenza, and Sheila Collins believe the liberation experience provides spiritual insight and use it to criticize tradition. Judith Plaskow and Mary Daly use feminist experience to construct new understandings of spirituality, rooted in feminist community.

According to the second model, women's traditional experiences, such as marriage and motherhood, although they have been distorted in patriarchy, can provide important clues for transforming patriarchal culture. Thinkers who focus on traditional experience believe that whatever sexist culture has rejected or denigrated must be revalued in a holistic feminist vision. Whatever is considered "feminine"—intuition, expression of feeling, concern for the personal dimensions of relationships—may be reappropriated from a feminist perspective. While some would argue that women's traditional experiences are simply a product of alienation, others believe that women's values are less alienated than men's. Women's body experiences—such as menstruation, pregnancy, lactation, and menopause, and the traditional association of women with nature that is based on these experiences—are also part of women's traditional experiences that many feminists wish to affirm. They argue that creating positive attitudes toward the female body is essential for women's liberation and that anything common to many women should be positively valued from a feminist perspective. Carol Christ's discussion of motherhood, Penelope Washbourn's discussion of menstruation, and the discussions of Goddess symbolism by Christ, Starhawk, and Zsuzsanna Budapest reclaim women's experience and women's bodies from a feminist perspective.

OTHER TENSIONS IN FEMINIST THEOLOGY

The poles of feminist and traditional experience are not the only tensions within feminist theology and spirituality. Feminists also hold very different views of the past, the human relationship to nature, the character of religious community, and central religious symbols. These tensions reflect different understandings of the nature of the alienation produced by sexism, of the sources of liberating vision, and of the future toward which feminism is striving. These tensions also call attention to a problem that runs through all feminist theology and that can be phrased as follows: "Is feminist theology genuinely liberating? Have those feminists who stand within Biblical traditions noted for their sexism adequately freed themselves from sexist theology? And have those feminists who reject biblical traditions adequately transcended the dualisms of patriarchal theology, or are they simply glorifying the denigrated side of the polarities that patriarchy created?"

RECONSTRUCTING THE PAST VERSUS
CREATING NEW TRADITIONS

Do feminists need the past—and if so, what past do they need? Feminist attitudes toward history provide a good example of the tensions within feminist theology and spiritual vision. While feminists agree on the general outlines of the critique of Jewish and Christian theology and the need to root theology in experience, they very much disagree on the reformability of tradition. For some, the vision of transcendence within tradition is seen as an authentic core of revelation pointing toward freedom from oppression, a freedom that they believe is articulated more clearly and consistently within tradition than without. Others believe that the prebiblical past or modern experience provide more authentic sources for feminist theology and vision.

While differing among themselves, thinkers of the first sort search tradition for positive and constructive alternatives to sexist theology. Jesus' so-called feminism,[9] Paul's statement that "in Christ there is no more male and female" (Gal. 3:28), and isolated instances of female or feminine imagery of God in the Bible and elsewhere are cited as possible bases for a critique of institutional sexism. These thinkers usually claim that we are inevitably rooted in our past and that the attempt to transcend history proposed by some feminists is fraught with danger. It is more sensible, they claim, to reform the past than to ignore it, because those who forget their history are doomed to repeat it. Because the term *reformist* has a venerable and specifiable meaning in the history of Western religion, we believe it is useful for describing those who are engaged in reforming traditions. Like the Protestants of the sixteenth century, these feminists believe they are calling the church and synagogue back to an essential core of Christian or Jewish truth and are cleansing traditions of historical deviations from that core.

Other feminists believe that the essential core of the traditions is so irreformably sexist that it is pointless to tinker with them in the hope of change. Emphasizing the symbolic portrayal of God as male within Christianity and Judaism and pointing to the ways in which institutional religion has supported sexism, they argue that the best way for women to free themselves from sexist traditions is to reject any loyalty to them. It is difficult to find a suitable term for those who reject biblical traditions. Some identify themselves as *post-Christian, post-Jewish, pagan, witch, Goddess worshipper,* or simply as members of the *womanspirit movement,* but none of these terms is accurate for the whole group. Sheila Collins and Carol Christ call this second group *revolutionaries,*[10] to emphasize that they claim no loyalty to biblical tradition. Yet the term *revolutionary* is misleading if it implies that the revolutionaries are more "radical" or have freed themselves more fully from the past than the reformists. Some revolutionaries claim to be followers of ancient prebiblical religious traditions, and thus to be even more "traditional" than followers of the biblical faiths. While rejecting the biblical past, they find the history of Goddess worship inspirational for feminist theology and spirituality. They argue that the Goddess symbol found in many traditions can aid modern women's liberation by providing an image of female power that can counteract the symbol of God as male. Merlin Stone, Sheila Collins, Carol Christ, Starhawk, and Zsuzsanna Budapest use the prebiblical past in constructing new feminist spiritual visions. Paradoxically, they can be charged, on the one hand, with not breaking sufficiently from the past, and, on the other, with distorting the past through romanticizing it.

Yet if both biblical and nonbiblical pasts hold dangers for feminists, to what sources can they appeal in creating theology and spirituality? Some revolutionaries believe woman's experience alone can serve as the basis for religious vision. But freedom from the past does not guarantee freedom from the influence of sexist culture. Naomi Goldenberg appeals to dreams and fantasies of contemporary women as sources of revelation. But (before she alters it in fantasy vision) the dream figure she considers in her essay is every bit as patriarchal as the Jewish or Christian God. Mary Daly appeals to the androgynous future called forth by God the Verb, but she creates a vision that is too abstract for many. Daly and Goldenberg have also begun to reclaim the ancient symbolism of Goddess, but this raises all the dangers that allegiance to the prebiblical past entails. Judith Plaskow (in "The Coming of Lilith") roots theological vision in the feminist present and future of sisterhood, but when she wants to do more than reflect on present experience she too turns to the retelling of an ancient story.

What can we conclude from this? Perhaps only that a relation to the past seems necessary to feminists who are beginning to create a new religious future. It may be that the real danger lies not in deriving insight from the past but in dealing with the past on *its* terms. This is the danger feminists are striving to avoid.

NATURE VERSUS FREEDOM

The traditional association of women and nature provides another example of the tensions and dilemmas of feminist theologians. Women's traditional roles have allowed them to maintain contact with nature and natural processes, while society as a whole has moved toward increasing alienation from nature. The sense of closeness to nature that some women experience in nature mysticism or in the cycles of their bodies, in menstruation, pregnancy, and birth have much to teach all women and men about the rootedness of the human condition in the natural order. It can even be argued that if women's sense of connection to nature had informed the culture creators of our society, Western culture might not have "progressed" to the ecological crisis we now endure.[11] But a focus on women's closeness to nature also has its dangers.[12] In traditional theology and philosophy, women have been equated with nature and men with freedom and transcendence. The new focus on women and nature elevates that which traditional theology and culture have denigrated. But it does not always offer resources to understand those elements of freedom and transcendence of nature that are also part of the human condition in general and feminist experience in particular. For, while modern feminist women may be reclaiming their bodies, they are not letting biology determine their life choices. Carol Christ, for example, celebrates female body experience and motherhood but is not herself a mother. Penelope Washbourn omits career choice from her discussion of the life crises of women, although it obviously was an important element in her own life. Clearly, the new spirituality must do more than reappropriate the despised body and traditional female experience. A fully adequate feminist theology must express the combination of rootedness in nature *and* freedom that feminists experience in their lives.

Although the problem of remaining bound to old dualisms seems particularly evident in the work of those who reclaim traditional women's experiences, theologians who focus on women's feminist experience also do not always transcend the terms of past theologies. In centering on those experiences of women that enable them to transcend old roles and stereotypes, these thinkers are bound negatively to the past. Plaskow's descriptions of the "yeah, yeah" experience and of sisterhood, Daly's visions of androgyny or God the Verb, and Aviva Cantor's interpretation of Passover as a celebration of liberation stress the freedom and creativity of women who move out of old roles. But the liberation derived from feminist experience is often defined largely as "freedom from" women's traditional experience of biologically defined roles. Theologies emphasizing freedom therefore also do not succeed in expressing the total experience of women as both free and rooted in nature nor do they offer a coherent vision of the future. Judith Plaskow's story "The Coming of Lilith" depicts symbolically—in the meeting of Eve and Lilith—what feminist theologians find more difficulty in expressing: the integration of the new feminist *and* traditional women's experience.

EQUALITY VERSUS FEMALE ASCENDENCY

Whether they work with biblical or other traditional experience or with new feminist experience alone, contributors to this volume are all engaged in creating a postpatriarchal religious future, different from the recent religious past. Yet they vary enormously in the paths they are creating toward that future and therefore, not surprisingly, in their visions of what that future will hold for women and men. They differ theologically in their visions of the community to which feminist theology points and in their vision of the most adequate symbolism for expressing feminist spiritual vision.

The differences among the contributors reflect the diversity of visions of the future in the feminist movement as a whole. In defining recent feminism in the United States, philosopher Marcia Keller notes that commitment to ending male domination is a value shared by all feminists but that feminists may be divided into those who favor full equality between the sexes and those who favor temporary or permanent ascendency of women and the female principle.[13] The line between these groups is not easy to draw, because some feminists call attention to women and the female principle as a temporary strategy for achieving eventual equality. But, granting this qualification, Keller's distinction is helpful in sorting out differences in religious vision among the contributors to this book. Those feminists who work within the biblical traditions tend to call for equality in religious rituals and symbolisms, while those whose theological or spiritual reflection is primarily rooted in the women's movement, especially in consciousness-raising groups, more often call for at least temporary ascendency of women and the female principle.

The contrast between those who advocate equality and those who advocate female ascendency can be most sharply drawn if we look at core symbolism. Most of the contributors to this volume agree that the identification of divinity with maleness characteristic of much of biblical tradition must be ended. But while some contributors, including Rita Gross, argue that "God-She" must be introduced alongside the Biblical "God-He," others, including Daly in "Why Speak About God?" prefer sex-transcendent or androgynous imagery. Still others call for a new emergence of the Goddess, but even this symbol may emerge in a female-ascendent or equalitarian context. Will the Goddess be the sole religious symbol in a new gender specific monotheism? Or will Goddess and God both be included in the new spiritual vision? In discussing the meaning of Goddess symbolism for women, Carol Christ leaves this question open. Starhawk and Budapest state that the overarching divine principle is more appropriately symbolized in female terms, as Goddess, while the male principle or God must remain secondary, the son and lover, but not the equal of his mother. Although these contrasts between female ascendency and equalitarian symbolism may be drawn, the lines between them often blur. Naomi Janowitz and Maggie Wenig, for example, introduce powerful and radical female symbolism into a traditional Jewish liturgy. It seems likely that their boldness was in part inspired by the women outside the biblical traditions who have been speaking about the Goddess.

The contrast between equality and female ascendency can also be seen in the religious or spiritual communities envisioned by different contributors. In their articles in this volume, Ruether, Trible, Fiorenza, McLaughlin, Gross, and Plaskow (in "Bringing a Daughter into the Covenant") implicitly or explicitly advocate the equality of women and men in a religious community that includes both sexes. Cantor, Wenig, and Janowitz advocate separate rituals for women within the framework of a religious community, Judaism, that includes women and men. Whether these Jewish celebrations for women only are temporary strategies or are intended as a permanent separation of the sexes may depend on the ability of Judaism to integrate the concerns of women into common rituals that women and men celebrate together. For the Orthodox Jewish, separation of the sexes may be a long-term solution, since tradition still requires Orthodox women to sit behind the *mechitzah,* or screen, during worship that includes men. Plaskow (in "The Coming of Lilith") and Goldenberg both describe communities in which women share and reflect on spiritual experience apart from men and outside of established religious communities but also do not state whether they envision permanent spiritual communities for women only. Starhawk writes out of a community that includes men, but in which priestesses and the Goddess are ascendent. Zsuzsanna Budapest writes out of a Dianic tradition for women only in which the Goddess is ascendent, but she believes traditions for men and women together and for men only are also valid. Of the contributors to the volume, only Budapest advocates the permanent ascendency of the female principle and worship for women only, but many others advocate at least a temporary focus on women's spirituality, women's communities, and female symbolism.

CREATIVE TENSIONS IN FEMINIST THEOLOGY

Some might wish to resolve these numerous tensions within feminist theology and vision; but we find them creative and exhilarating. Patriarchy is a many-headed monster, and it must therefore be attacked with all the strategies at our command. We would find it difficult to choose among the feminist views we have discussed the ones that have the greatest potential to transform religion and culture. The lines between reformist and revolutionary, reconstructor of received tradition and creator of new tradition, radical and conservative are difficult to draw. Some might argue that those who work within biblical traditions are so linked to the past that their visions can never be genuinely transforming. But then what is one to do with a thinker such as Fiorenza, who claims allegiance to tradition and yet rejects all sexist elements in the Bible? Her loyalty to biblical religion in one sense makes her a reformist, yet some people might consider her to be creating a new tradition. Similar examples are not hard to find. Budapest's rejection of biblical tradition and her vision of the Goddess sounds extremely radical, and yet she seeks to root her spiritual vision in a past more ancient than that of the Bible, which to some makes her conservative. Other contributors are even more difficult to categorize. Plaskow, Goldenberg, Washbourn, and Christ bracket the question of biblical tradition without rejecting it explicitly. The experiences and symbols they describe could be used either for radical reform and reconstruction of tradition or for creation of new traditions that they themselves do not clearly define. Some of the Jewish women who might be thought of as conservative in their commitment to Judaism could be considered radical in their commitment to female God symbolism and in their choice of a worshipping community for women only. Yet Starhawk, whose vision of the ascendency of Goddess and the female principle would be considered radical by some, celebrates in a community that includes men.

We believe that the diversity within feminist theology and spirituality is its strength. Each of these feminist positions has a contribution to make to the transformation of patriarchal culture. The fundamental commitment that feminists in religion share to end male ascendency in society and religion is more important than their differences. Time will tell which strategies will prove most effective in achieving the shared goal. What is clear is that, if feminists succeed, religion will never be the same again.

NOTES

1. For example, see Mary Daly, *The Church and the Second Sex* (New York: Harper & Row, 1968), and *Beyond God the Father* (Boston: Beacon Press, 1973); Rosemary Ruether, *Liberation Theology* (New York: Paulist Press, 1972), *New Woman/New Earth* (New York: Seabury Press, 1975) and Ruether, ed., *Religion and Sexism* (New York: Simon & Schuster, 1974); Sheila Collins, *A Different Heaven and Earth* (Valley Forge, Pa.: Judson Press, 1974); Judith Plaskow and Joan Arnold Romero, *Women and Religion*, rev. ed. (Missoula, Mont.: AAR and Scholars' Press, 1974); Elizabeth Clark and Herbert Richardson, eds., *Women and Religion* (New York: Harper & Row, 1977); Rita Gross, ed., *Beyond Androcentrism* (Missoula, Mont.: Scholars' Press, 1976); and Elizabeth Koltun, ed., *The Jewish Woman* (New York: Schocken Press, 1976).

2. Paul Tillich, *The Dynamics of Faith* (New York: Harper & Row, 1957).

3. For example, see Carl Jung, *Psychological Reflections,* Jolande Jacobi, ed. (New York: Harper & Row, 1961).

4. For example, see Naomi R. Goldenberg, "A Feminist Critique of Jung," *Signs,* 1976, *2* (2), 443–449, and her article in this volume.

5. Clifford Geertz, "Religion as a Cultural System," in William Lessa and Evon Vogt, eds., *Reader in Comparative Religion,* 2nd (rev.) ed. (New York: Harper & Row, 1972), pp. 204–216.

6. See Rosemary Ruether, "Motherearth and the Megamachine," reprinted in this volume.

7. Daly, *Beyond God the Father,* p. 8.

8. Muriel Rukeyser, "Käthe Kollwitz," *Rising Tides,* Laura Chester and Sharon Barba, eds. (New York: Pocket Books, 1973), p. 73.

9. See Leonard Swidler, "Jesus Was a Feminist," *The Catholic World 212* (1,270), January 1971, 177–183.

10. See Sheila Collins (1974), and Carol P. Christ, "The New Feminist Theology: A Review of the Literature," *Religious Studies Review* 1977, *3* (4), 203–212.

11. See Carol P. Christ, "Margaret Atwood: The Surfacing of Women's Spiritual Quest and Vision," *Signs, 2* (2), 1976, 316–330.

12. See Judith Plaskow, "Carol Christ on Margaret Atwood: Some Theological Reflections," *Signs, 2* (2), 1976, 331–339.

13. Marcia L. Keller, "Political-Philosophical Analysis of the U.S. Women's Liberation Movement," unpublished, 1977.

THE ESSENTIAL CHALLENGE:
DOES THEOLOGY SPEAK
TO WOMEN'S EXPERIENCE?

IN 1895, toward the end of a long and distinguished feminist career, Elizabeth Cady Stanton set about writing and editing *The Woman's Bible,* a series of commentaries on biblical passages pertaining to women. The project was a product of Stanton's firm conviction that the political and economic subordination of women has deep ideological and religious roots. The degradation of women is basic to the biblical view of creation and redemption, she felt. Therefore the emancipation of women is finally impossible unless the Bible is understood from a feminist perspective and repudiated as revelation. While Stanton thus saw a feminist biblical commentary as urgently necessary, her sister feminists did not share her estimate of its importance. In 1896, the twenty-eighth annual convention of the National-American Women Suffrage Association, which Stanton had cofounded, officially repudiated any connection with *The Woman's Bible.* It faded into oblivion, to be rediscovered by feminist scholars of religion in the last decade.

What must strike us today about *The Woman's Bible* is the depth and pertinence of the issues Stanton raises. Stanton was asking what feminists and religion scholars call "nonquestions."[1] She was questioning such deeply held convictions as to the order of things that it was difficult for others even to hear her. It must have taken tremendous courage for her to see and proclaim the biblical roots of sexism when so few people shared her vision.

The three articles in this section are products of this same "courage to see."[2] Reading or rereading them, one becomes aware of how recently it is that Stanton's nonquestions concerning the role of religion in perpetuating sexism have been squarely confronted. These essays raise the fundamental theological issues in women and religion: the importance of women's experience, the tenacity of dualistic thinking, the dangers of male God language. They raised them before the area had acquired any legitimacy, and yet two of them—Ruether's and Daly's—were written only in 1971.

Saiving's essay, a landmark in feminist theology, was ten years ahead of its time. Published in 1960 before the second wave of the women's movement, its author seems to have been aware of her own audacity in criticizing theology from the perspective of "feminine experience." "I am a student of theology," Saiving begins her article, "I am also a woman. Perhaps it strikes you as curious that I put these two assertions beside each other." Curious; it was revolutionary! In putting the two statements together, Saiving set forth what was to become the basic premise of all feminist theology: that the vision of the theologian is affected by the particularities of his or her experience as male or female.

Saiving develops this point in relation to the theologies of Reinhold Niebuhr and Anders Nygren. She argues that, in defining sin as pride and grace as sacrificial love, they not only fail to illumine women's experience, but they also reinforce what might be considered "women's sin" of self-forgetfulness and self-negation. She thus questions the claim of two major theologians to have established a *universal* definition of sin and grace. Their supposedly generic doctrines of "man" turn out on closer examination to be doctrines of male experience. She suggests that the sex of the theologian *matters*—and from this all later feminist work follows. She opened the door both to fuller criticism of "male" theology and to thorough exploration of theology from the perspective of women's experience.

While Saiving raised a fundamental issue for feminist thought, her work was not immediately followed by a burst of feminist writing. Her article was reprinted once, and then, like *The Woman's Bible,* was forgotten. For most of the 1960s there was little writing on women and religion. When we began graduate work in theology at Yale in the late 1960s, we were taught nothing about feminist or even feminine theology. When Rosemary Ruether came to speak at Yale in the spring of 1970, her presence seemed almost miraculous. We had read Saiving's essay and knew from our own experience that the material in our courses left out and belittled our experience as women. But we had never heard an articulate woman set out the problems that a purely male perspective had visited on Western theology and culture. That night Ruether outlined her important theory, also developed in her essay in this volume, that sexism is rooted in the dualistic world view that grew out of the dramatic religious changes that swept classical civilization in the first millenium B.C.E. The breakdown of tribal culture in that period led to the disruption of the holistic perspective that characterized early human societies. Woman and man, nature and culture, body and spirit, Goddess and God, once bound together in a total vision of world renewal, became split off from each other and ordered hierarchically. When male culture-creating groups appropriated the positive side of each of these dualisms for themselves, the age-old male–female polarity was given a newly oppressive significance. Women were identified with nature, body, the material realm, all of which were considered distinctly inferior to transcendent male spirit. A new language of female subordination was forged, a language that eventually was applied to other oppressed groups—such as the carnal Jew and the sexual Negro—and that was also used to justify exploitation of despised nature.

Ruether's argument at once specifies and broadens Saiving's claim that theology is a product of male experience, for it describes the nature of sexism and shows that it has deep roots in the Christian tradition. This analysis has profound implications for feminist thought. It suggests that the liberation of women is finally contingent on overcoming those dualisms that have for centuries molded Western consciousness. It links the women's movement with the movement for ecological sanity. It suggests that women—because their oppression is a model for the oppression of others—have a special role to play in the struggle for planetary liberation. And it implies that one key to the construction of a new holistic and world-affirming ethic may be the uplifting and reevaluation of those qualities dispised in women.

Although some of these implications have been amplified and explored by Ruether herself, aspects of her thought have been seized on by others and developed in new and original ways. While Ruether believes the Christian tradition has a liberating core that can be used to transform oppressive dualisms, Mary Daly used Ruether's analysis of hierarchal dualism to launch a full-scale attack on the Christian tradition. Daly entered the feminist theological arena in 1968 with the publication of her first major work in women and religion, *The Church and the Second Sex*. This book, a product of Daly's early—and brief— reformist period, described the history and nature of women's exclusion from full participation in the Catholic Church. Its thesis was that such exclusion, although real and deep seated, represented a distortion of the church's essential affirmation of the worth of every human being. The book was written in the hope that Catholicism would shuck off its sexist trappings and, in the spirit of modernization that began at Vatican II, move toward a future in which all persons could become whole.

Daly's *The Church and the Second Sex* was important because it articulated and legitimated the feelings of many women that something was wrong with religion's view of them. But it did not make the same important theoretical contributions to feminist thinking that Daly's more recent work did. The essay reprinted here represents both a stage in Daly's personal journey away from the church and a crucial breakthrough for feminist theology. Indeed, it contains two breakthroughs. First, the community out of which Daly speaks is no longer the church but the women's movement. Combining Saiving's claim that women's experience represents a new theological perspective with Ruether's argument that women are the oldest and primary oppressed group, Daly contends that women in the feminist movement constitute a messianic community, uniquely able to examine and challenge the oppressive tendencies of traditional religion.

Second, what Daly now finds oppressive in the Christian tradition is not individual sexist statements but the message implicit in its core *symbols*—God the Father, "the great patriarch in heaven," and the male Christ. In *The Church and the Second Sex,* she briefly considered the question of God's maleness[3] but focused chiefly on *ideas* about the place of women in the church. Here she is concerned with the power of symbols to shape experience independently of any conceptual explanation of a symbol's meaning. The maleness of God and Christ, she says, providing images of the "rightness" of male rule, reinforce and legitimate the power of males in society. Even if theologians insist that God is not male, the symbols convey their own meaning. "The medium is the message" as she puts it in *Beyond God the Father.*[4] It is not only the gender of God that Daly finds oppressive, however, but also *His* character and attributes. Borrowing Ruether's analysis of dualistic consciousness, Daly argues that the notion of a "Supreme Being" who is other than and infinitely superior to subservient humanity is the quintessential product of a patriarchal mentality that perceives everything in terms of higher–lower, good–evil, male–female. If women are to overcome their oppression, they must reject not only the male God but also all hierarchy and dualism, of which God language is simply an expression.

This argument challenges Christianity profoundly, for it says that not simply ideas and doctrines (as Saiving argues) but also its core symbolism have been molded (or warped) by a male perspective. If Daly is right, then the alternatives are two: Fundamentally transform this symbolism or abandon it altogether. In "After the Death of God the Father," Daly still holds out the possibility of an authentic Christian language that neither reifies transcendence nor makes an idol out of Christ. But in *Beyond God the Father* she takes the final step outside Christianity. In that book, she refuses to accept the possibility of a male messiah or to identify the nonobjectified God who is Be-ing with the male idol of the Christian tradition. This is a move that Ruether, with her more inclusive view of the liberation struggle, does not find necessary. For Ruether, the radical wing of the worldwide Christian community, which preaches a message of justice and liberation from oppression inspired by the prophets and Jesus, remains a viable community. For Daly, however, the iconoclastic and liberating perspective of feminism that began to emerge in "After the Death of God the Father" now becomes absolute. A new religious community arises, a community of women who, courageously asking basic nonquestions of our culture, reenvision and rename the cosmos.

NOTES

1. Mary Daly, *Beyond God the Father* (Boston: Beacon Press, 1973), p. 12.
2. Daly, 1973, p. 4.
3. Mary Daly, *The Church and the Second Sex* (New York: Harper & Row, 1968), pp. 138–141.
4. Daly, 1973, p. 72.

The Human Situation:
A Feminine View

VALERIE SAIVING

I am a student of theology; I am also a woman. Perhaps it strikes you as curious that I put these two assertions beside each other, as if to imply that one's sexual identity has some bearing on his theological views. I myself would have rejected such an idea when I first began my theological studies. But now, thirteen years later, I am no longer as certain as I once was that, when theologians speak of "man," they are using the word in its generic sense. It is, after all, a well-known fact that theology has been written almost exclusively by men. This alone should put us on guard, especially since contemporary theologians constantly remind us that one of man's strongest temptations is to identify his own limited perspective with universal truth.

I purpose to criticize, from the viewpoint of feminine experience, the estimate of the human situation made by certain contemporary theologians. Although the views I shall outline receive their most uncompromising expression in the writings of Anders Nygren and Reinhold Niebuhr, I believe that they represent a widespread tendency in

Valerie Saiving received her Ph.D. from the University of Chicago and teaches at Hobart and William Smith Colleges. She delivered the Dudleian Lecture at Harvard University in 1977 on "Feminism and Process Philosophy: A Feminist Appropriation of Whitehead's Thought," and her article "Androcentrism in Religious Studies" appeared in *The Journal of Religion*. This essay was originally published in *The Journal of Religion* (April, 1960), © 1960 by the University of Chicago, and is reprinted by permission of The University of Chicago Press.

contemporary theology to describe man's predicament as rising from
his separateness and the anxiety occasioned by it and to identify sin
with self-assertion and love with selflessness.

The human condition, according to many contemporary theologians,
is universally characterized by anxiety, for, while man is a creature,
subject to the limitations of all finite existence, he is different from
other creatures because he is free. Although his freedom is qualified by
his participation in the natural order, he is not simply bound by
inherited instinct to a repetitious livingout of the life pattern common
to all members of the species. Instead, he can stand apart from the
world and survey it, envision multiple possibilities and make choices,
elaborate his own private ends and imagine larger harmonies, destroy
given natural structures and create new ones in their place. This
freedom of man, which is the source of his historical and cultural
creativity, is also the source of his temptation to sin. For man's
freedom, which from another point of view can be called his individuality and his essential loneliness, brings with it a pervasive fear for the
survival of the self and its values. Sin is the self's attempt to overcome
that anxiety by magnifying its own power, righteousness, or knowledge. Man knows that he is merely a part of the whole, but he tries to
convince himself and others that he *is* the whole. He tries, in fact, to
become the whole. Sin is the unjustified concern of the self for its own
power and prestige; it is the imperialistic drive to close the gap between
the individual, separate self and others by reducing those others to the
status of mere objects which can then be treated as appendages of the
self and manipulated accordingly. Sin is not an occasional, isolated act
but pervades everything man does, even those acts which he performs
for the most pure and "unselfish" motives. For the human creature has
a marvelous capacity for blinding himself to the fact that, no matter
how altruistic his goals may be, he always inserts his own limited
individual goals into his attempts to achieve them.

Love is the precise opposite of sin. It is the true norm of human
existence and the one real solution to the fundamental predicament in
which man stands. Love, according to these theologians, is completely
self-giving, taking no thought for its own interests but seeking only the
good of the other. Love makes no value judgments concerning the
other's worth; it demands neither merit in the other nor recompense for
itself but gives itself freely, fully, and without calculation. Love is
unconditional forgiveness; concerning the one to whom it is given, it

beareth all things, believeth all things, hopeth all things, endureth all things. Love is personal; it is the concrete relatedness of an *I* to a *Thou*, in which the *I* casts aside all its particularities, all its self-affirmations, everything which separates it from the *Thou*, and becomes wholly receptive to the other.

It is important, I think, to emphasize that the foregoing analysis of the human situation and the definitions of love and sin which accompany it are mutually dependent concepts. The kind of love described is normative and redemptive precisely insofar as it answers to man's deepest need. If human nature and the human situation are not as described by the theologians in question, then the assertion that self-giving love is the law of man's being is irrelevant and may even be untrue. To the extent that contemporary theology has, in whole or in part, described the human condition inaccurately, to that same extent is its doctrine of love in question.

It is my contention that there are significant differences between masculine and feminine experience and that feminine experience reveals in a more emphatic fashion certain aspects of the human situation which are present but less obvious in the experience of men. Contemporary theological doctrines of love have, I believe, been constructed primarily upon the basis of masculine experience and thus view the human condition from the male standpoint. Consequently, these doctrines do not provide an adequate interpretation of the situation of women—nor, for that matter, of men, especially in view of certain fundamental changes now taking place in our own society.

But can we speak meaningfully about feminine experience as something fundamentally different from masculine experience? Is there such a thing as an underlying feminine character structure which always and everywhere differs from the basic character structure of the male? Are not all distinctions between the sexes, except the purely biological ones, relative to a given culture? Are we not all, men and women alike, members of a single species?

Of course it would be ridiculous to deny that there is a structure of experience common to both men and women, so that we may legitimately speak of the "human situation" without reference to sexual identity. The only question is whether we have described the human situation correctly by taking account of the experiences of both sexes. We know, too, that we can no longer make any hard-and-fast distinctions between the *potentialities* of men and women as such. The

twentieth century has witnessed the shattering of too many of our
traditional conceptions of sexual differences for us any longer to ignore
the tremendous plasticity of human nature. But perhaps the most
telling evidence of all that every distinction between the sexes above the
physiological level is purely arbitrary comes from the descriptions
given by cultural anthropologists of many primitive societies whose
ideas about the behavior appropriate to each sex are widely different
from, and in many instances contradictory to, those held in our own
tradition.

And yet, curiously enough, it is the anthropologists themselves who
have begun in recent years to question the assumption that the
characters of men and women are essentially alike in all respects. It is
even more startling to note that among them are two women of
unquestioned professional competence.

It was Ruth Benedict—who in *Patterns of Culture* stressed the
relativity of the character ideals held by various societies and the
inability of science to account for their diversity on a biological basis—
who also wrote these words: "To me it seems a very terrible thing to be
a woman." And again: "Nature lays a compelling and very distressing
hand upon woman, and she struggles in vain who tries to deny it or
escape it—life loves the little irony of proving it upon the very woman
who has denied it; she can only hope for success by working according
to Nature's conception of her makeup—not against them."[1]

Margaret Mead's concern with the problem of sex differentiation
has been expressed in much of her research and writing. In 1935, she
published *Sex and Temperament in Three Primitive Societies,*[2] in
which she came to the conclusion that there are no natural—that is to
say, innate—differences between the character traits of men and
women. Rather, the way any particular society defines masculinity and
femininity is by a purely arbitrary assignment to one or the other sex of
qualities to which members of either sex could be trained with equal
ease.

Fourteen years later, Margaret Mead published *Male and Female,*
in which she returned to the problem, but this time from a slightly
different perspective:

In every known society, mankind has elaborated the biological division of
labor into forms often very remotely related to the original biological differences that provided the original clues. . . . Sometimes one quality has been
assigned to one sex, sometimes to the other. . . . Whether we deal with small

matters or with large, with the frivolities of ornament and cosmetics or the sanctities of man's place in the universe, we find this great variety of ways, often flatly contradictory one to the other, in which the roles of the two sexes have been patterned.

But we always find the patterning. We know of no culture that has said, articulately, that there is no difference between men and women except in the way they contribute to the creation of the next generation; that otherwise in all respects they are simply human beings with varying gifts, no one of which can be exclusively assigned to either sex. . . .

So . . . we are faced with a most bewildering and confusing array of apparently contradictory evidence about sex differences. We may well ask: Are they important? Do real differences exist, in addition to the obvious anatomical and physical ones—but just as biologically based—that may be masked by the learnings appropriate to any given society, but which will nevertheless be there? Will such differences run through all of men's and all of women's behavior?[3]

Miss Mead answers this question in the affirmative, not because she has found new evidence which contradicts the evidence presented in her earlier book, but because she has put the question in a different way. Instead of asking the question most of us ask: "Are character differences between the sexes the result of heredity or environment, of biology or culture?" she asks, rather, whether there may not be certain basic similarities in the ways in which men and women in every culture have experienced what it means to be a man or to be a woman. Cultures may and do superimpose upon the fundamental meanings of sex membership other ideas which are irrelevant or contradictory to the basic structure of sexuality. Nevertheless, if such regularities do exist, then we may find that, underneath the specific additions which each culture has imposed, there remains a substratum or core of masculine and feminine orientations which, if too drastically contradicted by the superstructure, may threaten the very existence of the society and its members.

In my description of a few of these biocultural differences between masculine and feminine experience, I shall draw heavily upon Margaret Mead's analysis because I personally find it most illuminating. Nevertheless, I wish to make it clear that I am not attempting to summarize her thought, which is far too complex to present fully here, nor (since even anthropologists are not in agreement in these matters) do I present her as an authority. Primarily, what I shall say is based upon my own experience and observation as it has been clarified and substantiated by Miss Mead and by a number of other writers, including Helene Deutsch,[4] Erich Fromm,[5] and Theodor Reik[6] (psychoanalysts), Talcott Parsons[7] (sociologist), and Ashley Montagu[8] (anthropologist).

What, then, are the distinctions between the experiences of men and the experiences of women as they occur in any human society, and in what way do these contribute to the formation of differences between the masculine and the feminine character and orientation?

We must begin with the central fact about sexual differences: that in every society it is women—and only women—who bear children. Further, in every society the person closest to the infant and young child is a woman. This fact, based on the physiology of lactation, remains true even in our own culture, in which the formula has so largely replaced the mother's breast.

The close relationship between mother and infant plays the first and perhaps the most important role in the formation of masculine and feminine character, for it means that the person with whom the child originally identifies himself is a woman. Both male and female children must learn to overcome this initial identification by differentiating themselves from the mother. But the kind and degree of differentiation required of the boy are strikingly different from what is required of the girl. The little girl learns that, although she must grow up (become a separate person), she will grow up to be a woman, like her mother, and have babies of her own; she will, in a broad sense, merely take her mother's place. She learns, too, that she will attain womanhood quite naturally—merely by the maturation of her body. In fact, she already is a woman, if in miniature, and must therefore be protected against the premature exploitation of her femininity. And so the emphasis for the girl is upon the fact that she *is* a female and that all she needs to do to realize her full femininity is to wait.

The boy's process of differentiation from his mother is much more complex and difficult. He learns not only that he must grow up but that he must grow up to be a man; that men are different from women, since they do not have babies; and that he must therefore become quite a different sort of creature from his mother. Instead of imitating her, he must relinquish completely his original identification with her. He also finds that, while he is not and never will be a woman, neither is he yet a man. It will be many years before he can perform sexually as a man, and therefore he does not need to be guarded, like his sister, against sexual activity before he is ready for it. He is thus permitted far greater freedom than the girl. But this freedom has its drawbacks for him, since along with it goes a certain set of standards which he must meet before he will be judged to have achieved manhood. He must learn this or that skill, acquire this or that trait or ability, and pass this or that test of endurance, courage, strength, or accomplishment. He must *prove* himself to be a man. True, he has certain advantages over the girl, particularly in the fact that he has visible organs which demonstrate his sex. But, on the whole, the process of self-differentiation plays a stronger and more anxiety-provoking role in the boy's maturation than is normally the case for the girl. Growing up is not merely a natural process of bodily maturation; it is, instead, a challenge which he must meet, a proof he must furnish by means of performance, achievement, and activity directed toward the external world. And even so his reward for achieving manhood is not easily grasped in imagination. It is quite obvious to a child what motherhood is; it is not nearly so obvious what it means to be a father.

This early divergence between masculine and feminine sexual development is repeated, reinforced, and elaborated in later stages of the individual's life. For instance, the girl's history as a female is punctuated and authenticated by a series of definite, natural, and irreversible bodily occurrences: first menstruation, defloration, childbirth, menopause. Each of these events, to be sure, occasions anxiety for the girl and thus might seem to be the female equivalent of the constant anxiety regarding his maleness which besets the boy. Yet these physiological events which mark the woman's life have a reassuring aspect, too, for each of them is concrete, unmistakable proof of her femaleness. The boy's history will provide no such dramatic, once-for-all physical signals of his masculinity.

Even more significant are the differences between male and female roles in the various aspects of adult sexuality. The processes of impregnation, pregnancy, childbirth, and lactation have a certain passivity about them; they are things which *happen* to a woman more than things that she *does*. The sexual act itself, for example, has for her this basically passive quality. The woman, of course, *may* take an active role, but it is not necessary for her to do so, either to satisfy the man or to fulfil her reproductive function. In fact, she may be quite without desire or may even have strong feelings of revulsion, and yet she may, for any number of reasons, submit to the man—sometimes with sufficient grace so that he is completely unaware of her feelings. In the extreme case—rape—the passive structure of female sexuality unquestionably appears. The case is quite otherwise for the male, whose *active* desire and *active* performance in the sexual act is absolutely required for its completion. And here again the demand for performance is coupled with an inevitable anxiety; in order to prove his maleness, he *must* succeed in what he has undertaken—and it is possible for him to fail.

Considered in terms of its reproductive consequences, the sexual act has greatly different meanings for men and women. The male's part in the creation of a child seems indirect and is completed very quickly, while a woman's participation is direct, immediate, and prolonged. It is true that we now know as scientific fact what some primitive peoples have only suspected and others denied: that the man's role in reproduction is essential and that his genetic contribution is equal to the woman's. Yet the birth of a child is never an absolute guaranty to a man of his maleness, as it is to a woman of her femaleness. For, while there can be no doubt as to who is the mother of the child, "paternity remains, with all our modern biological knowledge, as inferential as it ever was, and considerably less ascertainable than it has seemed to be in some periods of history."[9] There is a sense, too, in which woman's biological creativity appears to present a challenge to a man; he perhaps feels his inability to bear children as a deficiency for which he must compensate by other kinds of creativity.

The man's sense of his own masculinity, then, is throughout characterized by uncertainty, challenge, and the feeling that he must again and again prove himself a man. It also calls for a kind of objective achievement and a greater degree of self-differentiation and self development than are required of the woman *as* woman. In a sense, masculinity is an endless process of *becoming,* while in femininity the emphasis is on *being.* Another way of putting the distinction is that woman is more closely bound to nature than is man. This has advantages and disadvantages for her as a human being. The advantages lie in her greater degree of natural security and the lesser degree of anxiety to which she is subject, both of which make it easier, all other things being equal, for her to enter into loving relationships in which self-concern is at a minimum. Yet if it is true, as Niebuhr says, that man stands at the juncture of nature and spirit, then woman's closeness to nature is a measure of the distance she must travel to reach spirit. That she, too, is a free human being is proved by the fact that she can reject the feminine role; but, having chosen it, she has chosen a kind of bondage which is not involved in a man's acceptance of his sexual identity.

For masculinity can with good reason be defined as the distance between spirit and nature. Because of his less direct and immediate role in the reproductive process, including nurture during the long period of human infancy, man is, in his greater freedom, necessarily subject to a kind of anxiety—and, consequently, to a kind of creative drive—which is experienced more rarely and less intensely by most women.

I have drawn the distinctions between masculine and feminine experience in the sharpest possible terms in order to clarify the divergence between them. But it is important to remind ourselves of the countless changes which have been rung on these basic themes in human societies. Every culture, we have said, superimposes upon the necessities of sexual roles a whole structure of masculine and feminine character traits. Many of these addenda are only tenuously related to the foundation on which they rest, and they may even be completely contradictory to that foundation. When this phenomenon is carried to its extreme, so that women, for example, are educated by their society to despise the functions of childbearing and nurture, then the society is in grave danger of bringing about its own destruction. Similarly, where procreation is valued so highly that men attempt to participate directly in the processes of pregnancy, birth, and the rearing of children to the exclusion of other kinds of creative activity, the social fabric again becomes dangerously weak. Both types of society have been discovered among preliterate peoples,[10] and, as we shall see, our own society has not escaped the tendency to overvalue the traits characteristic to one or the other sex.

The truth is, of course, that there is no impassable gulf between the ways in which men and women may look at themselves and at their world. Just as sexuality is not the whole of human existence, so the individual's sense of his own identity is not derived solely from his sexual role. Human beings of both sexes have certain basic experiences in common from earliest infancy—hunger and satiety, constriction and freedom, defenselessness and power, resentment and love. Men and women can and do learn from each other, too; women can be aggressive and ambitious, and men can be fatherly. Neither sex is exempt from anxiety, and both experience the temptations of passivity. Yet the individual's sense of being male or female, which plays such an important part in the young child's struggle for self-definition, can never be finally separated from his total orientation to life; in those cases—which are the majority—in which adult men and women accept and are able to actualize their respective sexual roles, the characterological tendencies based on sex membership are reinforced and strengthened. This is surely the reason why, although there have been women philosophers, musicians, and murderers, there have been no female Platos, Bachs, or Hitlers. It is also the reason why even those men who enjoy being fathers most fully can scarcely be imagined as finding complete self-fulfilment in fatherhood. "A woman, as Madame de Staël remarked, either has children or writes books."[11] As for men, Margaret Mead has observed:

In every known human society, the male's need for achievement can be recognized. Men may cook, or weave or dress dolls or hunt hummingbirds, but if such activities are appropriate occupations of men, then the whole society, men and women alike, votes them as important. When the same occupations are performed by women, they are regarded as less important. In a great number of human societies, men's sureness of their sex role is tied up with their right, or ability, to practice some activity that women are not allowed to practice. Their maleness, in fact, has to be underwritten by preventing women from entering some field or performing some feat. Here may be found the relationship between maleness and pride; that is, a need for prestige that will outstrip the prestige which is accorded to any woman. There seems no evidence that it is necessary for men to surpass women in any specific way, but rather that men do need to find reassurance in achievement, and because of this connection, cultures frequently phrase achievement as something that women do not or cannot do, rather than directly as something which men do well.

The recurrent problem of civilization is to define the male role satisfactorily enough—whether it be to build gardens or raise cattle, kill game or kill enemies, build bridges or handle bank shares—so that the male may in the course of his life reach a solid sense of irreversible achievement, of which his childhood knowledge of the satisfactions of childbearing have given him a glimpse. In the case of women, it is only necessary that they be permitted by the given social arrangements to fulfil their biological role, to attain this sense of irreversible achievement. If women are to be restless and questing, even in the face of childbearing, they must be made so through education. If men are ever to be at peace, ever certain that their lives have been lived as they were meant to be, they must have, in addition to paternity, culturally elaborated forms of expression that are lasting and sure. Each culture—in its own way—has developed forms that will make men satisfied in their constructive activities without distorting their sure sense of their masculinity. Fewer cultures have yet found ways in which to give women a divine discontent that will demand other satisfactions than those of childbearing.[12]

It seems to me that a more realistic appraisal of contemporary theological doctrines of sin and love is possible against this general background, for the prevalent theologies today were created by men who lived amid the tensions of a hypermasculine culture. What is usually called the "modern era" in Western civilization, stretching roughly from the Renaissance and Reformation up to very recent times and reaching the peak of its expression in the rise of capitalism, the industrial revolution, imperialism, the triumphs of science and technology, and other well-known phenomena of the eighteenth, nineteenth, and twentieth centuries—this modern era can be called the "masculine age par excellence," in the sense that it emphasized, encouraged, and set free precisely those aspects of human nature which are peculiarly significant to men. It placed the highest value on external achievement, on the creation of structures of matter and meaning, on self-differentiation and the separation of man from nature. By its emphasis on laissez-faire competition and economic uncertainty, on scientific and geographic explorations, on the widening of the gulf between family relationships, on the one hand, and the public life of business and politics, on the other—by these and many more innovations, the modern era presented a heightened challenge to men; and, by the same token, it increased their natural sense of insecurity and anxiety. It was a masculine era, too, in the degree to which it devalued the functions of women and children and the whole reproductive process. It thereby provoked a new restlessness in women, too.[13]

It is clear that many of the characteristic emphases of contemporary theology—its definition of the human situation in terms of anxiety, estrangement, and the conflict between necessity and freedom; its identification of sin with pride, will-to-power, exploitation, self-assertiveness, and the treatment of others as objects rather than persons; its conception of redemption as restoring to man what he fundamentally lacks (namely, sacrificial love, the I-Thou relationship, the primacy of the personal, and, ultimately, peace)—it is clear that such an analysis of man's dilemma was profoundly responsive and relevant to the concrete facts of modern man's existence. Insofar as modern woman, too, increasingly accepted the prevailing values of the age and took on the challenges and opportunities, risks and insecurities of participation in the masculine world, this theology spoke directly to her condition also. And, since the most striking features of modern culture were but heightened expressions of one aspect of the universal human situation, the adequacy of this theology as a description of man's fundamental predicament seemed assured.

As a matter of fact, however, this theology is not adequate to the universal human situation; its inadequacy is clearer to no one than to certain contemporary women. These women have been enabled, through personal experience and education, to transcend the boundaries of a purely feminine identity. They now stand closer to the juncture of nature and spirit than was possible for most women in the past. They believe in the values of self-differentiation, challenge, and adventure and are not strangers to that "divine discontent" which has always driven men. Yet these same women value their femininity also; they do not wish to discard their sexual identity but rather to gather it up into a higher unity. They want, in other words, to be both women *and* full human beings.

Many of these women, who were brought up to believe in the fundamental equality of the sexes and who were given the same kind of education and the same encouragement to self-realization as their male contemporaries, do not really discover until they marry and bear children—or, perhaps, have been forced to admit to themselves that they never will marry—that there are real differences between the masculine and feminine situations which cannot be blamed upon a cultural lag in the definitions of femininity, or upon the "selfishness" and "stupidity" of men. It is only at this point, when the ultimate actualization of their specific sexuality must be either accepted or given up for good, that they become aware of the deep need of almost every woman, regardless of her personal history and achievements or her belief in her own individual value, to surrender her self-identity and be included in another's "power of being." And, if she is fortunate enough to bear a child, she very soon discovers that the one essential, indispensable relationship of a mother to her child is the I-Thou relationship. In infancy, the very existence of the child depends upon the mother's ability to transcend her own patterns of thought, feeling, and physical need. As Margaret Mead puts it, "The mother who must learn that the infant who was but an hour ago a part of her own body is now a different individual, with its own hungers and its own needs, and that if she listens to her own body to interpret the child, the child will die, is schooled in an irreplaceable school."[14] At a later stage in the child's life, too, the essential relationship continues to be one of love. To take just one example—the least sentimental one, perhaps—the child, when he has learned to talk, is almost constantly absorbed in trying to understand the world around him. It is so full of strange and wonderful and lovely and terrifying things. He is full of questions, and upon his learning the true and adequate answers to them depends the whole process of acculturation upon which the uniqueness of human societies rests. But, in order to answer a child's eager questions, the mother must be able to transcend her own habitual patterns of thought; she must meet the child where *he* is at that moment. It is absolutely impossible to communicate with a young child without in some way abandoning one's own perspective and looking at the world through *his* eyes.

A mother who rejoices in her maternal role—and most mothers do most of the time—knows the profound experience of self-transcending love. But she knows, too, that it is not the whole meaning of life. For she learns not only that it is impossible to sustain a perpetual I–Thou relationship but that the attempt to do so can be deadly. The moments, hours, and days of self-giving must be balanced by moments, hours, and days of withdrawal into, and enrichment of, her individual selfhood if she is to remain a whole person. She learns, too, that a woman can give too much of herself, so that nothing remains of her own uniqueness; she can become merely an emptiness, almost a zero, without value to herself, to her fellow men, or, perhaps, even to God.

For the temptations of woman *as woman* are not the same as the temptations of man *as man*, and the specifically feminine forms of sin—"feminine" not because they are confined to women or because women are incapable of sinning in other ways but because they are outgrowths of the basic feminine character structure—have a quality which can never be encompassed by such terms as "pride" and "will-to-power." They are better suggested by such items as triviality, distractibility, and diffuseness; lack of an organizing center or focus; dependence on others for one's own self-definition; tolerance at the expense of standards of excellence; inability to respect the boundaries of privacy; sentimentality, gossipy sociability, and mistrust of reason—in short, underdevelopment or negation of the self.

This list of specifically feminine sins could be extended. All of them, however, are to be understood as merely one side of the feminine coin.

For just as man's distance from nature is the precondition of his creativity, on the one hand, and his self-concern, on the other, so does woman's closeness to nature have dipolar potentialities. Her sureness of her own femininity and thus of her secure place in the scheme of things may, if she accepts the feminine role with joy, enable her to be a source of strength and refreshment to her husband, her children, and the wider community. If she has been brought up to devalue her femininity, on the other hand, this same sense that for her "anatomy is destiny" may create an attitude of stolid and sterile resignation, a feeling that there is no use in trying. Again, the fact that her whole growth toward womanhood has the character of an inevitable process of bodily maturation rather than that of a challenge and a task may lead her to dissipate herself in activities which are merely trivial. Yet it is the same lack of creative drive which may make it possible for her to perform cheerfully the thousand-and-one routine tasks—the woman's work which is never done—which someone must do if life is to go on. Her capacity for surrendering her individual concerns in order to serve the immediate needs of others—a quality which is so essential to the maternal role—can, on the other hand, induce a kind of diffuseness of purpose, a tendency toward being easily distracted, a failure to discriminate between the more and the less important, and an inability to focus in a sustained manner on the pursuit of any single goal.[15] Her receptivity to the moods and feelings of others and her tendency to merge her selfhood in the joys, sorrows, hopes, and problems of those around her are the positive expressions of an aspect of the feminine character which may also take the negative forms of gossipy sociability, dependence on others (such as husband or children) for the definition of her values, or a refusal to respect another's right to privacy. And her capacity for forgiving love, for cherishing all her children equally without regard to beauty, merit, or intelligence, can also express itself in a kind of indiscriminate tolerance which suspects or rejects all objective criteria of excellence.

All this is not meant to constitute an indictment of the feminine character as such. I have no wish, certainly, to add to the burden of guilt which has been heaped upon women—by themselves as well as by men—for centuries. My purpose, indeed, as far as it concerns women in particular, is quite the opposite. It is to awaken theologians to the fact that the situation of woman, however similar it may appear on the surface of our contemporary world to the situation of man and however much it may be echoed in the life of individual men, is, at bottom, quite different—that the specifically feminine dilemma is, in fact, precisely the opposite of the masculine. Today, when for the first time in human history it really seems possible that those endless housewifely tasks—which, along with the bearing and rearing of children, have always been enough to fill the whole of each day for the average woman—may virtually be eliminated; today, when at last women might seem to be in a position to begin to be both feminine and fully developed, creative human beings; today, these same women are being subjected to pressures from many sides to return to the traditional feminine niche and to devote themselves wholly to the tasks of nurture, support, and service of their families. One might expect of theologians that they at least not add to these pressures. One might even expect them to support and encourage the woman who desires to be both a woman and an individual in her own right, a separate person some part of whose mind and feelings are inviolable, some part of whose time belongs strictly to herself, in whose house there is, to use Virginia Woolf's marvelous image, "a room of one's own." Yet theology, to the extent that it has defined the human condition on the basis of masculine experience, continues to speak of such desires as sin or temptation to sin. If such a woman believes the theologians, she will try to strangle those impulses in herself. She will believe that, having chosen marriage and children and thus being face to face with the needs of her family for love, refreshment, and forgiveness, she has no right to ask anything for herself but must submit without qualification to the strictly feminine role.

Perhaps, after all, the contemporary woman who wants to participate in the creative tasks of the world outside her home—those tasks upon which mankind has built all that is distinctively human, that is, history and culture—and yet remain a woman is attempting an impossible task. Perhaps the goal we should set ourselves is to rear our daughters in the older way, without too much formal education and without encouraging them to be independent, differentiated, free human beings of whom some contribution is expected other than the production of the next generation. If we could do this, our daughters might be able to find secure fulfilment in a simple femininity. After all, the division of labor between the sexes worked fairly well for thousands of years, and we may be only asking for trouble by trying to modify that structure.

And yet I do not think we can turn back this particular clock. Nor do I think that the feminine dilemma is of concern only to women. To understand it is important for men, too, not only because it is a loss to every man when a woman fails to realize her full self-identity, but because there is, it seems to me, a growing trend in contemporary life toward the feminizing of society itself, including men as well as women.

To document and explore this trend would require a lengthy exposition beyond the scope of the present paper. I can only refer here briefly to two recent analyses of contemporary Western culture which have impressed me greatly in this connection. Neither of these books— David Riesman's *The Lonely Crowd*[16] and Hannah Arendt's *The Human Condition*[17]—deals with the masculine–feminine theme as such. Yet both of them see a quite recent shift in the fundamental orientation of our present society, one which presages an era as different from what we call the "modern age" as the modern age differs from the medieval. And the analysis of each presents, in its own way, the picture of a society in which the character traits inherent in femininity are being increasingly emphasized, encouraged, and absolutized, just as the modern era raised the essentially masculine character traits to their highest possible power. Lionel Trilling has noted the same trend in our contemporary life and has characterized both its virtues and its dangers with great clarity:

Our culture is in process of revision, and of revision in a very good and right direction, in the direction of greater openness, greater socialization, greater cooperativeness, greater reasonableness. There are, to be sure, tendencies to be observed which go counter to this one, but they are not, I believe, so momentous as the development of the tendency toward social peace. It must always seem ill-natured to raise any question at all about this tendency. It goes against the grain to do so. . . . The American educated middle class is firm in its admiration of nonconformity and dissent. The right to be nonconformist, the right to dissent, is part of our conception of community. Everybody says so: in the weekly, monthly, quarterly magazines and in *The New York Times,* at the cocktail party, at the conference of psychiatrists, at the conference of teachers. How good this is, and how right! And yet, when we examine the content of our idea of nonconformity, we must be dismayed at the smallness of the concrete actuality this very large idea contains. The rhetoric is as sincere as it is capacious, yet we must sometimes wonder whether what is being praised and defended is anything more than the right to have had some sympathetic connection with Communism ten or twenty years ago. . . . We cannot really imagine nonconformity at all, not in art, not in moral or social theory, certainly not in the personal life—it is probably true that there never was a culture which required so entire an eradication of personal differentiation, so bland a uniformity of manner. Admiring nonconformity and loving community, we have decided that we are all nonconformists together. We assert the right of our egos to court adventure without danger and of our superegos to be conscientious without undue strain. We make, I think, what is in many ways a very attractive culture, but we really cannot imagine what it means to take an intellectual chance, or to make an intellectual mistake, or to have a real intellectual difference. You have but to read our novels to understand that we have a growing sense of the cooperative virtues and a diminishing sense of the self that cooperates.[18]

It is true that the kind of "selflessness" and "community" described here is hardly what the theologians who identify love with selflessness and community mean when they speak of the redemptive power of love. Yet there is no mistaking the fact that there is a strong similarity between theology's view that salvation lies in selfless love and contemporary man's growing tendency to avoid any strong assertion of the self as over against others and to merge his individual identity in the identities of others. In truth, the only element that is lacking in the latter picture is the theological presupposition of man's inherent sinfulness, the stubborn refusal of the individual human being to give up his individuality and separateness and to unite in harmonious love. But, if this refusal to become selfless is wholly sinful, then it would seem that we are obliged to try to overcome it; and, when it is overcome, to whatever extent this may be possible, we are left with a chameleon-like creature who responds to others but has no personal identity of his own.

If it is true that our society is moving from a masculine to a feminine orientation, then theology ought to reconsider its estimate of the human condition and redefine its categories of sin and redemption. For a feminine society will have its own special potentialities for good and evil, to which a theology based solely on masculine experience may well be irrelevant.

NOTES

1. Quoted by Clyde Kluckhohn in a review of Margaret Mead, *An Anthropologist at Work: Writings of Ruth Benedict* (Boston: Houghton Mifflin Co., 1959), *New York Times Book Review,* May 31, 1959.

2. New York: William Morrow & Co., 1935.

3. Margaret Mead, *Male and Female* (New York: New American Library, 1959, by arrangement with William Morrow & Co., [originally published in 1949]), pp. 16–17.

4. Helene Deutsch, *Psychology of Women* (New York: Grune & Stratton, 1944), Vols. I and II.

5. Erich Fromm, "Sex and Character," in Ruth Nanda Anshen (ed.), *The Family: Its Function and Destiny* (New York: Harper & Bros., 1949), chap. xix.

6. Theodor Reik, *Of Love and Lust* (New York: Grove Press, 1957, by arrangement with Farrar, Straus & Cudahy [originally published in 1949]).

7. Talcott Parsons, "The Social Structure of the Family," in Anshen (ed.), *op. cit.,* pp. 186–88.

8. Ashley Montagu, *The Natural Superiority of Women* (New York: Macmillan Co., 1953).

9. Mead, *Male and Female*, p. 125.

10. See, among others, Mead, *ibid., passim.*

11. Robert Briffault, *The Mothers* (New York: Macmillan Co., 1927), II, 443.

12. Mead, *Male and Female* pp. 125–26.

13. This point is discussed at some length by Ferdinand Lundberg and Marynia F. Farnham, M.D., *Modern Woman, the Lost Sex* (New York: Grosset & Dunlap, 1959, by arrangement with Harper & Bros. [originally published in 1947]).

14. Mead, *Male and Female,* p. 284.

15. "The tendency to identification sometimes assumes very valuable forms. Thus, many women put their qualities, which may be excellent, at the disposal of their object of identification. . . . They prefer to love and enjoy their own qualities in others. . . . There are women endowed with rich natural gifts that cannot, however, develop beyond certain limits. Such women are exposed to outside influences and changing identifications to such an extent that they never succeed in consolidating their achievements. Instead of making a reasonable choice among numerous opportunities at their disposal, they constantly get involved in confusion that exerts a destructive influence on their own lives and the lives of those around them" (Deutsch, *op. cit.,* pp. 132–33).

16. New York: Doubleday & Co., 1950, by arrangement with Yale University Press (originally published in 1950).

17. Chicago: University of Chicago Press, 1958.

18. Lionel Trilling, *Freud and the Crisis of Our Culture* (Boston: Beacon Press, 1955), pp. 50–53.

Motherearth and the Megamachine: A Theology of Liberation in a Feminine, Somatic and Ecological Perspective

ROSEMARY RADFORD RUETHER

Christianity, as the heir of both classical Neo-Platonism and apocalyptic Judaism, combines the image of a male, warrior God with the exaltation of the intellect over the body. The classical doctrine of Christ, which fused the vision of the heavenly messianic king with the transcendent *logos* of immutable Being, was a synthesis of the religious impulses of late antique religious consciousness, but precisely in their alienated state of development. These world-negating religions carried a set of dualities that still profoundly condition the modern world view.

Rosemary Radford Ruether received her Ph.D. from Claremont School of Theology and is Georgia Harkness Professor of Theology at Garrett Evangelical Seminary, Northwestern University. Long active in antiwar, radical Catholic, feminist, and civil rights groups, she is author of many books, including *Religion and Sexism, Liberation Theology,* and *New Woman/New Earth,* as well as countless articles. This essay is reprinted from *Christianity and Crisis* (April 12, 1972), copyright © 1972 by Christianity and Crisis, Inc., and from her *Liberation Theology,* Paulist Press, copyright © 1972 by the Missionary Society of St. Paul the Apostle in the State of New York.

All the basic dualities—the alienation of the mind from the body; the alienation of the subjective self from the objective world; the subjective retreat of the individual, alienated from the social community; the domination or rejection of nature by spirit—these all have roots in the apocalyptic–Platonic religious heritage of classical Christianity. But the alienation of the masculine from the feminine is the primary sexual symbolism that sums up all these alienations. The psychic traits of intellectuality, transcendent spirit, and autonomous will that were identified with the male left the woman with the contrary traits of bodiliness, sensuality, and subjugation. Society, through the centuries, has in every way profoundly conditioned men and women to play out their lives and find their capacities within this basic antithesis.

This antithesis has also shaped the modern technological environment. The plan of our cities is made in this image: The sphere of domesticity, rest, and childrearing where women are segregated is clearly separated from those corridors down which men advance in assault upon the world of "work." The woman who tries to break out of the female sphere into the masculine finds not only psychic conditioning and social attitudes but the structure of social reality itself ranged against her.

The physical environment—access to basic institutions in terms of space and time—has been shaped for the fundamental purpose of freeing one half of the race for the work society calls "productive," while the other half of the race remains in a sphere that services this freedom for work. The woman who would try to occupy both spheres at once literally finds *reality itself* stacked against her, making the combination of maternal and masculine occupations all but impossible without extraordinary energy or enough wealth to hire domestic help.

Thus, in order to play out the roles shaped by this definition of the male life-style, the woman finds that she must either be childless or have someone else act as her "wife" (i.e., play the service role for her freedom to work). Women's liberation is therefore *impossible* within the present social system except for an elite few. Women simply cannot be persons within the present system of work and family, and they can only rise to liberated personhood by the most radical and fundamental reshaping of the entire human environment in a way that redefines the very nature of work, family, and the institutional expressions of social relations.

Although widespread hopes for liberty and equality among all humans rose with the *philosophes* of the Enlightenment, hardly any of these ideologies of the French Revolution and the liberal revolutions of the nineteenth century envisioned the liberation of women. The bourgeoisie, the workers, the peasants, even the Negro slaves were more obvious candidates for liberation, while the subjugation of women continued to be viewed as an unalterable necessity of nature. When the most radical of the French liberals, the Marquis de Condorcet, included women in the vision of equality, his colleagues thought he had lost his senses and breached the foundations of the new rationalism. The ascendency of Reason meant the ascendency of the intellect over the passions, and this must ever imply the subjugation of women.

An embarrassed silence or cries of ridicule likewise greeted this topic when it was raised half a century later by another consistent libertarian, John Stuart Mill. Only after a long struggle from the nineteenth to the early twentieth century did women finally break down the barriers that separated them from the most basic rights to work, education, financial autonomy, and full citizenship—and even these freedoms are not universally secured today.

The reaction against and suppression of the Woman's Liberation Movement has been closely tied to reactionary cultural and political movements, and the emancipated woman has been the chief target of elitism, fascism, and neoconservatism of all kinds. The Romantic Movement traumatized Europe's reaction to the French Revolution, reinstated the traditional view of women in idealized form, while the more virulent blood-and-soil reactionaries of the nineteenth century expressed a more naked misogynism. Literary figures such as Strindberg and Nietzsche couldn't stress strongly enough their abhorrence of women. At the turn of the century, Freud codified all the traditional negative views of the female psychology, giving them scientific respectability for the new psychological and social sciences. These negative stereotypes have been a key element in the repression of the women's movement through the popular mass media.

In Nazism, the reactionary drive against the libertarian tradition culminated in a virulent revival of racism, misogynism, elitism, and military and national chauvinism. Its victims were Jews, Communists, Social Democrats, and libertarians of all kinds—and, finally, the nascent women's movement.

In America, the period from World War I to the 1960s was characterized by a successive revival of anti-Negro racism, anti-

Semitism, the destruction of the American Left, and finally the cold war militarization of society based on a fanatic anti-Communism. In this same period, a continuous reactionary pacification of the women's movement deprived women of many of their earlier gains in educational and professional fields

This modern backlash against the libertarian tradition seeks to reinstate attitudes and social relations whose psychic roots run back through the Judeo-Christian and classical cultures into the very foundations of civilization building. The cry for liberty, equality, and fraternity challenged the roots of the psychology whereby the dominant class measured its status in terms of the conquest of classes, nations, races, and nature itself.

Lewis Mumford, in his monumental work on the foundations of ancient civilization, *The Myth of the Machine,* and its supplementary volume on modern technological society, *The Myth of the Machine: The Pentagon of Power,* has shown how civilization has been founded on a subjugation of man to machinery. A chauvinist, paranoid psychology has directed men's productive energies into destruction rather than the alleviation of the necessities of all, thus aborting the promise of civilization. The subjugation of the female by the male is the primary psychic model for this chauvinism and its parallel expressions in oppressor–oppressed relationships between social classes, races and nations. It is this most basic symbolism of power that has misdirected men's psychic energy into the building of the Pentagon of Power, from the pyramids of ancient Egypt to the North American puzzle-palace on the Potomac.

The psychosocial history of the domination of women has not been explored with any consistency, so the effort to trace its genesis and development here can only be very general. However, it appears that in agricultural societies sexist and class polarization did not immediately reshape the religious world view. For the first two millennia of recorded history, religious culture continued to reflect the more holistic view of society of the neolithic village, where the individual and the community, nature and society, male and female, earth Goddess and sky God were seen in a total perspective of world renewal. The salvation of the individual was not split off from that of the community; the salvation of society was one with the renewal of the earth; male and female played their complementary roles in the salvation of the world. This primitive democracy of the neolithic village persisted in the divine pantheons of Babylonia, despite the social class stratification that now appeared.

In these early civilizations, this holistic world view was expressed in the public celebration of the new year's festival, wherein the whole society of humanity and nature experienced the annual death of the cosmos and its resurrection from primordial chaos. In this cult, the king, as the personification of the community, played the role of the God who dies and is reborn from the netherworld. His counterpart was a powerful feminine figure who was at once virgin and mother, wife and sister, and who rescued the dying God from the power of the underworld. The king united with her at the end of the drama to create the divine child of the new year's vegetation. The crisis and rebirth encompassed both society and nature: The hymns of rejoicing celebrated the release of the captives, justice for the poor, and security against invasion, as well as the new rain, the new grain, the new lamb and the new child.

Somewhere in the first millennium B.C., however, this communal world view of humanity and nature, male and female, carried over from tribal society started to break down, and the alienations of civilization began to reshape the religious world picture. This change was partly aggravated by the history of imperial conquest that swept the people of the Mediterranean into larger and larger social conglomerates where they no longer felt the same unity with the king, the soil or the society.

The old religions of the earth became private cults for the individual, no longer anticipating the renewal of the earth and society but rather expecting an otherworldly salvation of the individual soul after death. Nature itself came to be seen as an alien reality, and men now visualized their own bodies as foreign to their true selves, longing for a heavenly home to release them from their enslavement within the physical cosmos. Finally, earth ceased to be seen as man's true home.

Hebrew religion is significant in this history as the faith of a people who clung with particular tenacity to their tribal identity over against the imperial powers of civilization. Hebrew society inherited kingship and the new year's festival of the temple from their Canaanite neighbors. But Yahwism repressed the feminine divine role integral to this cult and began to cut loose the festival itself from its natural base in the renewal of the earth.

This desert people claimed the land as a divine legacy, but they imagined a manner of acquiring it that set them against the traditional cult of the earth. They took over the old earth festivals but reinterpreted them to refer to historical events in the Sinai journey. The messianic hopes of the prophets still looked for a paradisal renewal of earth and society, but this renewal broke the bonds of natural possibility and was projected into history as a future event.

So the pattern of death and resurrection was cut loose from organic harmonies and became instead an historical pattern of wrath and redemption. The feminine imagery of the cult was repressed entirely, although it survived in a new form in the symbol of the community as the bride of Yahweh in the Covenant. But the bride was subordinate and dependent to the male Lord of Hosts, who reigned without consort in the heavens, confronting his sometimes rebellious, sometimes repentant people with punishment or promises of national victory.

The hopes for a renewal of nature and society, projected into a once and for all historical future, now came to be seen as less and less realizable within history itself. And so the prophetic drive to free man from nature ended in the apocalyptic negation of history itself: a cataclysmic world destruction and angelic new creation.

In this same period of the first millennium B.C., we find in classical philosophy a parallel development of the alienation of the individual from the world. Like the prophets, the philosophers repudiated the old nature Gods in their sexual forms of male and female divinities, and maleness was seen as bodiless and intellectual.

For Plato, the authentic soul is incarnated as a male, and only when it succumbs to the body is it reincarnated in the body of a female and then into the body of some beast resembling the evil character into which it has fallen. The salvation of the liberated consciousness repudiates heterosexual for masculine love and mounts to heaven in flight from the body and the visible world. The intellect is seen as an alien, lonely species that originates in a purely spiritual realm beyond time, space, and matter, and has been dropped, either as into a testing place or, through some fault, into this lower material world. But space and time, body and mutability are totally alien to its nature. The body drags the soul down, obscuring the clarity of its knowledge, debasing its moral integrity. Liberation is a flight from the earth to a changeless, infinite world beyond. Again we see the emergence of the liberated consciousness in a way that alienates it from nature in a body-fleeing, world-negating spirituality.

Christianity brought together both of these myths—the myth of world cataclysm and the myth of the flight of the soul to heaven. It also struggled to correct the more extreme implications of this body-negating spirituality with a more positive doctrine of creation and incarnation. It even reinstated, in covert form, the old myths of the year cult and the virgin–mother Goddess.

But the dominant spirituality of the Fathers of the Church finally accepted the antibody, antifeminine view of late antique religious culture. Recent proponents of ecology have, therefore, pointed the finger at Christianity as the originator of this debased view of nature, as the religious sanction for modern technological exploitation of the earth.

But Christianity did not originate this view. Rather, it appears to correspond to a stage of development of human consciousness that coincided with ripening classical civilization. Christianity took over this alienated world view of late classical civilization, but its oppressive dualities express the basic alienations at work in the psychosocial channelization of human energy since the breakup of the communal life of earlier tribal society.

What we see in this development is a one-sided expression of the ego, claiming its transcendental autonomy by negating the finite matrix of existence. This antithesis is projected socially by identifying woman as the incarnation of this debasing threat of bodily existence, while the same polarized model of the psyche is projected politically upon suppressed or conquered social groups.

The emphasis upon the transcendent consciousness has literally created the urban earth, and both abstract science and revolution are ultimate products of this will to transcend and dominate the natural and social world that gave birth to the rebellious spirit. The exclusively male God who creates out of nothing, transcending nature and dominating history, and upon whose all-powerful wrath and grace man hangs as a miserable, crestfallen sinner, is the theological self-image and guilty conscience of this self-infinitizing spirit.

Today we recognize that this theology of rebellion into infinity has its counterpart in a world-destroying spirituality that projects upon the female of the race all its abhorrence, hostility and fear of the bodily powers from which it has arisen and from which it wishes to be independent. One can feel this fear in the threatened, repressively hostile energy that is activated in the dominant male society at the mere suggestion of the emergence of the female on an equal plane—as though equality itself must inevitably mean *his* resubjugation to preconscious submersion in the womb.

This most basic duality characterizes much recent theology. Karl Barth, despite his model of cohumanity as the essence of the creational covenant, insists on the relation of super- and subordination between men and women as an ordained necessity of creation. "Crisis" and "secular" theologians such as Bultmann and Gogarten continually stress the transcendence of history over nature, defining the Gospel as the freedom of the liberated consciousness to depart endlessly from natural and historical foundations into the contentless desert of pure possibility. Such theologians are happy to baptize modern technology as the expression of the freedom mediated by the Gospel to transcend and dominate nature.

Today, both in the West and among insurgent Third World peoples, we are seeing a new intensification of this Western mode of abstractionism and revolution. Many are convinced that the problems created by man's ravaging of nature can be solved only by a great deal more technological manipulation. The oppressed peoples who have been the victims of the domination of the elite classes now seek to follow much the same path of pride, transcending wrath, separatism and power in order to share in the benefits of independence and technological power already won by the dominant classes.

Yet, at the same time, nature and society are giving clear warning signals that the usefulness of this spirituality is about to end. Two revolutions are running in contrapuntal directions. The alienated members of the dominant society are seeking new communal, egalitarian life-styles, ecological living patterns, and the redirection of psychic energy toward reconciliation with the body. But these human potential movements remain elitist, privatistic, esthetic and devoid of a profound covenant with the poor and oppressed of the earth.

On the other hand, the aspirations of insurgent peoples rise along the lines of the traditional rise of civilization through group pride, technological domination of nature and antagonistic, competitive relationships between peoples. Such tendencies might be deplored by those who have so far monopolized technology and now believe they have seen the end of its fruitfulness, but they must be recognized as still relevant to the liberation of the poor and oppressed from material necessity and psychological dependency.

We are now approaching the denouement of this dialectic. The ethic of competitiveness and technological mastery has created a world divided by penis-missiles and countermissiles that could destroy all humanity a hundred times over. Yet the ethic of reconciliation with the earth has yet to break out of its snug corners of affluence and find meaningful cohesion with the revolutions of insurgent peoples.

The significance of the women's revolution, then, may well be its unique location in the center of this clash between the contrapuntal directions of current liberation movements. Women are the first and oldest oppressed, subjugated people. They too must claim for themselves the human capacities of intellect, will, and autonomous creative consciousness that have been denied them through this psychosocial polarization in its most original form.

Yet woman have also been identified with nature, the earth, and the body in its despised and rejected form. To simply reject this identification would be to neglect that part of ourselves we have been left to cultivate and to buy into that very polarization of which we have been the primary victims. The significance of our movement will be lost if we merely seek valued masculine traits at the expense of devalued feminine ones.

Women must be the spokesmen for a new humanity arising out of the reconciliation of spirit and body. This does not mean selling short our rights to the powers of independent personhood. Autonomy, world-transcending spirit, separatism as the power of consciousness raising, and liberation from an untamed nature and from subjugation to the rocket-ship male—all these revolutions are still vital to women's achievement of integral personhood. But we have to look beyond our own liberation from oppression to the liberation of the oppressor as well. Women should not buy into the masculine ethic of competitiveness that sees the triumph of the self as predicated upon the subjugation of the other. Unlike men, women have traditionally cultivated a communal personhood that could participate in the successes of others rather than seeing these as merely a threat to one's own success.

To seek the liberation of women without losing this sense of communal personhood is the great challenge and secret power of the women's revolution. Its only proper end must be the total abolition of the social pattern of domination and subjugation and the erection of a new communal social ethic. We need to build a new cooperative social order out beyond the principles of hierarchy, rule, and competitiveness.

Starting in the grass roots local units of human society where psychosocial polarization first began, we must create a living pattern of
mutuality between men and women, between parents and children,
among people in their social, economic, and political relationships and,
finally, between mankind and the organic harmonies of nature.

Such a revolution entails nothing less than a transformation of all
the social structures of civilization, particularly the relationship between work and play. It entails literally a global struggle to overthrow
and transform the character of power structures and points forward to
a new messianic epiphany that will as far transcend the world-rejecting
salvation myths of apocalypticism and Platonism as these myths
transcended the old nature myths of the neolithic village. Combining
the values of the world-transcending Yahweh with those of the world-
renewing Ba'al in a posttechnological religion of reconciliation with the
body, the woman and the world, its salvation myth will not be one of
divinization and flight from the body but of humanization and reconciliation with the earth.

Our model is neither the romanticized primitive jungle nor the
modern technological wasteland. Rather it expresses itself in a new
command to learn to cultivate the garden, for the cultivation of the
garden is where the powers of rational consciousness come together
with the harmonies of nature in partnership.

The new earth must be one where people are reconciled with their
labor, abolishing the alienation of the megamachine while inheriting its
productive power to free men for unalienated creativity. It will be a
world where people are reconciled to their own finitude, where the last
enemy, death, is conquered, not by a flight into eternity, but in that
spirit of St. Francis that greets "Brother Death" as a friend that
completes the proper cycle of the human soul.

The new humanity is not the will to power of a monolithic empire,
obliterating all other identities before the one identity of the master
race, but a polylinguistic appreciativeness that can redeem local space,
time, and identity. We seek to overcome the deadly Leviathan of the
Pentagon of Power, transforming its power into manna to feed the
hungry of the earth. The revolution of the feminine revolts against the
denatured Babel of concrete and steel that stifles the living soil. It does
not merely reject the spirit child born from the earth but seeks to
reclaim spirit for body and body for spirit in a messianic appearing of
the body of God.

After the Death of God the Father: Women's Liberation and the Transformation of Christian Consciousness

MARY DALY

The women's liberation movement has produced a deluge of books and articles. Their major task has been exposition and criticism of our male-centered heritage. In order to reveal and drive home to readers the oppressive character of our cultural institutions, it was necessary to do careful research, to trot out passages from leading philosophers, psychologists, statesmen, poets, historians, saints, and theologians which make the reader's hair stand on end by the blatancy of their misogynism. Part of the task also has been the tracing of the subtle psychological mechanisms by which society has held men up and women down. This method of exposition and analysis reached its crescendo within this past year when Kate Millet's *Sexual Politics*

Mary Daly holds a Ph.D. and Th.D. from the University of Fribourg, Switzerland, and teaches at Boston College. Author of *The Church and the Second Sex, Beyond God the Father,* and *Gyn/Ecology,* she is a noted feminist theorist. She has repudiated the Christian symbol system since writing this essay, which was originally published in *Commonweal* (March 12, 1971), and is reprinted with permission of Commonweal Publishing Co., Inc.

rocketed her into the role of American counterpart to Simone de Beauvoir.

As far as the level of creative research is concerned, that phase of the work is finished. The skeletons in our cultural closet have been hauled out for inspection. I do not mean to imply that there are not countless more of the same to be uncovered (just the other day I noticed for the first time that Berdyaev blandly affirms there is "something base and sinister in the female element." Etcetera). Nor do I mean that the task of communicating the message is over. Millions have yet to hear the news, let alone to grasp its import. Certainly it would be a mistake and a betrayal to trivialize the fact that our culture is so diseased. That has always been a major tactic in the fine art of suppressing the rage of women. No, what I am saying is that Phase One of critical research and writing in the movement has opened the way for the logical next step in creative thinking. We now have to ask how the women's revolution can and should change our whole vision of reality. What I intend to do here is to sketch some of the ways in which it can influence Western religious thoughts.

The Judaic-Christian tradition has served to legitimate sexually imbalanced patriarchal society. Thus, for example, the image of the Father God, spawned in the human imagination and sustained as plausible by patriarchy, has in turn rendered service to this type of society by making its mechanisms for the oppression of women appear right and fitting. If God in "his" heaven is a father ruling "his" people, then it is in the "nature" of things and according to divine plan and the order of the universe that society be male dominated. Theologian Karl Barth found it appropriate to write that woman is "ontologically" subordinate to man. Within this context, a mystification of roles takes place: the husband dominating his wife represents God himself. What is happening, of course, is the familiar mechanism by which the images and values of a given society are projected into a realm of beliefs, which in turn justify the social infrastructure. The belief system becomes hardened and objectified, seeming to have an unchangeable independent existence and validity of its own. It resists social change which would rob it of its plausibility. Nevertheless, despite the vicious circle, change does occur in society, and ideologies die, though they die hard.

As the women's revolution begins to have its effect upon the fabric of society, transforming it from patriarchy into something that never existed before—into a diarchal situation that is radically new—it will, I believe, become the greatest single potential challenge to Christianity to rid itself of its oppressive tendencies or go out of business. Beliefs and values that have held sway for thousands of years will be questioned as never before. It is also very possibly the greatest single hope for survival of religious consciousness in the West.

At this point, it is important to consider the objection that the liberation of women will only mean that new characters will assume the same old roles, but that nothing will change essentially in regard to structure, ideology, or values. This objection is often based upon the observation that the very few women in "masculine" occupations seem to behave very much as men do. This is really not to the point for it fails to recognize that the effect of tokenism is not to change stereotypes or social systems but to preserve these. What I am discussing here is an emergence of women such as has never taken place before. It is naive to assume that the coming of women into equal power in society generally and in the church in particular will simply mean uncritical acceptance of values formerly given priority by men. Rather, I suggest that it will be a catalyst for transformation of our culture.

The roles and structures of patriarchy have been developed and sustained in accordance with an artificial polarization of human qualities into the traditional sexual stereotypes. The image of the person in authority and the accepted understanding of "his" role have corresponded to the eternal masculine stereotype, which implies hyper-rationality, "objectivity," aggressivity, the possession of dominating and manipulative attitudes toward persons and environment, and the tendency to construct boundaries between the self (and those identified with the self) and "the other." The caricature of a human being which is represented by this stereotype depends for its existence upon the opposite caricature—the eternal feminine (hyperemotional, passive, self-abasing, etc.). By becoming whole persons, women can generate a counterforce to the stereotype of the leader as they challenge the artificial polarization of human characteristics. There is no reason to assume that women who have the support of their sisters to criticize the masculine stereotype will simply adopt it as a model for themselves. More likely they will develop a wider range of qualities and skills in themselves and thereby encourage men to engage in a comparably liberating procedure (a phenomenon we are beginning to witness already in men's liberation groups). This becoming of *whole* human beings will affect the values of our society, for it will involve a change in the fabric of human consciousness.

Accordingly, it is reasonable to anticipate that this change will affect the symbols which reflect the values of our society, including religious symbols. Since some of these have functioned to justify oppression, women and men would do well to welcome this change. Religious symbols die when the cultural situation that supported them ceases to give them plausibility. This should pose no problem to authentic faith, which accepts the relativity of all symbols and recognizes that fixation upon any of them as absolute in itself is idolatrous.

The becoming of new symbols is not a matter that can arbitrarily be decided around a conference table. Rather, they grow out of a changing communal situation and experience. This does not mean that theologically we are consigned to the role of passive spectators. We are called upon to be attentive to what the new experience of the becoming of women is revealing to us, and to foster the evolution of consciousness beyond the oppressiveness and imbalance reflected and justified by symbols and doctrines throughout the millennia of patriarchy.

This imbalance is apparent first of all in the biblical and popular image of the great patriarch in heaven who rewards and punishes according to his mysterious and arbitrary will. The fact that the effects of this image have not always been humanizing is evident to any perceptive reader of history. The often cruel behavior of Christians toward unbelievers and even toward dissenters among themselves is shocking evidence of the function of that image in relation to values and behavior.

Sophisticated thinkers, of course, have never intellectually identified God with an elderly parent in heaven. Nevertheless it is important to recognize that, even when very abstract conceptualizations of God are formulated in the mind, images have a way of surviving in the imagination in such a way that a person can function on two different and even apparently contradictory levels at the same time. Thus one can speak of God as spirit and at the same time imagine "him" as belonging to the male sex. Such primitive images can profoundly affect conceptualizations which appear to be very refined and abstract. Even the Yahweh of the future, so cherished by the theology of hope, comes through on an imaginative level as exclusively a He-God, and it is perhaps consistent with this that theologians of hope have attempted to develop a political theology which takes no explicit cognizance of the devastation wrought by sexual politics.

The widespread conception of the "Supreme Being" as an entity distinct from this world but controlling it according to plan and keeping human beings in a state of infantile subjection has been a not too subtle mask of the divine patriarch. The Supreme Being's plausibility, and that of the static world view which accompanies this projection, has, of course, declined. This was a projection grounded in specifically patriarchal infrastructures and sustained as subjectively real by the usual processes of generating plausibility. The sustaining power of the social infrastructures has been eroded by a number of developments in recent history, including the general trend toward democratization of society and the emergence of technology with the accompanying sense of mastery over the world and man's destiny. However, it is the women's movement which appears destined to play the key role in the overthrow of such oppressive elements in traditional theism, precisely because it strikes at the source of the imbalance reflected in traditional beliefs.

The women's movement will present a growing threat to patriarchal religion less by attacking it than by simply leaving it behind. Few of the leaders in the movement evince an interest in institutional religion, having recognized it as an instrument of their betrayal. Those who see their commitment to the movement as consonant with concern for the religious heritage are aware that the Christian tradition is by no means bereft of elements which foster genuine experiences and intimations of transcendence. The problem is that their liberating potential is choked off in the surrounding atmosphere of the images, ideas, values, and structures of patriarchy. What will, I think, become possible through the social change coming from radical feminism is a more acute and widespread perception of qualitative differences between those conceptualizations of God and of the human relationship to God which are oppressive in their implications and those which encourage self-actualization and social commitment.

The various theologies that hypostatize transcendence invariably use this "God" to legitimate oppression, particularly that of women. These are irredeemably antifeminine and therefore antihuman. In contrast to this, a more authentic language of transcendence does not hypostatize or objectify God and consequently does not lend itself to such use. So, for example, Tillich's way of speaking about God as ground and power of being would be very difficult to use for the legitimation of any sort of oppression. It grows out of awareness of that reality which is both transcendent and immanent, not reducible to or adequately represented by such expressions as *person, father, supreme being.* Awareness of this reality is not achieved by playing theological games but by existential courage. I am not saying that a liberated consciousness necessarily will use Tillich's language of transcendence. That of Whitehead, James, Jaspers, to mention a few—or an entirely new language—may do as well or better. But it remains true that the driving revelatory force which will make possible an authenticity of religious consciousness is courage in the face of anxiety.

Since the projections of patriarchal religion have been blocking the dynamics of existential courage by offering the false security of alienation—that is, of self-reduction to stereotyped roles—there is reason to see hope for the emergence of genuine religious consciousness in the massive challenge to patriarchy which is now in its initial stages. The becoming of women may be not only the doorway to deliverance from the omnipotent Father in all of his disguises—a deliverance which secular humanism has passionately fought for—but also a doorway to something; that is, the beginning for many of a more authentic search for transcendence; that is, for God.

The imbalance in Christian ideology resulting from sexual hierarchy is manifested not only in the doctrine of God but also in the notion of Jesus as the unique God-man. A great deal of Christian doctrine concerning Jesus has been docetic; that is, it has not really seriously accepted the fact that Jesus was a human being. An effect of the liberation of women will very likely be the loss of plausibility of Christological formulas which come close to reflecting a kind of idolatry in regard to the person of Jesus. As it becomes better understood that God is transcendent and unobjectifiable—or else not at all—it will become less plausible to speak of Jesus as the Second Person of the Trinity who "assumed" a human nature. Indeed, the prevalent emphasis upon the total uniqueness and supereminence of Jesus will, I think, become less meaningful. To say this is not at all to deny his extraordinary character and mission. The point is to attempt a realistic assessment of certain ways of using his image (which in all likelihood he himself would repudiate). It is still not uncommon for priests and ministers, when confronted with the issue of women's liberation, to assert that God become incarnate uniquely as a male, and then to draw arguments for male supremacy from this. Indeed, the tradition itself tends to justify such assertions. The underlying—and often explicit—assumption in the minds of theologians down through the centuries has been that the divinity could not have deigned to become incarnate in the "inferior" sex, and the "fact" that "he" did not do so reinforces the belief in masculine superiority. The transformation of society by the erosion of male dominance will generate serious challenges to such assumptions of the Christological tradition.

It will, I think, become increasingly evident that exclusively masculine symbols for the ideal of "incarnation" will not do. As a uniquely masculine divinity loses credibility, so also the idea of a unique divine incarnation in a human being of the male sex may give way in the religious consciousness to an increased awareness of the divine presence in all human beings, understood as expressing and in a real sense incarnating—although always inadequately—the power of being. The seeds of this awareness are already present, of course, in the traditional doctrine that all human beings are made to the image of God and in a less than adequate way in the doctrine of grace. Now it should become possible to work out with increasing realism the implication in both of these doctrines that human beings are called to self-actualization and to the creation of a community that fosters the becoming of women and men. This means that no completely adequate models can be taken from the past. It may be that we will witness a remythologizing of Western religion. Certainly, if the need for parental symbols for God persists, something like the Father-Mother God proposed by Mary Baker Eddy will be more acceptable to the new woman and the new man than the Father God of the past. A symbolism for incarnation of the divine in human beings may continue to be needed in the future, but it is highly unlikely that women or men will continue to find plausible that symbolism which is epitomized in the image of the Virgin kneeling in adoration before her own son. Perhaps this will be replaced by the emergence of bisexual imagery which is not hierarchical. The experience of the past brought forth a new Adam and a new Eve. Perhaps the future will bring a new Christ and a new Mary. For the present, it would appear that we are being called upon to recognize the poverty of all symbols and the fact of our past idolatry regarding them, and to turn to our own resources for bringing about the radically new in our own lives.

The manifestation of God in Jesus was an eschatological event whose fulfilled reality lies in the future. The Jesus of the Gospels was a free person who challenged ossified beliefs and laws. Since he was remarkably free of prejudice against women and treated them as equals insofar as the limitations of his culture would allow, it is certain that he would be working with them for their liberation today. This awakening of women to their human potentiality by creative action as they assume equal partnership with men in society can bring about a manifestation of God in themselves which will be the Second Coming of God incarnate, fulfilling the latent promise in the original revelation that men and women are made to the image of God.

BEHIND THE MASK

It should be evident, then, that women's liberation is an event that can challenge authoritarian, exclusive, and nonexistential notions of faith and revelation. Since women have been extraenvironmentals, to use a McLuhanish term; that is, since they have not been part of the authority structure which uses "faith" and "revelation" to reinforce the mechanisms of alienation, their emergence can effect a more widespread criticalness of idolatry which is often masked by these ideas. There could result from this a more general understanding of faith as a state of ultimate concern and commitment and a heightened sense of relativity concerning the symbols it uses to express this commitment. An awareness might also emerge—not merely in the minds of a theological elite, but in the general consciousness—that revelation is an ongoing experience.

The becoming of women implies also a transvaluation of values in Christian morality. As the old order is challenged and as men and women become freed to experience a wholeness of personality which the old polarizations impeded, the potentiality will be awakened for a change in moral consciousness which will go far beyond Nietzsche's merely reactionary rejection of Christian values.

Much of the traditional theory of Christian virtue appears to be the product of reactions on the part of men—perhaps guilty reactions—to the behavioral excesses of the stereotypic male. There has been theoretical emphasis upon charity, meekness, obedience, humility, self-abnegation, sacrifice, service. Part of the problem with this moral ideology is that it became generally accepted not by men but by women, who have hardly been helped by an ethic which reinforced their abject situation. This emphasis upon the passive virtues, of course, has not challenged exploitativeness but supported it. Part of the syndrome is the prevailing notion of sin as an offense against those in power, or against "God" (the two are often equated). Within the perspective of such a privatized morality, the structures themselves of oppression are not seen as sinful.

Consistent with all of this is the fact that the traditional Christian moral consciousness has been fixated upon the problems of reproductive activity in a manner totally disproportionate to its feeble political concern. This was summed up several years ago in Archbishop Roberts' remark that "if contraceptives had been dropped over Japan instead of bombs which merely killed, maimed, and shriveled up thousands alive there would have been a squeal of outraged protest from the Vatican to the remotest Mass center in Asia." Pertinent also is Simone de Beauvoir's remark that the church has reserved its uncompromising humanitarianism for man in the fetal condition. Although theologians today acknowledge that this privatized morality has failed to cope with the structures of oppression, few seriously face the possibility that the roots of this distortion are deeply buried in the fundamental and all-pervasive sexual alienation which the women's movement is seeking to overcome.

It is well known that Christians under the spell of the jealous God who represents the collective power of his chosen people can use religion to justify that "us and them" attitude which is disastrous in its consequences for the powerless. It is less widely understood that the projection of "the other"—easily adaptable to national, racial and class differences—has basically and primordially been directed against women. Even the rhetoric of racism finds its model in sexism.

The consciousness raising which is beginning among women is evoking a qualitatively new understanding of the subtle mechanisms which produce and destroy "the other," and a consequent empathy with all of the oppressed. This gives grounds for the hope that their emergence can generate a counterforce to the exploitative mentality which is destroying persons and the environment. Since the way men and women are seen in society is a prime determinant in the whole social system and ideology, radical women refuse to see their movement as simply one among others. What I am suggesting is that it might be the only chance for the turning of human beings from a course leading to the deterioration and perhaps the end of life on this planet.

Those who see their concern for women's liberation as consonant with an evolving Christianity would be unrealistic to expect much comprehension from the majority of male ecclesiastics. Such writers as Gordon Rattrey Taylor (*The Biological Time Bomb*), Robert Francoeur (*Utopian Motherhood*), and others keep beeping out the message that we are moving into a world in which human sexuality is no longer merely oriented to reproduction of the species—which means that the masculine and feminine mystiques are doomed to evaporate. Within the theological community, however, the predictable and almost universal response has been what one might call the ostrich syndrome. Whereas the old theology justified sexual oppression, the new theology for the most part simply ignores it and goes on in comfortable compatibility with it, failing to recognize its deep connection with such other major problems as war, racism, and environmental pollution. The work of fostering religious consciousness which is explicitly incompatible with sexism will require an extraordinary degree of creative rage, love, and hope.

THE PAST: DOES IT HOLD
A FUTURE FOR WOMEN?

THE first three essays in this volume argue that Western religion is profoundly sexist. Its ideas and doctrines, images and symbols, are products of male perceptions of reality and have legitimated and reinforced the subordination of women. Defending these claims, numerous feminist scholars have described and evaluated the oppression of women by patriarchal religion. They have trotted out negative statements about women, examined destructive images, and carefully appraised the impact of religion on women's lives. Articulating and giving substance to the charge that religion is sexist has been the first job of feminist theology.

Now that this charge has been established, however—and certainly by now it has—feminist thinkers face a more difficult task: that of giving voice to the religious experience of women, which has been suppressed for several thousand years. This task is multifaceted. Scholars must explore the hidden history of women in religion, understand present women's experience, and show how women's experience may transform religious ideas, structures, and practice. The essays in this section concern the hidden history of women. Believing that the history of interpretation of religious texts and artifacts has been skewed to focus on "his" story, the story of men, scholars in this section focus on "her" story, the story of religion from women's perspective. They discover a positive herstory of women within and outside patriarchal religious traditions. In describing areas of Western religion that have been neglected or forgotten, they broaden our knowledge of feminine religious symbolism and of women's participation in religious tradition.

But these articles are not simply compensatory. They also force us to reevaluate the paradigms through which we understand the past. As Sheila Collins points out in "Reflection on the Meaning of Herstory," studying herstory is radicalizing. Herstory locates the center of historical interest precisely in those areas tradition has ignored. Seeking to reexamine or rediscover the past, herstory takes seriously material that has been declared unimportant, heretical, or altogether outside the canon. In doing so, it disrupts notions of tradition as unfolding organically or magically along a given path. It widens our vision of reality and alters our understanding of the nature of authority and tradition. Herstory forces us to see the development and interpretation of tradition as a series of human choices, which may be imaginatively revoked to yield both a new understanding of the history of women and of the historical process.

This does not mean that all herstory is antitraditional: the herstorian may reexamine tradition in order to preserve it. The articles reprinted here represent the range of herstorical writing along a spectrum from the reinterpretation of traditionally canonical materials to the exploration of traditions completely outside canonical bounds. Phyllis Trible and Elisabeth Fiorenza, arguing for the liberating potential of biblical faith, represent one end of this spectrum. The essential biblical message, they claim, is not the sanctity of patriarchy but the liberation of men and women to relatedness with God. For Trible, the universality of the biblical message of salvation means that it must be possible to read and translate the Bible in nonsexist terms. Studying Hebrew scripture without the blinders of centuries of patriarchal interpretation, one can discover numerous passages in it that point beyond the contradictions of a male-dominated society to an intuition of the fundamental equality of male and female. Even the story of Adam and Eve, traditionally interpreted to show the subordination of women and long a mainstay of arguments for female inferiority, can be read as supporting equality if one approaches it without sexist presuppositions. Such a reading is true to the fundamental *intentionality* of biblical faith, Trible claims, if not to the achievements of Hebrew society.

Fiorenza also feels that the Bible points beyond patriarchy, but it is the *practice* of New Testament society she finds liberating, not the *intentionality* of the New Testament text. The gospel writers, she says, lived in a patriarchal culture and selected from among many traditions about Jesus, those they found relevant and acceptable to the contemporary Christian community. They seem to have played down traditions concerning the ministry of women, and to this extent, their intention was patriarchal. But, when we consider how much of the herstory of early Christianity must be lost to us, those references to women that survive suggest that women played an exceptional role in the primitive church. Women were found among the followers of Jesus; they were the first witnesses to the resurrection; they were prophets, apostles, and full participants in the missionary work of the early Christian community. Their role becomes clearest to us, Fiorenza argues, when we do not simply reread the text—as Trible does—but take into account sexist editing by its authors.

The arguments of Trible and Fiorenza are simultaneously radical and conservative. They are radical in that they transform traditional interpretations of biblical texts for new feminist purposes but conservative in that they assume that, once we understand the true meaning of scripture or reality to which it points, we are bound to find this meaning, or reality, authoritative and normative. This stance allows for creative reform of tradition, but it ignores the gap between biblical and modern problems and perspectives. Because this gap motivates feminist readings of tradition in the first place, it would seem necessary to take it into account even while bridging it.

Eleanor McLaughlin also assumes Christian tradition is

authoritative, but only if the locus of tradition is broadened and revised. What interests her as a church historian is not the "old story" of the church powerful and glorious, speaking through councils, popes, and scholastic theologians, but the spirituality of the church, its inner experience of religious quest, vision, and prayer. She finds that in the Middle Ages, the spiritual or virgin life provided women with opportunities for wholeness, self-expression, and even authority, a kind of "virginal feminism," which sharply contrasted with their roles both in the church hierarchy and in patriarchal marriage. Excluding them from its bureaucracy, the church nevertheless empowered women to participate on an equal footing with men in the life of holiness and thus to bring to theology and prayer the language of their own experience. The literature of medieval spirituality actually includes significant works by women. Defining spirituality as a central part of the Christian tradition therefore allows McLaughlin to move beyond the reinterpretation of what male biblical writers and theologians have said about women to an exploration of women's own religious experience.

The articles by Pagels and Stone widen the purview of herstory still further by turning to female images and roles in traditions beyond the pale of the Jewish and Christian canons. Thus Pagels focuses on gnostic "heresy" and finds in certain gnostic texts rejected by the early church an understanding of God and humanity quite at variance with the orthodox Christian position. Images of God as both male and female, Father and Mother, Source and Silence, were correlated for some gnostic Christians with a view of human nature as dyadic or androgynous, consisting of male and female components. Struck by the power of this imagery and its attendant understanding of humanity, and recognizing that these gnostics considered themselves Christians, Pagels is led to wonder what caused the church to repudiate them. One factor in an explanation, she argues, may be the gnostics' derivation of concrete social consequences from their conceptions of God and humanity. Much to the horror of certain orthodox thinkers, women played important roles in these "heretical" groups—teaching, healing, baptizing, prophesying, and even acting as bishops. Pagels suggests that the orthodox rejection of gnosticism may in part have represented a rejection of the prominence of women and female symbolism in gnostic communities. If she is correct, then the subordination of women and female symbolism in mainstream Christianity cannot be excused as a natural outgrowth of patriarchal society but must be seen as the result of a complex, at least partly conscious, political process in which men consolidated their power within the church.

The issue of the suppression of female power and symbolism suggested by the gnostic materials is raised more sharply by the demise of Goddess worship—which once was, Stone suggests, a nearly universal phenomenon. In prehistoric and early historic sanctuaries and dwellings, in cultures in all parts of the globe, female deities were adored as healers and warriors, purveyors of wisdom and creators of the earth. The ancient Near East was no exception. Behind the biblical polemic against "abominations of the Canaanites," one discovers the Great Goddess who flourished and ruled for thousands of years before the Hebrews settled in the area. The connection between female symbolism and female religious and social leadership remains speculative. The earliest Goddess-worshipping peoples left no written records. The data on primitive matriarchies are controversial, and Stone avoids using the term matriarchy. But—Stone argues in the book from which this excerpt comes—much evidence suggests that women held more power and prestige in the Goddess-worshipping cultures of the ancient Near East than they did in the Hebrew culture that is the basis of Judaism and Christianity. The suppression of "idolatry" in biblical traditions meant, perhaps intentionally, the suppression of female imagery and authority. Like Pagels, Stone suggests that, as herstorians look not only within tradition but delve behind and under it, they will discover images of female power very different from those offered by patriarchal religion. Whether or not these images are directly appropriable, they perform the crucial herstorical task of expanding our sense of both female and religious possibilities.

Reflections on the Meaning of Herstory

SHEILA COLLINS

"History, therefore, is nothing but a compilation of the
depositions made by assassins with respect to their victims and
themselves."

—SIMONE WEIL[1]

History, Simone Weil pointed out in *The Need for Roots,* has always
been written by the conquerors. To the extent that history represents
the world view and value system of those who have "won," it is to that
extent a distortion of the totality of reality systems which could be
extant at any period of time. . . .

Women's herstory seeks to open up to purview the vast panorama of
human experience, so that reality systems may be seen in their
relationship to one another. Just as colors assume differing hues
depending on the colors they are surrounded by, so Judeo-Christian
history and its authority systems take on a different gestalt when
juxtaposed with the world view they sought to extinguish.

The development of herstory involves the ability to see through the

Sheila Collins received her M.A. from Columbia University, has taught at Union
Theological Seminary, Pacific School of Religion, and New York Theological Seminary,
and is currently Director of United Methodist Voluntary Services in New York. She has
been active in the women's movement, the peace movement, and in Southern Africa
solidarity work. Her articles on women and religion, class, and social ethics have
appeared in *Christianity and Crisis* and *Cross Currents;* her poetry is anthologized in
Half a Winter to Go. This essay is abridged from her book *A Different Heaven and
Earth,* © 1974 by Judson Press, and is reprinted by permission of Judson Press.

cracks of the present reality system or "world construction," to use Peter Berger's term, to distinguish the outlines of another. During the course of his apprenticeship to Don Juan, Carlos Castaneda (in *The Teachings of Don Juan, A Separate Reality*) is asked by the old Indian sorcerer to concentrate on the interstices between the leaves of a tree, rather than on the leaves. When he does this, the spaces themselves assume an objectivity, a reality they hadn't had for him previously. Herstory is somewhat like the space between the leaves; it is the forest which could not be seen by patriarchal historians because they had been concentrating so hard on the trees.

What happens when we begin to crack the prevailing reality system to discover new layers beneath and around it? . . . Certain affirmations can be made and certain inferences can be drawn.

The first affirmation is that the imperialism of the historical event as the authority for faith has been broken. Herstory relativizes history as it points to the fallibility of men and institutions to report accurately and fully on the events in which they are immersed. Herstory focuses light on the hidden assumptions and agreements, the disguised structure of language and emotion, and the cultural biases and accretions which determine the telling of patriarchal history. By the same token, herstory realizes its own agreements and assumptions but declares these at the outset, so that at least it cannot be accused of being devious.

In relativizing history, herstory undermines the authority of biblical revelation to be the exclusive channel of truth. It shows that the rise of monotheism and the development of what has been lauded as the "ethical impulse" in religious history were not won without great sacrifice; namely, the rejection of the body as a vehicle for the sacred, the subjugation of women and like "others" whose experience did not fit the right categories, and the rape of the earth.

The herstorian recognizes and affirms the noble impulse, the thrust of promise and fulfillment which lies behind the biblical epic, but laments some of the ways in which this impulse was translated. She is therefore not likely to find in particular biblical passages, events, or people that completeness of intent that the tradition claims for itself, but looks before, behind, beyond, and even outside the tradition as well as at it for her affirmation. . . .

Once the imperialism of the historical event has been relativized, the feminist herstorian is free to choose from the tradition those points of insight and affirmation which speak most forcefully to her own experience and that of her sisters. She is also freed to explore the rich heritage of myth and symbol—both biblical and extrabiblical—and to allow it to speak to her, rather than accepting an interpretation of it as given by Scripture or authority. . . .

As the herstory of women relativizes the imperialism of history as fact, event, or narrative, it also widens the historical lens. That is, it establishes a more inclusive range and depth of meanings which human societies have elaborated and which can have transforming power for us. In order to develop a comprehensive anthropology of *homo religiosus,* we cannot simply begin with the revelation of Yahweh to the Israelites because that "revelation" was predicated on the debasement of woman and of the natural world. As Christian and Jewish women, we have participated in that definition of ourselves at the expense of our *selves.* We have become our own oppressors.

We must begin, then, as far back as artifact, myth, legend, and unconscious memory will take us in order to understand ourselves fully as religious beings; and we must look seriously at those religious impulses which lay outside the boundaries defined by the Judeo-Christian tradition.

Some exciting things begin to happen when we dare to go beyond the stated boundaries in order to discover more of ourselves. First, the exclusivity of the linear view of history dissolves, and other paradigms begin to assume an ontological and existential importance for us; for example, the cyclical view of history becomes once again a possibility. When the historical lens is widened, we realize how fallible the Western linear view of history has been. No longer can history be conceived as a progressively upward movement from savagery and ignorance toward civilization and enlightenment. We see it as a much more complex and convoluted process. Whether or not one assigns one age to a higher rank than another depends upon the particular world view one holds. In questioning the value assumptions undergirding the Western theological–historical tradition, women also question the place assigned to certain events and movements on the scale of historical justice.

Who can say, for example, that the "pagans" were more ignorant or more savage than the Israelites? Yet it is precisely this assumption which forms the silent agreements upon which Christian theology rests. When the role, condition, and freedom of women is weighed in the balance, we would probably have to assign the pagans a more enlightened position than the postexilic Hebrews or the medieval Christian church. Likewise, on what basis do we assign the "Old Religion"—the witch cults of the peasant masses of medieval times—to a place of ignominy in the pageant of history while exonerating the efforts of the Christian church to stamp out this aberrant movement? Some claim that the attitude toward the natural world which is expressed in Genesis 1 (man is to "subdue" the earth) is "better" than the reverence for life which was expressed in the lamentations of Ishtar or in the mysteries at Eleusis. Idolatry, then, exists in the eyes of the critical beholder, rather than in the eyes of the worshiper. Were the images constructed by the Judeo-Christian church—"God, the Father," the untainted virgin, the all-sacrificing mother, Jesus, the "Logos"—any less subject to idolatrous use than the figures of Astarte, Ishtar, and Demeter through whom the forces of mystery, transcendence, and the organic unity of life were mediated for the pagans?

Without being fully conscious of it, women today are recovering or rediscovering the pre-Judeo-Christian understanding of themselves as women. The interest in exploring our own bodies and our sexuality frankly and openly, the decision by many women to have children regardless of whether they are married, the fierce insistence on defining ourselves in ourselves and not simply in relation to men, and the deep empathy for the organic world which I see among many feminists today all have their echoes in the ancient matriarchal world view. In addition, there is a self-conscious exploration into ancient myth, symbol, and archetype going on among feminist artists, writers, psychologists, and theologians. In their experience the ancient mother Goddesses are being resurrected and are demonstrating that their transformative and integrative powers are equal to that of the Christian Christ.

There is at work among women today a powerful religious force which cannot be fully explained in Christian terminology. It is inadequate to say that women want to return to the ancient world view. Such a desire would be both stupid and impractical. But there is a sense in which we are beginning to understand and incorporate the deep psychic meanings which that world view expressed and which have been continually suppressed in Western culture, in order to go on to a new synthesis. Women today are able to incorporate these meanings with a self-consciousness which the ancients did not possess, immersed as they were in a struggle for survival.

Thus, we are involved in a kind of cyclical return to our origins and are going beyond them to a new understanding of future possibility. The paradigm which expresses this process is more like that of a sprung spring than an enclosed circle, for we never simply return to the beginning as it was. We incorporate that beginning from the vantage point of greater understanding, which then allows us to go on to incorporate ever larger meanings. A diagram of the paradigm might look something like this:

Each intersection of lines is thus the beginning and end of one circle or loop and the beginning of still another. . . .

Another paradigm for the historical process, which is made possible by a consideration of herstory, is that of radical discontinuity. This paradigm presents more problems for us in light of the evidence pointing to the efficacy of the cyclic or sprung spring paradigm, but there is some justification for being open to this possibility. Elizabeth Gould Davis's speculations lead to a consideration of this possibility. Based on the assumptions of Immanuel Velikovsky that somewhere around the tenth millennium B.C. a worldwide shifting of the poles occurred, Ms. Davis speculates that the mythical kingdom of Atlantis, the race of Amazons, the mysterious knowledge of the Druids, the inexplicable existence of stone monoliths around the world, and the early evidence of belief in a mother Goddess all point to the preexistence of an advanced technological civilization ruled by women—a civilization which was eventually destroyed by the world cataclysms which myth and recent archaeological discoveries record.[2] There is also a sense in which the technological breakthroughs in the biomedical field which have been made in the last few years present us with the possibility of a truly radical future, as radical as the patriarchal age must have been from the matriarchal. The development of cloning, test-tube babies, genetic manipulation, and the like presages a totally different kind of human animal and community. Radical discontinuity is indeed a possibility.

Since feminist women have least to lose from a break with the old system, we are more open to a radically discontinuous future. The question we must ask ourselves is "Will we allow this future to overtake us, as we allowed the patriarchal revolution, or will we have some voice in its direction?"...

NOTES

1. Simone Weil, *The Need for Roots,* trans. Arthur Wills (New York: Harper & Row, 1971), p. 225.
2. See Elizabeth Gould Davis, *The First Sex* (New York: Putnam, 1971), pp. 22, 48–59, 93.

Eve and Adam:
Genesis 2-3 Reread

PHYLLIS TRIBLE

On the whole, the Women's Liberation Movement is hostile to the Bible, even as it claims that the Bible is hostile to women. The Yahwist account of creation and fall in Genesis 2-3 provides a strong proof text for that claim. Accepting centuries of (male) exegesis, many feminists interpret this story as legitimating male supremacy and female subordination.[1] They read to reject. My suggestion is that we reread to understand and to appropriate. Ambiguity characterizes the meaning of 'adham in Genesis 2-3. On the one hand, man is the first creature formed (2:7). The Lord God puts him in the garden "to till it and keep it," a job identified with the male (cf. 3:17-19). On the other hand, 'adham is a generic term for humankind. In commanding 'adham not to eat of the tree of the knowledge of good and evil, the Deity is speaking to both the man and the woman (2:16-17). Until the differentiation of female and male (2:21-23), 'adham is basically androgynous: one creature incorporating two sexes.

Concern for sexuality, specifically for the creation of woman, comes last in the story, after the making of the garden, the trees, and the

Phyllis Trible received her Ph.D. from Union Theological Seminary and Columbia University. She teaches at Andover Newton Theological School and is author of *God and the Rhetoric of Sexuality*. Her articles on feminism and biblical faith have appeared in *Soundings, Journal of the American Academy of Religion,* and *Religion in Life*. This essay is reprinted by permission from *Andover Newton Quarterly* 13 (March, 1973).

animals. Some commentators allege female subordination based on this order of events.[2] They contrast it with Genesis 1:27 where God creates *'adham* as male and female in one act.[3] Thereby they infer that whereas the Priests recognized the equality of the sexes, the Yahwist made woman a second, subordinate, inferior sex.[4] But the last may be first, as both the biblical theologian and the literary critic know. Thus the Yahwist account moves to its climax, not its decline, in the creation of woman.[5] She is not an afterthought; she is the culmination. Genesis 1 itself supports this interpretation, for there male and female are indeed the last and truly the crown of all creatures. The last is also first where beginnings and endings are parallel. In Hebrew literature, the central concerns of a unit often appear at the beginning and the end as an *inclusio* device.[6] Genesis 2 evinces this structure. The creation of man first and of woman last constitutes a ring composition whereby the two creatures are parallel. In no way does the order disparage woman. Content and context augment this reading.

The context for the advent of woman is a divine judgment: "It is not good that *'adham* should be alone; I will make him a helper fit for him" (2:18). The phrase needing explication is "helper fit for him." In the Old Testament the word *helper* (*'ezer*) has many usages. It can be a proper name for a male.[7] In our story, it describes the animals and the woman. In some passages, it characterizes Deity. God is the helper of Israel. As helper Yahweh creates and saves.[8] Thus *'ezer* is a relational term; it designates a beneficial relationship; and it pertains to God, people, and animals. By itself, the word does not specify positions within relationships; more particularly, it does not imply inferiority. Position results from additional content or from context. Accordingly, what kind of relationship does *'ezer* entail in Genesis 2:18, 20? Our answer comes in two ways: (1) The word *neged,* which joins *'ezer,* connotes equality: a helper who is a counterpart.[9] (2) The animals are helpers, but they fail to fit *'adham.* There is physical, perhaps psychic, rapport between *'adham* and the animals, for Yahweh forms (*yasar*) them both out of the ground (*'adhamah*). Yet their similarity is not equality. *'Adham* names them and thereby exercises power over them. No fit helper is among them. And thus the narrative moves to woman. . . . God is the helper superior to man; the animals are helpers inferior to man; woman is the helper equal to man.

Let us pursue the issue by examining the account of the creation of woman ([verses] 21–22). This episode concludes the story even as the creation of man commences it .... The ring composition suggests an interpretation of woman and man as equals. To establish this meaning, structure and content must mesh. They do. In both episodes, Yahweh alone creates. For the last creation the Lord God "caused a deep sleep (*tardemah*) to fall upon the man." Man has no part in making woman; he is out of it. He exercises no control over her existence. He is neither participant nor spectator nor consultant at her birth. Like man, woman owes her life solely to God. For both of them, the origin of life is a divine mystery. Another parallel of equality is creation out of raw materials: dust for man and a rib for woman. Yahweh chooses these fragile materials and in both cases processes them before human beings happen. As Yahweh shapes dust and then breathes into it to form man, so Yahweh takes out the rib and then builds it into woman.[10] To call woman "Adam's rib" is to misread the text, which states carefully and clearly that the extracted bone required divine labor to become female, a datum scarcely designed to bolster the male ego. Moreover, to claim that the rib means inferiority or subordination is to assign the man qualities over the woman which are not in the narrative itself. Superiority, strength, aggressiveness, dominance, and power do not characterize man in Genesis 2. By contrast, he is formed from dirt; his life hangs by a breath which he does not control; and he himself remains silent and passive while the Deity plans and interprets his existence.

The rib means solidarity and equality. *'Adham* recognizes this meaning in a poem:[11]

> This at last is bone of bones
>   and flesh of my flesh.
> She shall be called *'ishshah* [woman]
>   because she was taken out of *'ish* [man]. (2:23)

The pun proclaims both the similarity and the differentiation of female and male. Before this episode the Yahwist has used only the generic term *'adham*. No exclusively male reference has appeared. Only with the specific creation of woman (*'ishshah*) occurs the first specific terms for man as male (*'ish*). In other words, sexuality is simultaneous for woman and man. The sexes are interrelated and interdependent. Man as male does not precede woman as female but happens concurrently with her. Hence, the first act in Genesis 2 is the creation of androgyny (2:7), and the last is the creation of sexuality (2:23).[12] Male embodies

female, and female embodies male. The two are neither dichotomies
nor duplicates. The birth of woman corresponds to the birth of man
but does not copy it. Only in responding to the female does the man
discover himself as male. No longer a passive creature, *'ish* comes alive
in meeting *'ishshah.*

Some read into the poem a naming motif. The man names the
woman and thereby has power and authority over her.[13] But again
. . . reread. Neither the verb nor the noun *name* is in the poem. We
find instead the verb *qara'*, to call: "She shall be called woman." Now,
in the Yahwist primeval history this verb does not function as a
synonym or parallel or substitute for *name*. The typical formula for
naming is the verb *to call* plus the explicit object *name*. This formula
applies to Deity, people, places, and animals. For example, in Genesis
4 we read:

> Cain built a city and *called* the *name* of the city after the
> *name* of his son Enoch. (v. 17)
> And Adam knew his wife again, and she bore a son and
> *called* his *name* Seth. (v. 25)
> To Seth also a son was born and he *called* his *name*
> Enoch. (v. 26a)
> At that time men began to *call* upon the *name* of the Lord.
> (v. 26b)

Genesis 2:23 has the verb *call* but does not have the object *name*. Its
absence signifies the absence of a naming motif in the poem. The
presence of both the verb *call* and the noun *name* in the episode of the
animals strengthens the point:

So out of the ground the Lord God formed every beast of the field and every
bird of the air, and brought them to the man to see what he would *call* them;
and whatever the man *called* every living creature, that was its *name*. The man
gave *names* to all cattle, and to the birds of the air, and to every beast of the
field. (2:19-20)

In calling the animals by name, *'adham* establishes supremacy over
them and fails to find a fit helper. In calling woman, *'adham* does not
name her and does find in her a counterpart. Female and male are
equal sexes. Neither has authority over the other.[14]

A further observation secures the argument: *Woman* itself is not a
name. It is a common noun; it is not a proper noun. It designates
gender; it does not specify person. *'Adham* recognizes sexuality by the

words *'ishshah* and *'ish*. This recognition is not an act of naming to assert the power of male over female. Quite the contrary. But the true skeptic is already asking: What about Genesis 3:20, where "the man called his wife's name Eve"? We must wait to consider that question. Meanwhile, the words of the ancient poem as well as their context proclaim sexuality originating in the unity of *'adham*. From this one (androgynous) creature come two (female and male). The two return to their original unity as *'ish* and *'ishshah* become one flesh (2:24):[15] another instance of the ring composition.

Next the differences which spell harmony and equality yield to the differences of disobedience and disaster. The serpent speaks to the woman. Why to the woman and not to the man? The simplest answer is that we do not know. The Yahwist does not tell us anymore than he explains why the tree of the knowledge of good and evil was in the garden. But the silence of the text stimulates speculations, many of which only confirm the patriarchal mentality which conceived them. Cassuto identifies serpent and woman, maintaining that the cunning of the serpent is "in reality" the cunning of the woman.[16] He impugns her further by declaring that "for the very reason that a woman's imagination surpasses a man's, it was the woman who was enticed first." Though more gentle in his assessment, von Rad avers that "in the history of Yahweh religion, it has always been the women who have shown an inclination for obscure astrological cults" (a claim which he does not document).[17] Consequently, he holds that the woman "confronts the obscure allurements and mysteries that beset our limited life more directly than the man does," and then he calls her a "temptress." Paul Ricoeur says that woman "represents the point of weakness," as the entire story "gives evidence of a very masculine resentment." [18] McKenzie links the "moral weakness" of the woman with her "sexual attraction" and holds that the latter ruined both the woman and the man.[19]

But the narrative does not say any of these things. It does not sustain the judgment that woman is weaker or more cunning or more sexual than man. Both have the same Creator, who explicitly uses the word *good* to introduce the creation of woman (2:18). Both are equal in birth. There is complete rapport, physical, psychological, sociological, and theological, between them: bone of bone and flesh of flesh. If there be moral frailty in one, it is moral frailty in two. Further, they are equal in responsibility and in judgment, in shame and in guilt, in redemption and in grace. What the narrative says about the nature of woman it also says about the nature of man.

Why does the serpent speak to the woman and not to the man? Let a female speculate. If the serpent is "more subtle" than its fellow creatures, the woman is more appealing than her husband. Throughout the myth, she is the more intelligent one, the more aggressive one, and the one with greater sensibilities.[20] Perhaps the woman elevates the animal world by conversing theologically with the serpent. At any rate, she understands the hermeneutical task. In quoting God, she interprets the prohibition ("neither shall you touch it"). The woman is both theologian and translator. She contemplates the tree, taking into account all the possibilities. The tree is good for food; it satisfies the physical drives. It pleases the eyes; it is esthetically and emotionally desirable. Above all, it is coveted as the source of wisdom *(haskîl)*. Thus the woman is fully aware when she acts, her vision encompassing the gamut of life. She takes the fruit, and she eats. The initiative and the decision are hers alone. There is no consultation with her husband. She seeks neither his advice nor his permission. She acts independently.

By contrast, the man is a silent, passive, and bland recipient: "She also gave some to her husband, and he ate." The narrator makes no attempt to depict the husband as reluctant or hesitating. The man does not theologize; he does not contemplate; he does not envision the full possibilities of the occasion. His one act is belly oriented, and it is an act of quiescence, not of initiative. The man is not dominant; he is not aggressive; he is not a decision maker. Even though the prohibition not to eat of the tree appears before the female was specifically created, she knows that it applies to her. She has interpreted it, and now she struggles with the temptation to disobey. But not the man, to whom the prohibition came directly (2:16). He follows his wife without question or comment, thereby denying his own individuality. If the woman be intelligent, sensitive, and ingenious, the man is passive, brutish, and inept. These character portrayals are truly extraordinary in a culture dominated by men. I stress their contrast not to promote female chauvinism but to undercut patriarchal interpretations alien to the text.

The contrast between woman and man fades after their acts of disobedience. They are one in the new knowledge of their nakedness (3:7). They are one in hearing and in hiding. They flee from the sound of the Lord God in the Garden (3:8). First to the man come questions of responsibility (3:9, 11), but the man fails to be responsible: "The woman whom Thou gavest to be with me, she gave me fruit of the tree, and I ate" (3:12). Here the man does not blame the woman; he does not say that the woman seduced him;[21] he blames the Deity. The verb which he uses for both the Deity and the woman is *ntn* (cf. 3:6). . . . This verb neither means nor implies seduction in this context or in the lexicon. Again, if the Yahwist intended to make woman the temptress, he missed a choice opportunity. The woman's response supports the point. "The serpent beguiled me, and I ate" (3:13). Only here occurs the strong verb *nsh'*, meaning to deceive, to seduce. God accepts this subject-verb combination when, immediately following the woman's accusation, Yahweh says to the serpent, "Because you have done this, cursed are you above all animals" (3:14).

Though the tempter (the serpent) is cursed,[22] the woman and the man are not. But they are judged, and the judgments are commentaries on the disastrous effects of their shared disobedience. They show how terrible human life has become as it stands between creation and grace. We misread if we assume that these judgments are mandates. They describe; they do not prescribe. They protest; they do not condone. Of special concern are the words telling the woman that her husband shall rule over her (3:16). This statement is not license for male supremacy, but rather it is condemnation of that very pattern.[23] Subjugation and supremacy are perversions of creation. Through disobedience, the woman has become slave. Her initiative and her freedom vanish. The man is corrupted also, for he has become master, ruling over the one who is his God-given equal. The subordination of female to male signifies their shared sin.[24] This sin vitiates all relationships: between animals and human beings (3:15); mothers and children (3:16); husbands and wives (3:16); people and the soil (3:17–18); humanity and its work (3:19). Whereas in creation man and woman know harmony and equality, in sin they know alienation and discord. Grace makes possible a new beginning.

A further observation about these judgments: they are culturally conditioned. Husband and work (childbearing) define the woman; wife and work (farming) define the man. A literal reading of the story limits both creatures and limits the story. To be faithful translators, we must recognize that women as well as men move beyond these culturally defined roles, even as the intentionality and function of the myth move beyond its original setting. Whatever forms stereotyping takes in our own culture, they are judgments upon our common sin and disobedience. The suffering and oppression we women and men know now are marks of our fall, not of our creation.

At this place of sin and judgment, "the man calls his wife's name Eve" (3:20), thereby asserting his rule over her. The naming itself faults the man for corrupting a relationship of mutuality and equality. And so Yahweh evicts the primeval couple from the Garden, yet with signals of grace.[25] Interestingly, the conclusion of the story does not specify the sexes in flight. Instead the narrator resumes use of the generic and androgynous term *'adham* with which the story began and thereby completes an overall ring composition (3:22- 24).

Visiting the Garden of Eden in the days of the Women's Movement, we need no longer accept the traditional exegesis of Genesis 2-3. Rather than legitimating the patriarchal culture from which it comes, the myth places that culture under judgment. And thus it functions to liberate, not to enslave. This function we can recover and appropriate. The Yahwist narrative tells us who we are (creatures of equality and mutuality); it tells us who we have become (creatures of oppression); and so it opens possibilities for change, for a return to our true liberation under God. In other words, the story calls female and male to repent.

NOTES

1. *See inter alia,* Kate Millett, *Sexual Politics* (New York: Doubleday, 1970), pp. 51–54; Eva Figes, *Patriarchal Attitudes* (Greenwich, Conn.: Fawcett, 1970), pp. 38f; Mary Daly, "The Courage to See," *The Christian Century,* September 22, 1971, p. 1110; Sheila D. Collins, "Toward a Feminist Theology," *The Christian Century,* August 2, 1972, p. 798; Lilly Rivlin, "Lilith: The First Woman," *Ms.,* December 1972, pp. 93, 114.

2. Cf. E. Jacob, *Theology of the Old Testament* (New York: Harper & Bros., 1958), pp. 172f; S. H. Hooke, "Genesis," *Peake's Commentary on the Bible* (London: Thomas Nelson, 1962), p. 179.

3. E.g., Elizabeth Cady Stanton observed that Genesis 1:26–28 "dignifies woman as an important factor in the creation, equal in power and glory with man," while Genesis 2 "makes her a mere afterthought" *(The Woman's Bible,* Part I [New York: European Publishing Company, 1895], p. 20). See also Elsie Adams and Mary Louise Briscoe, *Up Against the Wall, Mother . . .* (Beverly Hills: Glencoe Press, 1971), p. 4.

4. Cf. Eugene H. Maly, "Genesis," *The Jerome Biblical Commentary* (Englewood Cliffs, N.J.: Prentice-Hall, 1968), p. 12: "But woman's existence, psychologically and in the social order, is dependent on man."

5. See John L. McKenzie, "The Literary Characteristics of Gen. 2-3," *Theological Studies,* Vol. 15 (1954), p. 559; John A. Bailey, "Initiation and the Primal Woman in Gilgamesh and Genesis 2-3," *Journal of Biblical Literature,* June 1970, p. 143. Bailey writes emphatically of the remarkable importance and position of the woman in Genesis 2-3, "all the more extraordinary when one realizes that this is the only account of the creation of woman as such in ancient Near Eastern literature." He hedges, however, in seeing the themes of helper and naming (Genesis 2:18-23) as indicative of a "certain subordination" of woman to man. These reservations are unnecessary; see below. Cf. also Claus Westermann, *Genesis, Biblischer Kommentar* ¼ (Neukerchener-Vluyn: Newkirchener Verlag, 1970), p. 312.

6. James Muilenburg, "Form Criticism and Beyond," *Journal of Biblical Literature,* March 1969, pp. 9f; Mitchell Dahood, "Psalm I," *The Anchor Bible* (New York: Doubleday, 1966), *passim* and esp. p. 5.

7. See 1 Chronicles 4:4; 12:9; Nehemiah 3:19.

8. See Psalm 121:2, 124:8; 146:5; 33:20; 115:9-11; Exodus 18:4; Deuteronomy 33:7, 26, 29.

9. L. Koehler and W. Baumgartner, *Lexicon in Veteris Testamenti Libros* (Leiden: E. J. Brill, 1958), pp. 591f.

10. The verb *bnh* (to build) suggests considerable labor. It is used of towns, towers, altars, and fortifications, as well as of the primeval woman (Koehler-Baumgartner, op. cit., p. 134). In Genesis 2:22, it may mean the fashioning of clay around the rib (Ruth Amiran, "Myths of the Creation of Man and the Jericho Statues," *BASOR,* No. 167 [October 1962], p. 24).

11. See Walter Brueggemann, "Of the Same Flesh and Bone (Gen. 2:23a)," *Catholic Biblical Quarterly,* October 1970, pp. 532-42.

12. In proposing as primary an androgynous interpretation of *'adham,* I find virtually no support from (male) biblical scholars. But my view stands as documented from the text, and I take refuge among a remnant of ancient (male) rabbis (see George Foot Moore, *Judaism* [Cambridge, Mass.: Harvard University Press, 1927]), I, 453; also Joseph Campbell, *The Hero with a Thousand Faces* (Meridian Books, The World Publishing Company, 1970), pp. 152ff., 279f.

13. See e.g., G. von Rad, *Genesis* (Philadelphia: Westminster Press, 1961), pp. 80-82; John H. Marks, "Genesis," *The Interpreter's One-Volume Commentary on the Bible* (Nashville: Abingdon Press, 1971), p. 5; Bailey, op. cit., p. 143.

14. Cf. Westermann, op. cit., pp. 316ff.

15. Verse 24 probably mirrors a matriarchal society (so Von Rad, op. cit., p. 83). If the myth were designed to support patriarchy, it is difficult to explain how this verse survived without proper alteration. Westermann contends, however, that an emphasis on matriarchy misunderstands the point of the verse, which is the total communion of woman and man (ibid., p. 317).

16. U. Cassuto, *A Commentary on the Book of Genesis,* Part I (Jerusalem: Magnes Press, n.d.), pp. 142f.

17. Von Rad, op. cit., pp. 87f.

18. Ricoeur departs from the traditional interpretation of the woman when he writes: *"Eve n'est donc pas la femme en tant que 'deuxieme sexe'; toute femme et tout homme sont Adam; tout homme et toute femme sont Eve."* But the fourth clause of his sentence obscures this complete identity of Adam and Eve: *"toute femme peche 'en Adam, tout homme est seduit 'en Eve."* By switching from an active to a passive verb, Ricoeur makes only the woman directly responsible for both sinning and seducing. (Paul Ricoeur, Finitude et Culpabilite, II. *La Symbolique du Mal,* Aubier, Editions Montaigne [Paris: 1960]. Cf. Paul Ricoeur, *The Symbolism of Evil* [Boston: Beacon Press, 1969], p. 255).

19. McKenzie, op. cit., p. 570.

20. See Bailey, op. cit., p. 148.

21. See Westermann, op. cit., p. 340.

22. For a discussion of the serpent, see Ricoeur, *The Symbolism of Evil,* op. cit., pp. 255– 60.

23. Cf. Edwin M. Good, *Irony in the Old Testament* (Philadelphia: Westminster Press, 1965), p. 84, note 4: "Is it not surprising that, in a culture where the subordination of woman to man was a virtually unquestioned social principle, the etiology of the subordination should be in the context of man's primal sin? Perhaps woman's subordination was not unquestioned in Israel." Cf. also Henricus Renckens, *Israel's Concept of the Beginning* (New York: Herder & Herder, 1964), pp. 127f.

24. *Contra* Westermann, op. cit., p. 357.

25. Von Rad, op. cit., pp. 94, 148.

Women in the Early Christian Movement

ELISABETH SCHÜSSLER FIORENZA

In the last century, one of the main arguments against the women's movement was derived from the Bible. Antifeminist preachers and writers maintained that the subjugation of women was divinely ordained and revealed in the Bible. Whenever women protested against political discrimination and civil degradation or whenever they argued against the inequality in the Church they were referred to the Bible: woman was made after man; she brought sin and death into the world; she has therefore to be dependent for everything on her husband. It is not possible for woman to achieve equality with man because this is against divine law and biblical revelation.

The objections against woman's equality were, however, not confined to the nineteenth century. Even today the Bible is still invoked by anti-ERA groups or fundamentalist preachers. The Catholic charismatic movement insists that the subordination of woman and the headship of man is divinely ordained in the New Testament. The appearance of Marabel Morgan's book *The Total Woman* gave the

Elisabeth Schüssler Fiorenza received her Th.D. from the University of Munster, Germany, and now teaches at Notre Dame University. Active in various Christian feminist groups, she has written several books on New Testament exegesis and feminist theology, including *Der Vergessene Partner, Priester für Gott,* and *The Apocalypse;* her articles have appeared in *Theological Studies, The Liberating Word,* and *Women Priests.* This essay was originally published in *New Catholic World* (November–December, 1976), under the title "Women in the New Testament," and is reprinted with permission.

debate new publicity. She claims not only that the subordination of women is revealed in the Bible but also that women can achieve happiness only if they live according to the biblical teachings on womanhood.

Those supporting the liberation of women also invoke the authority of the Bible. Throughout the centuries, the teaching of Galatians 3:28 that in Christ there is no longer Jew or Greek, slave or free, male or female represented the "magna charta" for the equality of women in the Christian community. In the last century as well as today, many claimed that the Bible teaches woman's equality....

Elizabeth Cady Stanton, one of the main leaders of the women's movement in the nineteenth century, proposed to scrutinize and list in a book all biblical passages that referred to women. She gathered a group of women, including three ordained ministers, in order to present an accurate account and feminist critique of women's role and image in the Bible. Stanton and her committee were not only concerned about the fact that the Bible was used against the women's movement but also about the fact that many women because of such teachings would abandon religious faith altogether.

One of the committee, Ursula Gestefeld, who was convinced that the Bible teaches the equality of men to women, spelled out the hermeneutic (from the Greek, meaning "interpretive") principle: "If the question is asked 'What is your authority for this view of the Bible?' the answer is 'I have none but the internal evidence of the book itself.' " Elizabeth Cady Stanton states in her introduction: "The Bible cannot be accepted or rejected as a whole; its teachings are varied and its lessons differ widely from each other." In maintaining verbal inspiration of all passages, the Church has made the Bible into a fetish. Each text should be read and accepted or rejected on its own merits. In response to the appearance of the *Woman's Bible* (1895 and 1898), Frances E. Willard spelled out one of the most decisive feminist insights: "I think that men have read their own selfish theories into the book, that theologians have not in the past sufficiently recognized the progressive quality of its revelation, nor adequately discriminated between its records as history and its principles of ethics and religion."

THE INTERPRETATION OF THE NEW TESTAMENT

The debate around the *Woman's Bible* has spelled out exegetical insights which are generally accepted in contemporary biblical interpretation. The discussion of the interpretation of historical texts has underlined that a value-free, objectivistic historiography is not possible. All interpretations of texts depend on the presuppositions, prejudices, and questions of those who attempt to exegete them. Since most biblical scholars and historians are men, they usually study and preach the New Testament from a male point of view. Scholars not only translate the New Testament texts into a masculinized language but also interpret them from a patriarchal perspective. Insofar as we single out "the place of women" in the Bible as a special problem, we reflect our own cultural perspective, which assumes that male existence is the standard expression of human existence and sees and defines "woman" always as the "other" in relation to men. In such a perspective, only the role of women becomes a special problem, whereas the role of men and the patriarchal, ecclesial, and sexist societal structures remain unexamined. In a play with words, feminist authors have therefore pointed out that history is rightly called "his story" recorded and interpreted from the point of view of cultural and religious male dominance. The interpretation of the New Testament texts and the reconstruction of the history of early Christianity suffer from such a one-sided perspective.

Scholars have amply demonstrated that the biblical authors did not intend to write a report of historical facticity or a history in the modern sense of "what actually happened" but that they, like all ancient writers, wanted to point out the meaning and importance of what had happened. They wrote, moreover, the Gospels, for the Christians of their own time, and addressed their questions and problems. They selected from the rich flow of traditions about Jesus those stories and sayings that appeared to be significant for their own faith and community. How they did this can be seen from the way that Matthew and Luke incorporated into their own Gospel accounts the Gospel of Mark. Since the New Testament authors selected traditional materials and sources from their own theological point of view, we must assume that many words and stories about Jesus and his first followers have been lost. Since the New Testament authors lived in a patriarchal culture, they attempted to make the Christian message acceptable to the Jews as well as the pagans of their time. We can see from the study of the Christian apologists or Fathers of the second century that because of their apologetic and missionary interests they played down the role of women in the Christian community in order not to be ridiculed as belonging to an effeminate religion. Finally the early Christian writers wrote against other Christian groups and directions, e.g., the Gnostics or Montanists, who accorded women a greater role in the life and preaching of the Christian community.

If we take into consideration all these circumstances influencing the New Testament authors, we can easily see that they transmit only a fraction of the possibly rich tradition on the role of women in the ministry of Jesus and in the earliest Christian communities. Most of the genuine Christian "herstory" is, therefore probably lost. We cannot reasonably expect to find extensive documentation for the role of women in early Christianity. The few, but remarkable, surviving traces have to be recaptured not only from the bias of contemporary interpreters but also sifted out from the patriarchal records of the New Testament authors themselves.

If we study the New Testament texts from such a perspective, we are astonished how much they tell us about the role of women in the early Church. Students or participants of Bible groups often have never heard of Mary Magdalene or Prisca and their role in the early Christian movement. If it is the first time that they hear of the role of women in the New Testament, they are genuinely surprised about the richness of the New Testament traditions about women.

THE JESUS MOVEMENT

Studies of the sociocultural conditions of the beginning Christian movement show that it cannot be justifiably argued that Jesus as a Jew of the first century could not have had women disciples. The circle of followers around Jesus did not belong to the establishment of their society or religion, but were a group of outsiders, since there were many sectarian groups in the Judaism of the time. The Jesus group did not accept the values and institutions of their Jewish society and milieu but often stood in opposition to them. Jesus and his disciples, for example, did not live an ascetic life-style like John the Baptist and his followers. The Jesus group rejected the religious purity laws and attracted the outcasts of their society as well as those who were for various reasons ostracized from their religious community. In distinction to the community at Qumran or the Pharisees, the Jesus movement in Palestine was not an exclusive but an inclusive group. Jesus did not call into his fellowship the righteous, pious, or highly influen-

tial persons of the community but invited those who did not belong—
tax collectors, sinners, and women. He promised God's Kingdom not to
the rich, the established, and the pious, but to the poor, the destitute,
and the prostitutes. This inclusive character of Jesus' message and
movement made it possible for women to become his disciples. All four
Gospels note that women were found in the fellowship of Jesus and
that they were the most courageous of all his disciples (cf. Mk. 14:60:
15:40f par.).

This inclusive character of the Jesus movement made it possible
later to invite Gentiles of all nations into the Christian community,
which transcended Jewish as well as Hellenistic cultural and religious
boundaries. In this new community, status distinctions were abolished,
and neither fixed structures nor institutionalized leadership was present. These Christians understood themselves as the eschatological
community and the representatives of the "new creation." They all had
received the Holy Spirit and all were empowered by the Spirit to
proclaim the great deeds of God in Jesus Christ. This witness of the
Christians, according to most of the New Testament writings, had to
be proved and verified through the "walking in the Spirit" or through
the praxis of agape love. "Love, joy, peace, patience, kindness, goodness, faithfulness, gentleness, self-control" (Gal. 5:25f) were not "feminine" virtues but the "fruits" of the new life in the Spirit.

THE BAPTISMAL CONFESSION

The new self-understanding of the early Christian movement is
expressed in Galatians 3:28. In the new, Spirit-filled community of
equals all distinctions of race, religion, class, and gender are abolished.
All are equal and one in Jesus Christ. Exegetes more and more agree
that Galatians 3:28 represents a pre-Pauline baptismal confession
which Paul quotes in Galatians to support his view that in the
Christian community any distinction between Jews and Gentiles is
eradicated. By reciting this baptismal formula, the newly initiated
Christians expressed their Christian self-understanding over and
against the societal-religious creeds of their surrounding Greco-Roman
culture. It was a well-known tenet of Hellenistic society that a man
had to be grateful that he was born a human being and not a beast, a
man and not a woman, a Hellene and not a barbarian. This Hellenistic
conviction was adopted by Judaism and found its way into the

synagogue liturgy. Three times daily an adult male Jew thanked God for not having made him a Gentile, a woman, or a slave. In the second century, Rabbi Judah comments that a Jew is thankful to be a man because as a male he has more opportunities to fulfill the divine commandments than a woman who was because of familial obligations exempted from many religious duties. Over and against this societal-religious pattern shared by Gentiles and Jews alike, the Christians affirmed at their baptism that all religious-patriarchal distinctions were abolished in Jesus Christ. It is important to note that Galatians 3:28 does not yet extol the same male standard, as later Gnostic writings do. Whereas according to various Gnostic texts a woman had to become "male" and "like men" in order to become a full disciple and elect Christian, Galatians 3:28 does not propose maleness as the form and standard of the new life in the Spirit. Since the terms "Jew and Greek" and "slave and free" imply the abolishment of social-religious distinctions in the Christian community, we can safely assume that the pair "male and female" are to be understood in the same social-religious sense. This new self-understanding of the Christian community allowed not only Gentiles and slaves to assume leadership in the Christian movement but also women. Women were not marginal figures in this community but exercised leadership as apostles, prophets, and missionaries.

WOMEN AS APOSTLES AND PROPHETS

The leadership of apostles was most decisive for the early Christian communities, as the controversies of Paul with his opponents indicate. Paul does not limit apostleship to the twelve, since he himself was not one of them. According to Paul all those Christians were apostles who fulfilled two conditions: they had to be (1) eyewitnesses to the resurrection and (2) commissioned by the resurrected Lord to missionary work (cf. 1 Cor. 9:4). Luke's requirements for apostleship are somewhat different. He maintains that only those Christians were eligible to replace Judas who had accompanied Jesus in his ministry and had also witnessed the resurrection (Acts 1:21). According to all four Gospels, women fulfilled these criteria of apostleship that Paul and Luke have spelled out. They accompanied Jesus from Galilee to Jerusalem, and they witnessed his death. Moreover, according to all criteria of historical authenticity women were the first witnesses of the resurrection. This fact could not have been imagined in Judaism or invented by the primitive Church. The opposite is true. All four Gospels attempt to downplay the fact of the women's witness, and Luke clearly excludes them, insofar he adds "maleness" as an additional qualification for apostleship. Since the Gospels do not leave these women anonymous but identify them by name, it is obvious that they must have played an important role in the Christian movement in Palestine. Their leader appears to have been Mary of Magdala. All four Gospels transmit her name, whereas the names of the other women vary. She has, moreover, a position equaling that of Peter in the apocryphal gospel literature. Thus, according to the Gospel traditions, women were the primary apostolic witnesses for the fundamental events of the early Christian preaching: they were witnesses of Jesus' ministry, his suffering and death, his burial and his resurrection. They were moreover, sent to proclaim the message of the resurrection.

An unbiased reading of Romans 16:7 provides us with one instance in the New Testament where a woman is called *apostle*. There is no valid reason to understand the name Junia as a short form of the male name Junianus, since Junia was a well-known name for women at the time. Andronicus and Junia are a missionary couple, like Aquila and Prisca. Both are fellow prisoners of Paul. They had been converted to Christianity before Paul and are outstanding figures among the "apostles."

Prophets played an eminent role within the early Christian community, for from the very beginning they functioned as inspired spokespersons of the resurrected Lord and their authority was seen as based on divine revelations. Not only does Paul repeatedly mention the prophets directly after the apostles but he even values the gift of prophecy higher than that of speaking in tongues. Despite the existence of false prophets, the prophets still had great authority in the community at the end of the first century, as Revelation and the Didache indicate.

Luke asserts that the Spirit of prophecy is given to women as well as to men (Acts 2:17f). He specificially mentions the four daughters of Philip as renowned Christian prophets (Acts 21:9). Paul takes it for granted that women prophesy and have liturgical functions: he just insists that they do it in a "proper way" (1 Cor. 11:2–16). We know from Revelation that at the end of the first century a woman was the head of a prophetic school in the community of Thyatira (Rv. 2:20ff).

We do not know her real name, because the author of Revelation called her only by the slanderous name "Jezebel." However, he could not deny that she still held great authority in the community and was not the head of a heretical group. It appears that her authority and fellowship was similar to that of the author of Revelation.

THE LEADERSHIP OF WOMEN IN THE EARLY CHRISTIAN MISSION

A survey of the scattered references to the participation of women in the early Christian missionary endeavor shows that the missionary work of women was equal to that of men like Barnabas, Apollos, or Paul. Women were among the wealthy and prominent converts (cf. Acts 17:4, 12). As patronesses, they exercised decisive influence on the missionary enterprise which was similar to that of Jewish or proselyte women in the religious propaganda of Judaism. Since they were baptized, often together with their whole household, it was common sense that they had the leadership in the house churches. In Philemon 2, Paul greets Apphia, "our sister," who together with Philemon and Archippus was a leader of the house church in Colossae. The church in Philippi began with the conversion of the businesswoman Lydia from Thyatira (Acts 16:14f). The author of Colossians refers to Nympha of Laodicea and "the church in her house" (Col. 4:15). Paul twice sends greetings to the missionary couple Prisca and Aquila and to "the church in their house" (1 Cor. 16:19: Rom. 16:5). He was compelled to write the first letter to the community at Corinth because of the inquiry of certain persons from the household of a woman Chloe (1 Cor. 1:11).

The missionary work of women was not initiated by Paul, but he attests that it was equal to his own. Paul commends Mary, Tryphena, Tryphosa, and Persis because they have "labored" hard in the Lord (Rom. 16:6, 12). Paul uses the same Greek verb that he usually employs to characterize his own missionary work, the evangelizing and teaching of others and of himself. In Philippians 4:2f., Paul explicitly states that Euodia and Syntyche have "contended" side by side with him. As in an athletic competition, women have contended with Paul, Clemens, and the rest of Paul's comissionaries in the cause of the Gospel. Paul considers the impact of both women on the community of Philippi so great that their dissensions might be a serious threat to the existence of this community. Romans 16 mentions two of the most prominent women in the Pauline churches. The first, Phoebe, receives the titles *diakonos* and *prostatis*. Exegetes take pains to downplay the significance of both titles because they are given to a woman. Whenever Paul uses the title *diakonos* for himself or another male leader, scholars translate it as "minister" or "deacon," whereas in the case of Phoebe they render it as "servant" or "deaconess." But 1 Corinthians 3:5, 9 proves that Paul uses the title as exchangeable with *synergos* (missionary coworker). As a comissionary with Paul, Phoebe receives, like other missionaries, a letter of recommendation. The second title of Phoebe, *prostatis,* is usually translated as "helper" or "patroness" even though in the literature of the time it has the connotation of leading officer, president, governor, or superintendent. The verb form of the noun is used in 1 Thessalonians 5:12 which admonishes the community to respect those "who labor among you and are over you in the Lord." In 1 Timothy 3:4–5; 5:17, the verb characterizes the functions of the bishop, deacons, or elders. Phoebe had, therefore, a leadership role in the community of Cenchreae and was a person with authority for many and for Paul as well.

Prisca, together with her husband Aquila, was a comissionary of Paul, Barnabas, Titus, or Apollos. Since her name is mentioned four times out of six before that of her husband, she must have been the leading figure. Paul calls the couple his coworkers and stresses that not only he but "all the churches of the Gentiles" give thanks to them. Their house was a missionary center in Corinth (1 Cor. 16:19), Ephesus (Acts 18:18), and Rome (Rom. 16:5). Since Luke concentrates in Acts on the great missionary Paul, he mentions the couple only in passing, but his remarks indicate that he and his sources know more about them than he relates. That he speaks of the couple at all is an indication that they were so important for the early Christian mission that he could not overlook them.

Much of women's "her-story" in early Christianity is lost. The few references which survived in the New Testament records are like the tip of an iceberg indicating what we have lost. Yet at the same time they show how great the influence of women was in the early Christian movement. Indeed women's leadership in the primitive Church was exceptional not only by the standards of Judaism and the Greco-Roman world, but also by those of the later Christian Church.

The Christian Past: Does it Hold a Future for Women?

ELEANOR L. McLAUGHLIN

This essay has two ends in view: the first is methodological, raising the general problems of relevance and revisionism in Church historical studies today. The second aim is substantive and illustrates my methodological thesis, that the study of the Christian past can be usable and prophetic for those who seek to realize the biblical promise that in Christ all are one, Jew and Greek, bond and free, male and female. The introduction sets forth an argument for new questions, new approaches, in the field of Church history. What then follows is a sampling of the new wine that will appear if our methodological wineskins are renewed, an illustration of the thesis that Christian tradition under certain conditions and at certain times was radically supportive of women and informed by women's experience.

Church history has not been widely regarded as a discipline pushing at the frontiers of Christian redefinition and prophetic witness in the twentieth century. Certainly among the student population of the past decade, historical studies of every sort have experienced a sharp decline

Eleanor McLaughlin is Associate Professor of Church History at Andover-Newton Theological School. Episcopal representative at the Faith and Order Commission of the National Council of Churches, and Chairwoman of the Commission on Women and Ministry of the Diocese of Massachusetts, her articles on women in the middle ages have appeared in *Religion and Sexism, Male and Female,* and *The St. Luke's Journal of Theology.* This essay appeared in longer form in the *Anglican Theological Review* (57) January, 1975, 600 Haven Street, Evanston, Illinois 60201.

as the demand for immediate and obvious relevance has been raised. In particular, the movements for human liberation, those of the black people, women, and the Third World, are placing a premium on future, change-oriented studies. It is not surprising that women within the churches who seek a just voice and role in the traditionally male dominated, hierarchically organized Christian community have found in the history of the church a depressing litany of theological justifications for the oppressive customs of patriarchal societies, of misogyny and neglect intensified by theological images, and ecclesiastical structures and practices that reflected and reinforced the androcentric character of theological and secular definitions of human nature. The tradition seems to have been created by and interpreted by men.[1] Therefore, Christian women in and outside of the seminaries who are hoping for change today often find the Christian past and its study to be a repository of all that must be overcome and discarded if the Church is to begin to reflect that promise in Galatians 3:28. All too often the history of the church has been written as if it were identical with the story of popes, bishops, priests, abbots, and kings. When women find their way into the narrative, it is as queen or temptress; daughter of Eve; the fascinatingly dramatic witch; or Mary, ever virgin and her saintly imitators whose merits seem so destructive to the twentieth-century woman. The deeply antihistorical bias of many Christian women who seek wholeness within the church is fully understandable if one spends any time with the traditional and even the most recent studies of church history. Just as one looks in vain for the important role played by nuns in the religious life of pre-Reformation Christendom in standard histories of monasticism, so Sr. Marie Augusta Neal has pointed out that the most recent histories of Christianity in America, Protestant and Roman Catholic, ignore the existence of the women's movement in their discussions of the churches in the 1970s.[2]

Understandable as this bias is against Christian tradition and the study of the Christian past, I wish to take a methodological stand beyond the antihistoricism of radical Christian feminism while at the same time rejecting the irrelevance, incompleteness, and admittedly often unconscious sexism of much of traditional church history. This alternative or revisionist approach to the Christian past seeks to set forth a history that is at once *responsible*—that is, grounded in the historicist rubric of dealing with the past on its own terms—and *usable*.

I mean by the search for a usable past—a phrase recognized by historians who lived through the 1960s—an examination of Christian history with a new set of questions that arise out of commitments to wholeness for women and for all humanity. Following from new questions, this is a history that redresses omissions and recasts interpretations.

To be conscious of my commitments and the questions that follow from them does not preclude the recognition that the study of a past age generates its own questions and problems; but such a self-consciousness does underline the fact that all historians have a "politics," a canon of selectivity within the broad spectrum outlined by our adherence to "fairness" to the sources.

A revisionist history of the Christian tradition first lays bare the typological image of the woman that dominates most of our sources, an image as arbitrary and fear-filled and destructive as the image of the heretic that appears in inquisitorial record and popular chronicle. This kind of revisionist church history, already beginning to be written,[3] is, however, but half of the task. We must push further if the new church history is to be both responsible and truly usable, for a partial rewriting of history is ultimately a disservice to the present, if only because it can be so easily dismissed.

My historical judgment and theological understanding tell me it is unlikely that the Christian tradition has been unrelievedly destructive of only one half of humanity. Accordingly, I ask whether, in addition to the negative image of woman and the male image of God, the tradition holds ideals or moments of realization of human wholeness that can call forth the *renovatio* in Christian history that has so often been a source of radical change, renewal, reformation.

What should this new sort of church history look like? Eileen Power, reflecting the mental revolution wrought by Marx (although citing Lord Acton) and her own interests as an economic historian, bade us to turn from kings, parliaments, wars, and treaties to the "kitchens of history." She was referring to the need to abandon our class bias toward the history of elites, but it is interesting that a generation ago she used the symbol of the woman's world to refer to the hidden history of the "unnamed masses of people, now sleeping in unknown graves."[4] Following this advice, the revisionist church historian would turn from popes, councils, decretals, the *Corpus Iuris Canonici,* and the *Summae Theologiae,* from the church in her magisterial might, teaching, preaching, ordaining, and maintaining, to the church at prayer, experiencing, seeking, listening, savoring, and witnessing. It is in this world of spirituality that *women* are found who speak and write, who made history and shaped a tradition that we need to rediscover—and by "we" I mean not only all women but also all who value the integrity of the historical record. We must let those women speak, those images that affirm the wholeness of women, but not as simplistic or authoritative patterns for present or future. This revisionist history should not produce the old "famous women of the past" genre. Rather, it should be a careful, historical, critical analysis of those times and situations in the past when, patriarchal and androcentric institutions notwithstanding, the Christian tradition fostered the being, experience, and authority of women. Such a history may give us some insight into what has happened today, some sense of possible alternatives, and, for those who still find the Christian past in any way normative, some urgency for radical change.

The general outlines of the thesis, that Christian faith and institutions have been in certain times and under certain conditions radically supportive of women and informed by women's experience, will be illustrated primarily from the history of spirituality of the high and late Middle Ages. . . . Evidence is beginning to accumulate that in the religious life—that is, the regular life of Christian virginity—women in the Middle Ages could find a sphere of activity, of self-expression, even of authority and jurisdiction, that stands in sharp contrast to the limited picture of the woman found in formal theology, legal structures of church and society, and the reality of patriarchal marriage. This generalization can be substantiated by looking at the history of monastic institutions from Anglo-Saxon times that saw the work of Christian women missionaries like Leoba,[5] the beloved companion of Boniface; and great abbesses like Hilda of Whitby, ruling over a double monastery of men and women, friend of kings and bishops; to the period of religious renewal of the twelfth century when one finds women without the religious life, both regulars and semiregular Beguines, playing a formative role in the religious awakening of the high Middle Ages.[6]

Yet I feel there is a danger in focusing our attention on institutional history, for it asks fundamentally the question of political power. Not only were relatively few women in positions of administrative authority, but it is also possible that the place where women speak and shape tradition, what for us might be a usable past, is not to be sought among the powerful in the usual bureaucratic sense of that word. From this standpoint, books such as Joan Morris' *The Lady was a Bishop*[7] do not represent the kind of history that most needs to be written at this time. The most significant criticism of that book is not that it is badly documented or misleading in its tendentious spirit, but that prince bishops or abbots or abbesses, be they male or female, ruling over hundreds of serfs and disposing of countless benefices, are in a real sense the old story of the church conforming to the world of a feudal landed aristocracy. What is far more significant, certainly in terms of the life of the ordinary Christian woman of the twelfth through the fifteenth centuries, and perhaps more meaningful for us, is the as yet hardly written history of the leadership of women in the evolution of medieval spirituality. It is this literature of prayer, of visions, and the lives of the saints, which reveal something of the inner existence of Christian women, and often in their own words. From these sources, the historian can recover a sense of a time when women stood beside men in relatively equal numbers as the spiritual elite and models of Christian piety, a time when women's experience and the language of women's experience informed prayer and even theological formulation, a time when women and men in the religious life, partners and pilgrims in a common search for God, could relate to each other within the structures of the church as equals in a true mutuality of shared goals. To illustrate these themes, glimpses of a feminist heritage in the Christian tradition, I will look at two quite different documents: the *Life* of Christina of Markyate and the *Revelations of Divine Love* of Julian of Norwich. Both of these women in their lives and work illustrate a concrete historical realization of the equality of souls before God; their relationships with men and their self-understanding give evidence of the way in which Christian tradition could stand opposed to the structures of patriarchal society, the way in which women were empowered by that tradition.

Christina of Markyate was an English anchoress living in the first half of the twelfth century. The editor of her anonymous *Life* feels that, despite the likelihood that a churchman wrote this biography, the wealth of detail, especially of this woman's inner life and feeling, give us good reason to believe that Christina herself must have dictated the text.[8] Both the external details of her life and the language and character of her piety illustrate the thesis I am proposing: that in the context of the search for Christian perfection, a woman could find space in medieval Christianity to function as a person of authority and wholeness.

Christina was the daughter of a well-to-do middle-class family, betrothed and married by her parents to a suitable young man over her strong objection, for she had prior to this parental decision vowed herself to the service of Christ in perpetual virginity. Symbolic of her decision, she had discarded her baptismal name, Theodora, and named herself Christina, belonging to Christ. She proceeded to resist every pressure of family, the rejected betrothed, and even her bishop, whose assistance against Christina's stubbornness the father had purchased. The issues in this initial confrontation are made clear in the text. Her father complains, "Why must she depart from tradition? Why should she bring dishonor on her father? Her life of poverty will bring the whole of the nobility into disrepute."[9] Her parents lament that she is making of them the laughing stock of the neighborhood. Before her father bribes the bishop, who initially has supported Theodora, turned Christina, in her decision to preserve her virginity for God, the irate father complains, "You are even made mistress over me.... The Bishop has praised you to the skies and declared that you are freer than ever. So come and go as I do and live your own life as you please."[10] It is her religious commitment that gives her this freedom and independence to define her own life and even take her own name. She cites Matthew 19:29: "Everyone who leaves houses or brothers or sisters or mother or father or wife or children for my name's sake shall receive an hundredfold." Christina's resourcefulness in dealing with the spurned boy is equally remarkable as we are told of her escape from him and his crowd of rowdy friends by hanging by her fingertips from a ledge behind the curtains that enveloped the bed intended to be the place of his triumph.[11] The marriage was never consummated. Reminiscent of the citation from Jerome in which the holy woman becomes, as it were, a man (vir),[12] is Christina's escape disguised as a boy, saying to herself, "Why delay, fugitive? Why do you respect your feminine sex? Put on manly courage and mount the horse like a man."[13] Although this would seem to imply that Christina has thoroughly internalized the tradition's identity of sanctity with maleness, one must at the same time recognize how she was able to resist the enormous pressures of family and society, to make an independent decision for a life of her own choosing out of the strength afforded by her loyalty to a Lord not of this earth. And, except when corrupted by bribery, the church supported her legally and structurally in the decision. When the church gave in to the pressures of the world, she resisted the bishop's authority, citing scripture and the priority of Christ's claim on her life.

Even more striking in its opposition to the socially acceptable relationship between the sexes is the life that Christina led from the time of her escape from father and betrothed. She chose the existence of an anchoress, a female hermit, rather than that of a nun in community, a decision that was particularly popular in the twelfth century in England and the continent. But she did not live alone, for she found refuge in a hermitage already established by the recluse Roger, where, in separate cells, each shared a life of common prayer and meditation. It is this spiritual relationship between a man and woman that is so instructive for us in its unhierarchical nature, its astonishing degree of mutuality and equality. Although officially Christina placed herself under Roger's guidance and authority, for he was her senior in years and spiritual experience, the picture of their relationship which emerges in the *Life* is of a true spiritual companionship.

We read that Christina and Roger, by God's intent catch sight of each other at prayer:

> The fire namely which had been kindled by the spirit of God and burned in each one of them cast its sparks into their hearts by the grace of that mutual glance; and so made one in heart and soul in chastity and charity in Christ, they were not afraid to dwell together under the same roof.[14]
>
> By encouraging each other to strive after higher things, their holy affection grew day by day, like a large flame springing from two brands joined together. . . . And so their great progress induced them to dwell together.[15]

This relationship was not one of master and pupil; each supported and instructed the other in a common pilgrimage.[16] There are here . . . undoubtedly parallels to be found [to] the patristic institution of the *virgines subintroductae,* spiritual friendships between men and women pursuing together the life of Christian perfection. The foundation of all these instances of equality and mutuality between Christian women and men was the freeing and revolutionary conviction that beyond sexuality, in Christ, there was neither male nor female.

In the spiritual life, Christina recognized herself and was recognized by men and the society around her as a figure of authority, in every way equal, if not holier and thus more powerful in the realm of the spirit than her male coreligious. That power is symbolized by her fame as a healer, the bishops and pilgrims who streamed to her cell from all over Europe, the many requests that she leave to become abbess of eminent religious houses.

A second way in which the woman's experience was affirmed within medieval Christianity was in her relationship to the transcendent. This is illustrated by the language of Christina's piety and the imagery of the visions of Mary and Jesus through which she encountered the divine. It is interesting that one of the principal appearances of Jesus is not only as her spouse—there is relatively little of the "bride of Christ" language—but as a little child.

For in the guise of a small child, He came to the arms of his sorely tried spouse and remained with her a whole day, not only being felt but also seen. So the maiden took Him in her hands, gave thanks and pressed Him to her bosom. And with immeasurable delight she held Him at one moment to her virginal breast, at another she felt His presence within her flesh. Who shall describe the abounding sweetness with which the servant was filled by this condescension of her creator? From that moment, the fire of lust was so completely extinguished that never afterwards could it be revived.[17]

The roles of mother and bride, lover and beloved, are intermingled in this passage in a way that frees this frankly erotic spirituality from the rigidly hierarchical and submissive structures of the marriage metaphor. Furthermore, this erotic spirituality also provided a set of symbols and metaphors by which women could express their relationship to the transcendent in language that reflected the dominant experiences of women, in those times, the experiences of mothering and nurturing, in which roles women functioned in a preindustrial society as independent and authoritative figures.

Equally affirmative of women's experience is the language used to describe Christina's relationship with Mary, who appeared to her more frequently than Jesus. By Mary's intervention, she had escaped the pursuit of her betrothed, Burthred, and then the Virgin appeared to comfort Christina, a woman soothing another woman, just that moment freed from the threat of rape; the divine acting in a sisterly fashion.[18]

The *Life* of Christina of Markyate is unusual in many ways, and one might dismiss many of these observations if one were not able to discover in the literature of medieval spirituality of different times and places parallels to the affirmations of women's spiritual authority and experience which that biography reveals.

Julian of Norwich was another English recluse, living in the last half of the fourteenth century, a mystic, a spiritual director, and a woman of literary as well as spiritual gifts. We do not know whether she was ever a professed nun. She may well have been granted these graces as a pious laywoman, after which she sought a more perfect life as an anchoress. We do see that the medieval church provided a place for such a woman. In the little group of rooms that made up her "cell," a prophetic spirit such as Christina or Julian could pursue personal holiness and shape the world through her work as spiritual advisor to the humble as well as the mighty. Julian's *Revelations of Divine Love* records her experience of God and her theological reflection on that experience. Julian was a woman doing theology.

Again, I focus not on Julian's personal authority among Christians of her own day, even though that is a fact of the hidden history of the church that needs to be recovered. Instead, I wish to turn to an examination of her religious language, for her words illustrate powerfully the way in which the tradition could reflect and affirm women's being and experience and in turn be shaped by that experience.

Julian's piety is Christocentric, a theology of love that found its supreme expression in the incarnation. What is surprising and liberating is the language of that God experience. The first point that may be made is that Julian, while naturally recognizing the male sex of the historical Jesus, finds the cohumanity by which she shared his human nature not in maleness, but in the capacity of suffering, a capacity beyond but not excluding sexuality.[19] Far more affecting than this abstract observation is her continual use of the name "Mother Jesus" and the association of mothering metaphors with the action of both Jesus and the Godhead. The startling language should not be described but rather heard in our ears, so unaccustomed are we to these feelings in the context of prayer.

The human mother will suckle her child with her own milk, but our beloved Mother, Jesus, feeds us with himself, and with most tender courtesy, does it by means of the Blessed Sacrament, the precious food of all true life. . . . The human mother may put her child tenderly to her breast, but our tender Mother

Jesus simply leads us into his blessed breast through his open side, and there gives us a glimpse of the Godhead and heavenly joy, the inner certainty of eternal bliss.[20]

He is also our mother in whom "we grow and develop," our mother in mercy and grace, "he reforms and restores us." So does our mother "function as a kindly nurse who has no other business than to care for the wellbeing of her charge."[21] In addition to this naming and description of Christ's work as modes of mothering, there is an explicit reciprocal honoring and elevating of the concrete life of real mothers by associating God's action with the details of human mothering.

A kind, loving mother who understands and knows the needs of her child will look after it tenderly because it is the nature of a mother to do so. As the child grows older, she changes her methods—but not her love. Older still, she allows the child to be punished so that its faults are corrected and its virtues and graces are developed. This way of doing things, with much else that is right and good is our Lord at work in those who are doing them. Thus he is our Mother in nature, working by his grace in our lower part, for the sake of the higher. . . . Like this I could see that our indebtedness, under God to fatherhood and motherhood—whether it be human or divine—is fully met in truly loving God.[22]

All human relationships are taken up in this new sense of God, "rejoicing to be our Father, rejoicing too to be our Mother; and rejoicing yet again to be our true Husband, with our soul his beloved wife. And Christ rejoices to be our Brother and our Savior too."[23] Significantly, the only relationship missing is that of sisterhood. But Julian would have had to add another line to that hymn, "Our Father by whose Name, all Fatherhood is known."

From the model of these human relationships, in this case, female, mothering models, Julian tells us how God acts, and how we should act.

His desire is that we should do what a child does: for when a child is in trouble or is scared it runs to mother for help as fast as it can. Which is what He wants us to do, saying with the humility of a child, "Kind, thoughtful, dearest Mother, do be sorry for me. I have got myself into a filthy mess and am not a bit like you . . . ." Even if we do not feel immediate relief, we can still be sure that he behaves like a wise mother. If he sees it is better for us to mourn and weep he lets us do so, with pity and sympathy, of course and for the right length of time—because he loves us. And he wants us to copy the child who always and naturally trusts mother's love through thick and thin![24]

Is there not in this vision of God's action an acceptance of human trial and error? God is like a good mother, who has confidence that the child will grow through her mistakes. In other words, this God is a wise mother who looks forward to adulthood for her child, whose end goal is maturity and not dependence. Is that reading too much into Julian? In any case, the theological possibilities are shifted by the change in metaphor. Julian's language and her decision to model the actions of God on the experience of motherhood rather than fatherhood, kingship, and knighthood is unusual, but not without precedent in the tradition. Both Anselm and Bernard spoke of the motherhood of Jesus—this is an aspect of the history of medieval spirituality that needs to be lifted out of obscurity.

What conclusions or suggestions can we draw from these samples of spirituality, patristic, and medieval that have been set forth here? A first observation has to do with the structures and values of medieval Christianity, which produced a hierarchical order according to function and dignity. The ordinary Christian folk, laywomen and laymen, were confronted by two distinct religious hierarchies: first, the secular clergy, necessary for salvation as dispensers of the sacraments, but thoroughly and notoriously involved in the world and all its works. This bureaucracy, from parish priest to pope, was open to baptized free persons of the male sex only. The second group, the religious, those under the threefold vow of monastic life, stood higher still in the spiritual scheme of things, and this *ordo* was populated by *both* men and women. Beyond these neat distinctions was the category of holiness or sainthood, which cut across every *ordo,* for there were kings and prostitutes, robbers and queens, among the saints. However, sainthood was the special calling of the religious, that vocation and institution within the church that was open to women as well as men. The point to be made here, is that in medieval Christianity the highest religious and moral values of the society were exemplified not typically by the all-male clerical bureaucracy, but by the religious and those whom the people called the *saints,* categories in which women as well as men took an equal and active place. Holiness, not administrative or sacramental power, was at least in theory, and often in fact, the functional norm in medieval Christian society, and all agreed holiness was no respecter of sex. To be sure the mass was celebrated by men only, but the spiritual power to heal and save lay with the intercession of Mary or the local holy man or woman, be they living or part of the communion of the saints. In the twentieth-century church, even in those communions where the regular life still exists, there is no widely recognized institutionalized place for the publicly acknowledged pursuit of holiness, an enterprise by definition within the tradition open equally to women and men. What moral authority the church still exercises in this post-Christian world is mediated by the descendants of that all-male secular, clerical order. The clericalism already evident by the thirteenth century, reinforced by modern bureaucratism and professionalism today defines the church in terms of that male hierarchy. In the Middle Ages, in contrast, women stood beside men among the saints and holy ones as models of Christian living. In this sense, women played a role in medieval Christianity that at least in the Protestant tradition was quite obviously lost with the attack on the regular life, religious celibacy, and Catholic doctrines of sanctification.

A second observation is that in the preindustrial world the family was the economic unit of production, and the birthing and rearing of children was a task of overriding importance that dominated physically and spiritually the lives of most women. Medieval society valued that task, and its religion had come to reflect those female values and experiences in a way quite foreign both to the patristic theologians and the theologies and liturgies of our own day. That woman's world suffused not the formal school theology, but popular spirituality and prayer, especially that of women. This meant that the theological language, again not of the *Summae*, or formal liturgy, but of popular piety, often reflected the real-life experiences of women in a way that is not the case today. Indeed, it is probable that medieval piety reflected the real life of both men and women in a fashion not to be seen in our world outside of the black churches and the sects and free churches. What is women's experience today and how can it be lifted up and reflected in religious language?

A third observation is that the examples produced here demonstrate that a result of this grounding of God language in the life of women as well as men was an opening up of metaphor and naming that broke through the androcentric and patriarchal tradition to a vision of God as mother, nurse, nurturer, and midwife as well as father, king, and lord. Despite the historical reality of patriarchal family and a male-dominated warrior society, the realm of the transcendent included not only a Virgin Mother but a Mother–Father God, at least in certain corners of the tradition.

This androgynous character of the transcendent at once gave dignity and worth to the world of women. Could this happen once again?

This essay was introduced with a plea for a revisionist history·of the Christian tradition, a rewriting of church history in the light of current questions that would be at once responsible and usable. Such a history, by giving us a richer, more complex understanding of where we have come from, could enable us to move with greater freedom and hope in the future. Beside the now well-documented classical Christian stereotype of the female: misbegotten male, daughter of Eve, temptress, insatiable harlot, nagging, unfaithful, garrulous wife, we have found it possible to set another *persona*—the seeker after God, model of human holiness and divine action, wholly equal with her brother in the pursuit of Christian perfection. This does not necessarily provide an exact model for our future; rather, it functions as a generator of questions and challenges. It does remind us that within the Christian tradition there has existed from the beginning a powerful revolutionary egalitarian principle, that in Christ there is neither Jew nor Greek, slave nor free, male nor female. Medieval people, clerical or lay, did not cite Galatians 3:28 very often, but the ideal and institution of religious virginity provided a place where women and men pursued friendship with God and with each other as true equals before a common Lord. The recovery of that history restores to us a part of our tradition long hidden, a tradition in which women in their pursuit of wholeness or holiness were empowered and empowering members of their society despite the overwhelming patriarchal and androcentric presuppositions and structures of that age. If this be a usable past, it is the task now of those women who seek an authentic experience of self, in relation to that one who makes whole, to discover what changes in our own world and church will enable us once again to act with power and healing, as did the saints of old.

NOTES

1. The best presentation of this position is Mary Daly, *Beyond God the Father* (Boston: Beacon Press, 1973).

2. Sr. Marie Augusta Neal, "Women in Religion: A Sociological Perspective: 1974," *Sociological Inquiry*, 45(4): 33–39.

3. See the collection of essays in Rosemary R. Ruether, ed., *Religion and Sexism:*

Images of Women in the Jewish and Christian Traditions (New York: Simon & Schuster, 1974).

4. Eileen Power, *Medieval People* (New York: Doubleday, 1955), p. 16.

5. Rudolf, Monk of Fulda, *The Life of St. Leoba,* in Charles H. Talbot, ed., *Anglo-Saxon Missionaries in Germany* (New York: Sheed and Ward, 1954), pp. 205–226.

6. See Ernest W. McDonnell, *The Beguines and Beghards in Medieval Culture* (New Brunswick, N.J.: Rutgers University Press, 1954).

7. Joan Morris, *The Lady Was a Bishop* (New York: Macmillan Company, 1973).

8. Charles H. Talbot, trans. and ed., *The Life of Christina of Markyate: A Twelfth-Century Recluse* (Oxford: Clarendon Press, 1959), p. 6.

9. Talbot, *Life of Christina,* p. 59.

10. Talbot, *Life of Christina,* pp. 65–67.

11. Talbot, *Life of Christina,* p. 53.

12. St. Jerome, *Lettres,* ed. and trans. Jerome Labourt, 8 vols. (Para Les Belles Lettres: 1949–1963) 4: 71; Ep. x, ad Lucinum, "from a spouse she has become your sister, from a woman, a man, from a subject, an equal . . . under the same yoke she hastens with you towards the Kingdom of Heaven."

13. Talbot, *Life of Christina,* p. 93.

14. Talbot, *Life of Christina,* pp. 101–103.

15. Talbot, *Life of Christina,* p. 103.

16. Roger was described as her teacher, who trained her by word and example (Talbot, *Life of Christina,* p. 105) but he also spoke of her relationship as a metaphor that made of him her mother! He calls her his "Sunday" daughter, "whom . . . he loved more than all the others whom he had begotten or nursed in Christ" (Talbot, *Life of Christina,* p. 107).

17. Talbot, *Life of Christina,* p. 119.

18. Talbot, *Life of Christina,* p. 77.

19. Julian of Norwich, *Revelations of Divine Love,* trans. and ed., Clifton Walters (Baltimore, Md.: Penguin, 1966) p. 160.

20. Julian, *Revelations,* p. 170.

21. Julian, *Revelations,* pp. 166, 173.

22. Julian, *Revelations,* pp. 170–171.

23. Julian, *Revelations,* p. 151.

24. Julian, *Revelations,* pp. 172–173.

What Became of God the Mother? Conflicting Images of God in Early Christianity

ELAINE H. PAGELS

Unlike many of his contemporaries among the deities of the ancient Near East, the God of Israel shares his power with no female divinity, nor is he the divine Husband or Lover of any.[1] He scarcely can be characterized in any but masculine epithets: King, Lord, Master, Judge, and Father.[2] Indeed, the absence of feminine symbolism of God marks Judaism, Christianity, and Islam in striking contrast to the world's other religious traditions, whether in Egypt, Babylonia, Greece, and Rome or Africa, Polynesia, India, and North America. Jewish, Christian, and Islamic theologians, however, are quick to point out that God is not to be considered in sexual terms at all. Yet the actual language they use daily in worship and prayer conveys a different message and gives the distinct impression that God is thought of in exclusively *masculine* terms. And while it is true that Catholics

Elaine H. Pagels received her Ph. D. from Harvard University and now teaches at Barnard College, Columbia University. She is author of *The Johannine Gospel in Gnostic Exegesis* and *The Gnostic Paul.* Her articles have appeared in *Harvard Theological Review, Journal for Biblical Literature,* and *Journal of the American Academy of Religion.* This essay originally appeared in *Signs* (Vol. 2, no. 2), © 1976 by The University of Chicago, and is reprinted by permission of The University of Chicago Press.

revere Mary as the mother of Jesus, she cannot be identified as divine in her own right: if she is "mother of God," she is not "God the Mother" on an equal footing with God the Father.

Christianity, of course, added the trinitarian terms to the Jewish description of God. And yet of the three divine "Persons," two—the Father and Son—are described in masculine terms, and the third—the Spirit—suggests the sexlessness of the Greek neuter term *pneuma*. This is not merely a subjective impression. Whoever investigates the early development of Christianity—the field called "patristics," that is, study of "the fathers of the church"—may not be surprised by the passage that concludes the recently discovered, secret *Gospel of Thomas:* "Simon Peter said to them [the disciples], 'Let Mary be excluded from among us, for she is a woman, and not worthy of Life.' Jesus said, 'Behold I will take Mary, and make her a male, so that she may become a living spirit, resembling you males. For I tell you truly, that every female who makes herself male will enter the Kingdom of Heaven.' "[3] Strange as it sounds, this only states explicitly what religious rhetoric often assumes: that the men form the legitimate body of the community, while women will be allowed to participate only insofar as their own identity is denied and assimilated to that of the men.

Further exploration of the texts which include this *Gospel*—written on papyrus, hidden in large clay jars nearly 1,600 years ago—has identified them as Jewish and Christian gnostic works which were attacked and condemned as "heretical" as early as A.D. 100—150. What distinguishes these "heterodox" texts from those that are called "orthodox" is at least partially clear: they abound in feminine symbolism that is applied, in particular, to God. Although one might expect, then, that they would recall the archaic pagan traditions of the Mother Goddess, their language is to the contrary specifically Christian, unmistakably related to a Jewish heritage. Thus we can see that certain gnostic Christians diverged even more radically from the Jewish tradition than the early Christians who described God as the "three Persons" or the Trinity. For, instead of a monistic and masculine God, certain of these texts describe God as a dyadic being, who consists of *both* masculine and feminine elements. One such group of texts, for example, claims to have received a secret tradition from Jesus through James, and significantly, through Mary Magdalene.[4] Members of this group offer prayer to *both* the divine Father amd

Mother: "From Thee, Father, and through Thee, Mother, the two immortal names, Parents of the divine being, and thou, dweller in heaven, mankind of the mighty name."[5] Other texts indicate that their authors had pondered the nature of the beings to whom a single, masculine God proposed, "Let us make mankind in our image, after our likeness" (Gen. 1:26). Since the Genesis account goes on to say that mankind was created "male and female" (1:27), some concluded, apparently, that the God in whose image we are created likewise must be both masculine and feminine—both Father and Mother.

The characterization of the divine Mother in these sources is not simple since the texts themselves are extraordinarily diverse. Nevertheless, three primary characterizations merge. First, a certain poet and teacher, Valentinus, begins with the premise that God is essentially indescribable. And yet he suggests that the divine can be imagined as a Dyad consisting of two elements: one he calls the Ineffable, the Source, the Primal Father; the other, the Silence, the Mother of all things.[6] Although we might question Valentinus's reasoning that Silence is the appropriate complement of what is Ineffable, his equation of the former with the feminine and the latter with the masculine may be traced to the grammatical gender of the Greek words. Followers of Valentinus invoke this feminine power, whom they also call "Grace" (in Greek, the feminine term *charis*), in their own private celebration of the Christian eucharist: they call her "divine, eternal Grace, She who is before all things."[7] At other times they pray to her for protection as the Mother, "Thou enthroned with God, eternal, mystical Silence."[8] Marcus, a disciple of Valentinus, contends that "when Moses began his account of creation, he mentioned the Mother of all things at the very beginning, when he said, 'In the beginning, God created the heavens and the earth,' "[9] for the word *beginning* (in Greek, the feminine *arche*) refers to the divine Mother, the source of the cosmic elements. When they describe God in this way, different gnostic writers have different interpretations. Some maintain that the divine is to be considered masculo-feminine—the "great male-female power." Others insist that the terms are meant only as metaphors—for, in reality, the divine is *neither* masculine nor feminine. A third group suggests that one can describe the Source of all things in *either* masculine or feminine terms, depending on which aspect one intends to stress.[10] Proponents of these diverse views agree, however, that the divine is to be understood as consisting of a harmonious, dynamic relationship of opposites—a concept that may be akin to the eastern view of *yin* and *yang* but remains antithetical to orthodox Judaism and Christianity.

A second characterization of the divine Mother describes her as Holy Spirit. One source, the *Secret Book of John,* for example, relates how John, the brother of James, went out after the crucifixion with "great grief," and had a mystical vision of the Trinity: "As I was grieving . . . the heavens were opened, and the whole creation shone with an unearthly light, and the universe was shaken. I was afraid . . . and behold . . . a unity in three forms appeared to me, and I marvelled: how can a unity have three forms?" To John's question, the vision answers: "It said to me, 'John, John, why do you doubt, or why do you fear? . . . I am the One who is with you always: I am the Father; I am the Mother; I am the Son.' "[11] John's interpretation of the Trinity—as Father, Mother, and Son—may not at first seem shocking but is perhaps the more natural and spontaneous interpretation. Where the Greek terminology for the Trinity, which includes the neuter term for the spirit (*pneuma*), virtually requires that the third "Person" of the Trinity be asexual, the author of the *Secret Book* looks to the Hebrew term for spirit, *ruah*—a feminine word. He thus concludes, logically enough, that the feminine "Person" conjoined with Father and Son must be the Mother! Indeed, the text goes on to describe the Spirit as Mother: "the image of the invisible virginal perfect spirit. . . . She became the mother of the all, for she existed before them all, the mother-father [matropater]."[12] This same author, therefore, alters Genesis 1:2 ("the Spirit of God moved upon the face of the deep") to say, "the Mother then was moved."[13] The secret *Gospel to the Hebrews* likewise has Jesus speak of "my Mother, the Spirit."[14] And in the *Gospel of Thomas,* Jesus contrasts his earthly parents, Mary and Joseph, with his divine Father—the Father of Truth—and his divine Mother, the Holy Spirit. The author interprets a puzzling saying of Jesus in the New Testament ("whoever does not hate his father and mother is not worthy of me") by adding: "Whoever does not love his father and his mother in my way cannot be my disciple; for my [earthly] mother gave me death but my true Mother gave me the Life."[15] Another secret gnostic gospel, the *Gospel of Phillip,* declares that whoever becomes a Christian "gains both a father and a mother."[16] The author refers explicitly to the feminine Hebrew term to describe the Spirit as "Mother of many."[17]

If these sources suggest that the Spirit constitutes the maternal element of the Trinity, the *Gospel of Phillip* makes an equally radical suggestion concerning the doctrine that later developed as the virgin birth. Here again the Spirit is praised as both Mother and Virgin, the counterpart—and consort—of the Heavenly Father: "If I may utter a mystery, the Father of the all united with the Virgin who came down"[18]—that is,. with the Holy Spirit. Yet because this process is to be understood symbolically, and not literally, the Spirit remains a virgin! The author explains that "for this reason, Christ was 'born of a virgin' "—that is, of the Spirit, his divine Mother. But the author ridicules those "literal-minded" Christians who mistakenly refer the virgin birth to Mary, Jesus' earthly mother, as if she conceived apart from Joseph: "Such persons do not know what they are saying; for when did a female ever impregnate a female?"[19] Instead, he argues, virgin birth refers to the mysterious union of the two divine powers, the Father of the All with the Holy Spirit.

Besides the eternal, mystical Silence, and besides the Holy Spirit, certain gnostics suggest a third characterization of the divine Mother as Wisdom. Here again the Greek feminine term for wisdom, *sophia,* like the term for spirit, *ruah,* translates a Hebrew feminine term, *hokhmah.* Early interpreters had pondered the meaning of certain biblical passages, for example, Proverbs: "God made the world in Wisdom." And they wondered if Wisdom could be the feminine power in which God's creation is "conceived"? In such passages, at any rate, Wisdom bears two connotations: first, she bestows the Spirit that makes mankind wise; second, she is a creative power. One gnostic source calls her the "first universal creator";[20] another says that God the Father was speaking to her when he proposed to "make mankind in our image."[21] The *Great Announcement,* a mystical writing, explains the Genesis account in the following terms: "One Power that is above and below, self-generating, self-discovering, its own mother; its own father; its own sister; its own son: Father, Mother, unity, Root of all things."[22] The same author explains the mystical meaning of the Garden of Eden as a symbol of the womb: "Scripture teaches us that this is what is meant when Isaiah says, 'I am he that formed thee in thy mother's womb' [Isaiah 44:2]. The Garden of Eden, then, is Moses' symbolic term for the womb, and Eden the placenta, and the river which comes out of Eden the navel, which nourishes the fetus."[23] This teacher claims that the Exodus, consequently, symbolizes the exodus from the womb, "and the crossing of the Red Sea, they say, refers to the blood." Evidence for this view, he adds, comes directly from "the cry of the newborn," a spontaneous cry of praise for "the glory of the primal being, in which all the powers above are in harmonious embrace."[24]

The introduction of such symbolism in gnostic texts clearly bears implications for the understanding of human nature. The *Great Announcement,* for example, having described the Source as a masculo-feminine being, a "bisexual Power," goes on to say that "what came into being from that Power, that is, humanity, being one, is found to be two: a male-female being that bears the female within it."[25] This refers to the story of Eve's "birth" out of Adam's side (so that Adam, being one, is "discovered to be two," an androgyne who "bears the female within him"). Yet this reference to the creation story of Genesis 2—an account which inverts the biological birth process, and so effectively denies the creative function of the female—proves to be unusual in gnostic sources. More often, such sources refer instead to the first creation account in Genesis 1:26–27. ("And God said, let us make mankind in Our image, after Our image and likeness . . . in the image of God he created him: male and female he created them"). Rabbis in Talmudic times knew a Greek version of the passage, one that suggested to Rabbi Samuel bar Nahman that "when the Holy One . . . first created mankind, he created him with two faces, two sets of genitals, four arms, and legs, back to back: Then he split Adam in two, and made two backs, one on each side."[26] Some Jewish teachers (perhaps influenced by the story in Plato's *Symposium*) had suggested that Genesis 1:26–27 narrates an androgynous creation—an idea that gnostics adopted and developed. Marcus (whose prayer to the Mother is given above) not only concludes from this account that God is dyadic ("Let *us* make mankind") but also that "mankind, which was formed according to the image and likeness of God [Father and Mother] was masculo-feminine."[27] And his contemporary, Theodotus, explains: "the saying that Adam was created 'male and female' means that the male and female elements together constitute the finest production of the Mother, Wisdom."[28] We can see, then, that the gnostic sources which describe God in both masculine and feminine terms often give a similar description of human nature as a dyadic entity, consisting of two equal male and female components.

All the texts cited above—secret "gospels," revelations, mystical teachings—are among those rejected from the select list of twenty-six that comprise the "New Testament" collection. As these and other writings were sorted and judged by various Christian communities, every one of these texts which gnostic groups revered and shared was rejected from the canonical collection as "heterodox" by those who called themselves "orthodox" (literally, straight-thinking) Christians. By the time this process was concluded, probably as late as the year A.D. 200, virtually all the feminine imagery for God (along with any suggestion of an androgynous human creation) had disappeared from "orthodox" Christian tradition.

What is the reason for this wholesale rejection? The gnostics themselves asked this question of their "orthodox" attackers and pondered it among themselves. Some concluded that the God of Israel himself initiated the polemics against gnostic teaching which his followers carried out in his name. They argued that he was a derivative, merely instrumental power, whom the divine Mother had created to administer the universe, but who remained ignorant of the power of Wisdom, his own Mother: "They say that the creator believed that he created everything by himself, but that, in reality, he had made them because his Mother, Wisdom, infused him with energy, and had given him her ideas. But he was unaware that the ideas he used came from her: he was even ignorant of his own Mother."[29] Followers of Valentinus suggested that the Mother herself encouraged the God of Israel to think that he was acting autonomously in creating the world; but, as one teacher adds, "It was because he was foolish and ignorant of his Mother that he said, 'I am God; there is none beside me.' "[30] Others attribute to him the more sinister motive of jealousy, among them the *Secret Book of John:* "He said, 'I am a jealous God, and you shall have no other God before me,' already indicating that another god does exist. For if there were no other god, of whom would he be jealous? Then the Mother began to be distressed."[31] A third gnostic teacher describes the Lord's shock, terror, and anxiety "when he discovered that he was not the God of the universe." Gradually his shock and fear gave way to wonder, and finally he came to welcome the teaching of Wisdom. The gnostic teacher concluded: "This is the meaning of the saying, 'The fear of the Lord is the beginning of wisdom.' "[32]

All of these are, of course, mythical explanations. To look for the actual, historical reasons why these gnostic writings were suppressed is an extremely difficult proposition, for it raises the much larger question of how (i.e., by what means and what criteria) certain ideas, including those expressed in the texts cited above, came to be classified as heretical and others as orthodox by the beginning of the third century. Although the research is still in its early stages, and this question is far from being solved, we may find one clue if we ask whether these secret groups derived any practical, social consequences from their conception of God—and of mankind—that included the feminine element? Here again the answer is yes and can be found in the orthodox texts themselves. Irenaeus, an orthodox bishop, for example, notes with dismay that women in particular are attracted to heretical groups—especially to Marcus's circle, in which prayers are offered to the Mother in her aspects as Silence, Grace, and Wisdom; women priests serve the eucharist together with men; and women also speak as prophets, uttering to the whole community what "the Spirit" reveals to them.[33] Professing himself to be at a loss to understand the attraction that Marcus's group holds, he offers only one explanation: that Marcus himself is a diabolically successful seducer, a magician who compounds special aphrodisiacs to "deceive, victimize, and defile" these "many foolish women!" Whether his accusation has any factual basis is difficult, probably impossible, to ascertain. Nevertheless, the historian notes that accusations of sexual license are a stock-in-trade of polemical arguments.[34] The bishop refuses to admit the possibility that the group might attract Christians—especially women—for sound and comprehensible reasons. While expressing his own moral outrage, Tertullian, another "father of the church," reveals his fundamental desire to keep women out of religion: "These heretical women—how audacious they are! They have no modesty: they are bold enough to teach, to engage in argument, to enact exorcisms, to undertake cures, and, it may be, even to baptize!"[35] Tertullian directs yet another attack against "that viper"—a woman teacher who led a congregation in North Africa.[36] Marcion had, in fact, scandalized his "orthodox" contemporaries by appointing women on an equal basis with men as priests and bishops among his congregations.[37] The teacher Marcillina also traveled to Rome to represent the Carpocratian group, an esoteric circle that claimed to have received secret teaching from Mary, Salome, and Martha.[38] And among the Montanists, a radical prophetic circle, the prophet Philumene was reputed to have hired a male secretary to transcribe her inspired oracles.[39]

Other secret texts, such as the *Gospel of Mary Magdalene* and the

Wisdom of Faith, suggest that the activity of such women leaders challenged and therefore was challenged by the orthodox communities who regarded Peter as their spokesman. The *Gospel of Mary* relates that Mary tried·to encourage the disciples after the crucifixion and to tell them what the Lord had told her privately. Peter, furious at the suggestion, asks, "Did he then talk secretly with a woman, instead of to us? Are we to go and learn from *her* now? Did he love her more than us?" Distressed at his rage, Mary then asks Peter: "What do you think? Do you think I made this up in my heart? Do you think I am lying about the Lord?" Levi breaks in at this point to mediate the dispute: "Peter, you are always irascible. You object to the woman as our enemies do. Surely the Lord knew her very well, and indeed, he loved her more than us." Then he and the others invite Mary to teach them what she knows.[40] Another argument between Peter and Mary occurs in *Wisdom of Faith.* Peter complains that Mary is dominating the conversation, even to the point of displacing the rightful priority of Peter himself and his brethren; he urges Jesus to silence her—and is quickly rebuked. Later, however, Mary admits to Jesus that she hardly dares to speak freely with him, because "Peter makes me hesitate: I am afraid of him, because he hates the female race." Jesus replies that whoever receives inspiration from the Spirit is divinely ordained to speak, whether man or woman.[41]

As these texts suggest, then, women were considered equal to men, they were revered as prophets, and they acted as teachers, traveling evangelists, healers, priests, and even bishops. In some of these groups, they played leading roles and were *excluded* from them in the orthodox churches, at least by A.D. 150–200. Is it possible, then, that the recognition of the feminine element in God and the recognition of mankind as a male and female entity bore within it the explosive social possibility of women acting on an equal basis with men in positions of authority and leadership? If this were true, it might lead to the conclusion that these gnostic groups, together with their conception of God and human nature, were suppressed only because of their positive attitude toward women. But such a conclusion would be a mistake—a hasty and simplistic reading of the evidence. In the first place, orthodox Christian doctrine is far from wholly negative in its attitude toward women. Second, many other elements of the gnostic sources diverge in fundamental ways from what came to be accepted as orthodox Christian teaching. To examine this process in detail would require a much more extensive discussion than is possible here. Nevertheless, the evidence does indicate that two very different patterns of sexual attitudes emerged in orthodox and gnostic circles. In simplest form, gnostic theologians correlate their description of God in both masculine and feminine terms with a complementary description of human nature. Most often they refer to the creation account of Genesis 1, which suggests an equal (or even androgynous) creation of mankind. This conception carries the principle of equality between men and women into the practical social and political structures of gnostic communities. The orthodox pattern is strikingly different: it describes God in exclusively masculine terms and often uses Genesis 2 to describe how Eve was created from Adam and for his fulfillment. Like the gnostic view, the orthodox also translates into sociological practice: by the late second century, orthodox Christians came to accept the domination of men over women as the proper, God-given order—not only for the human race, but also for the Christian churches. This correlation between theology, anthropology, and sociology is not lost on the apostle Paul. In his letter to the disorderly Corinthian community, he reminds them of a divinely ordained chain of authority: As God has authority over Christ, so the man has authority over the woman, argues Paul, citing Genesis 2: "The man is the image and glory of God, but the woman is the glory of man. For man is not from woman, but woman from man; and besides, the man was not created for the woman's sake, but the woman for the sake of the man."[42] Here the three elements of the orthodox pattern are welded into one simple argument: the description of God corresponds to a description of human nature which authorizes the social pattern of male domination.

A striking exception to this orthodox pattern occurs in the writings of one revered "father of the church," Clement of Alexandria. Clement identifies himself as orthodox, although he knows members of gnostic groups and their writings well; some scholars suggest that he was himself a gnostic initiate. Yet his own works demonstrate how all three elements of what we have called the "gnostic pattern" could be worked into fully "orthodox" teaching. First, Clement characterizes God not only in masculine but also in feminine terms: "The Word is everything to the child, both father and mother, teacher and nurse.... The nutriment is the milk of the father ... and the Word alone supplies us children with the milk of love, and only those who suck at this breast are truly happy.... For this reason seeking is called sucking; to those infants who seek the Word, the Father's loving breasts supply milk."[43] Second, in describing human nature, he insists that "men and women share equally in perfection, and are to receive the same instruction and discipline. For the name 'humanity' is common to both men and women; and for us 'in Christ there is neither male nor female.' "[44] Even in considering the active participation of women with men in the Christian community Clement offers a list—unique in orthodox tradition—of women whose achievements he admires. They range from ancient examples, like Judith, the assassin who destroyed Israel's enemy, to Queen Esther, who rescued her people from genocide, as well as others who took radical political stands. He speaks of Arignole the historian, of Themisto the Epicurean philosopher, and of many other women philosophers, including two who studied with Plato and one trained by Socrates. Indeed, he cannot contain his praise: "What shall I say? Did not Theano the Pythagoran make such progress in philosophy that when a man, staring at her, said, 'Your arm is beautiful,' she replied, 'Yes, but it is not on public display.' "[45] Clement concludes his list with famous women poets and painters.

If the work of Clement, who taught in Egypt before the lines of orthodoxy and heresy were rigidly drawn (ca. A.D. 160–80) demonstrates how gnostic principles could be incorporated even into orthodox Christian teaching, the majority of communities in the western empire headed by Rome did not follow his example. By the year A.D. 200, Roman Christians endorsed as "canonical" the pseudo-Pauline letter to Timothy, which interpreted Paul's views: "Let a woman learn in silence with full submissiveness. I do not allow any woman to teach or to exercise authority over a man; she is to remain silent, *for* [note Gen. 2!] Adam was formed first, then Eve and furthermore, Adam was not deceived, but the woman was utterly seduced and came into sin."[46] How are we to account for this irreversible development? The question deserves investigation which this discussion can only initiate. For example, one would need to examine how (and for what reasons) the zealously patriarchal traditions of Israel were adopted by the Roman (and other) Christian communities. Further research might disclose how social and cultural forces converged to suppress feminine symbolism—and women's participation—from western Christian tradition. Given such research, the history of Christianity never could be told in the same way again.

NOTES

1. Where the God of Israel is characterized as husband and lover in the Old Testament (OT), his spouse is described as the community of Israel (i.e., Isa. 50:1, 54:1–8; Jer. 2:2–3, 20–25, 3:1–20; Hos. 1–4, 14) or as the land of Israel (cf. Isa. 62:1–5).
2. One may note several exceptions to this rule: Deut. 32:11; Hos. 11:1; Isa. 66:12 ff; Num. 11:12.
3. *The Gospel according to Thomas* (hereafter cited as *ET*), ed. A. Guillaumount, H. Ch. Puech, G. Quispel, W. Till, Yassah 'Abd-al-Masih (London: Collins, 1959), logion 113–114.
4. Hippolytus, *Refutationis Omnium Haeresium* (hereafter cited as *Ref*), ed. L. Dunker, F. Schneidewin (Göttingen, 1859), 5.7.
5. Ref, 5.6.
6. Irenaeus, *Adversus Haereses* (hereafter cited as *AH*), ed. W. W. Harvey (Cambridge, 1857), 1.11.1.
7. Ibid., 1.13.2.
8. Ibid., 1.13.6.
9. Ibid., 1.18.2.
10. Ibid., 1.11.5–21.1, 3; *Ref,* 6.29.
11. *Apocryphon Johannis* (hereafter cited as *AJ*), ed. S. Giversen (Copenhagen: Prostant Apud Munksgaard, 1963), 47.20–48.14.
12. *AJ*, 52.34–53.6.
13. Ibid., 61.13–14.
14. Origen, *Commentary on John*, 2.12; *Hom. On Jeremiah*, 15.4.
15. *ET, 101.* The text of this passage is badly damaged; I follow here the reconstruction of G. MacRae of the Harvard Divinity School.
16. *L'Evangile selon Phillipe* (hereafter cited as *EP*), ed. J. E. Ménard (Leiden: Brill, 1967), logion 6.
17. *EP,* logion 36.
18. Ibid., logion 82.
19. Ibid., logion 17.
20. *Extraits de Théodote* (hereafter cited as *Exc*), ed. F. Sagnard, Sources chrétiennes 23 (Paris: Sources chrétiennes, 1948).
21. *AH,* 1.30.6.
22. *Ref,* 6.17.
23. Ibid., 6.14.
24. *AH,* 1.14.7–8.
25. *Ref,* 6.18.
26. Genesis Rabba 8.1, also 17.6; cf. Levitius Rabba 14. For an excellent discussion of androgyny, see W. Meeks, "The Image of the Androgyne: Some Uses of a Symbol in Earliest Christianity," *History of Religions* 13 (1974): 165–208.
27. *AH,* 1.18.2.
28. *Exc,* 21.1.

29. *Ref,* 6.33.
30. *AH,* 1.5.4; *Ref,* 6.33.
31. *AJ,* 61.8–14.
32. *Ref,* 7.26.
33. *AH,* 1.13.7.
34. Ibid., 1.13.2–5.
35. Tertullian, *De Praescriptione Haereticorum* (hereafter cited as *DP),* ed. E. Oethler (Lipsius, 1853–54), p. 41.
36. *De Baptismo* 1. I am grateful to Cyril Richardson for calling my attention to this passage and to the three subsequent ones.
37. Epiphanes, *De Baptismo,* 42.5.
38. *AH,* 1.25.6.
39. *DP,* 6.30.
40. *The Gospel according to Mary,* Codex Berolinensis, BG, 8502,1.7.1–1.19.5, ed., intro., and trans. G. MacRae, unpublished manuscript.
41. *Pistis Sophia,* ed. Carl Schmidt (Berlin: Academie-Verlag, 1925), 36 (57), 71 (161).
42. 1 Cor. 11:7–9. For discussion, see R. Scroggs, "Paul and the Eschatological Woman," *Journal of the American Academy of Religion* 40 (1972): 283–303; R. Scroggs, "Paul and the Eschatological Woman: Revisited," *Journal of the American Academy of Religion* 42 (1974): 532–37; and E. Pagels, "Paul and Women: A Response to Recent Discussion," *Journal of the American Academy of Religion* 42 (1972): 538–49.
43. Clement Alexandrinus, *Paidegogos,* ed. O. Stählin (Leipzig, 1905), 1.6.
44. Ibid., 1.4.
45. Ibid., 1.19.
46. 2 Tim. 2:11–14.

When God Was a Woman

MERLIN STONE

INTRODUCTION

Though we live amid high-rise steel buildings, formica countertops, and electronic television screens, there is something in all of us, women and men alike, that makes us feel deeply connected with the past. Perhaps the sudden dampness of a beach cave or the lines of sunlight piercing through the intricate lace patterns of the leaves in a darkened grove of tall trees will awaken from the hidden recesses of our minds the distant echoes of a remote and ancient time, taking us back to the early stirrings of human life on the planet. For people raised and programmed on the patriarchal religions of today, religions that affect us in even the most secular aspects of our society, perhaps there remains a lingering, almost innate memory of sacred shrines and temples tended by priestesses who served in the religion of the original supreme deity. In the beginning, people prayed to the Creatress of Life, the Mistress of Heaven. At the very dawn of religion, God was a woman. Do you remember?

For years, something has magnetically lured me into exploring the legends, the temple sites, the statues, and the ancient rituals of the female deities, drawing me back in time to an age when the Goddess

Merlin Stone received her M.A. from California College of Arts and Crafts. She is author of *When God Was a Woman* and is working on a collection of Goddess and heroine rituals and legends from all over the world. Her articles on Goddess religion have appeared in *Spare Rib, Heresies,* and *The Lunar Calendar.* This selection, reprinted from *When God Was a Woman,* by Merlin Stone, © 1976, was originally published as *The Paradise Papers* in Great Britain. It is used by permission of the publishers, The Dial Press and Quartet Books Limited.

was omnipotent, and women acted as Her clergy, controlling the form and rites of religion.

Perhaps it was my training and work as a sculptor that first exposed me to the sculptures of the Goddess found in the ruins of prehistoric sanctuaries and the earliest dwellings of human beings. Perhaps it was a certain romantic mysticism, which once embarrassed me, but to which I now happily confess, that led me over the years into the habit of collecting information about the early female religions and the veneration of female deities. Occasionally I tried to dismiss my fascination with this subject as overly fanciful and certainly disconnected from my work (I was building electronic sculptural environments at the time). Nevertheless, I would find myself continually perusing archaeology journals and poring over texts in museum or university library stacks.

As I read, I recalled that somewhere along the pathway of my life I had been told—and accepted the idea—that the sun, great and powerful, was naturally worshiped as male, while the moon, hazy, delicate symbol of sentiment and love, had always been revered as female. Much to my surprise, I discovered accounts of Sun Goddesses in the lands of Canaan, Anatolia, Arabia, and Australia, while Sun Goddesses among the Eskimos, the Japanese, and the Khasis of India were accompanied by subordinate brothers who were symbolized as the moon.

I had somewhere assimilated the idea that the earth was invariably identified as female, Mother Earth, the one who passively accepts the seed, while heaven was naturally and inherently male, its intangibility symbolic of the supposedly exclusive male ability to think in abstract concepts. This too I had accepted without question—until I learned that nearly all the female deities of the Near and Middle East were titled Queen of Heaven, and in Egypt not only was the ancient Goddess Nut known as the heavens but her brother-husband Geb was symbolized as the earth.

Most astonishing of all was the discovery of numerous accounts of the female Creators of all existence, divinities who were credited with bringing forth not only the first people but the entire earth and the heavens above. There were records of such Goddesses in Sumer, Babylon, Egypt, Africa, Australia, and China.

In India, the Goddess Sarasvati was honored as the inventor of the original alphabet, while in Celtic Ireland the Goddess Brigit was esteemed as the patron deity of language. Texts revealed that it was the

Goddess Nidaba in Sumer who was paid honor as the one who initially invented clay tablets and the art of writing. She appeared in that position earlier than any of the male deities who later replaced Her. The official scribe of the Sumerian heaven was a woman. But most significant was the archaeological evidence of the earliest examples of written language so far discovered; these were also located in Sumer, at the temple of the Queen of Heaven in Erech, written there over five thousand years ago. Though writing is most often said to have been invented by *man,* however that may be defined, the combination of the above factors presents a most convincing argument that it may have actually been woman who pressed those first meaningful marks into wet clay.

In agreement with the generally accepted theory that women were responsible for the development of agriculture, as an extension of their food-gathering activities, there were female deities everywhere who were credited with this gift to civilization. In Meşopotamia, where some of the earliest evidences of agricultural development have been found, the Goddess Ninlil was revered for having provided Her people with an understanding of planting and harvesting methods. In nearly all areas of the world, female deities were extolled as healers, dispensers of curative herbs, roots, plants, and other medical aids, casting the priestesses who attended the shrines into the role of physicians of those who worshiped there.

Some legends described the Goddess as a powerful, courageous warrior, a leader in battle. The worship of the Goddess as valiant warrior seems to have been responsible for the numerous reports of female soldiers, later referred to by the classical Greeks as the Amazons. More thoroughly examining the accounts of the esteem the Amazons paid to the female deity, it became evident that women who worshiped a warrior Goddess hunted and fought in the lands of Libya, Anatolia, Bulgaria, Greece, Armenia, and Russia and were far from the mythical fantasy so many writers of today would have us believe.

I could not help noticing how far removed from contemporary images were the prehistoric and most ancient historic attitudes toward the thinking capacities and intellect of woman, for nearly everywhere the Goddess was revered as wise counselor and prophetess. The Celtic Cerridwen was the Goddess of Intelligence and Knowledge in the pre-Christian legends of Ireland, the priestesses of the Goddess Gaia provided the wisdom of divine revelation at pre-Greek sanctuaries, while the Greek Demeter and the Egyptian Isis were both invoked as lawgivers and sage dispensers of righteous wisdom, counsel, and justice. The Egyptian Goddess Maat represented the very order, rhythm, and truth of the Universe. Ishtar of Mesopotamia was referred to as the Directress of People, the Prophetess, the Lady of Vision, while the archaeological records of the city of Nimrud, where Ishtar was worshiped, revealed that women served as judges and magistrates in the courts of law.

The more I read, the more I discovered. The worship of female deities appeared in every area of the world, presenting an image of woman that I had never before encountered. As a result, I began to ponder upon the power of myth and eventually to perceive these legends as more than the innocent childlike fables they first appeared to be. They were tales with a most specific point of view.

Myths present ideas that guide perception, conditioning us to think and even perceive in a particular way, especially when we are young and impressionable. Often they portray the actions of people who are rewarded or punished for their behavior, and we are encouraged to view these as examples to emulate or avoid. So many of the stories told to us from the time we are just old enough to understand deeply affect our attitudes and comprehension of the world about us and ourselves. Our ethics, morals, conduct, values, sense of duty, and even sense of humor are often developed from simple childhood parables and fables. From them, we learn what is socially acceptable in the society from which they come. They define good and bad, right and wrong, what is natural and what is unnatural among the people who hold the myths as meaningful. It was quite apparent that the myths and legends that grew from, and were propagated by, a religion in which the deity was female, and revered as wise, valiant, powerful, and just, provided very different images of womanhood from those which we are offered by the male-oriented religions of today.

[As she begins to consider the power of myth, Stone is led to examine the effects of the myth of Eve on our image of femaleness. She then observes that the archetypal woman in Goddess-worshiping religions is very different from Eve—and that many of the closest neighbors of the early Hebrews worshiped the Goddess.]

WHO WAS SHE?

It was not long before the various pieces of evidence fell into place and the connections began to take form. And then I understood.

Ashtoreth, the despised "pagan" deity of the Old Testament was (despite the efforts of biblical scribes to disguise her identity by repeatedly using the masculine gender) actually Astarte—the Great Goddess, as She was known in Canaan, the Near Eastern Queen of Heaven. Those heathen idol worshipers of the Bible had been praying to a woman God–elsewhere known as Innin, Inanna, Nana, Nut, Anat, Anahita, Istar, Isis, Au Set, Ishara, Asherah, Ashtart, Attoret, Attar, and Hathor—the many-named Divine Ancestress. Yet each name denoted, in the various languages and dialects of those who revered Her, the Great Goddess. Was it merely coincidence that during all those years of Sunday School I never learned that Ashtoreth was female?

Even more astonishing was the archaeological evidence which proved that Her religion had existed and flourished in the Near and Middle East for thousands of years before the arrival of the patriarchal Abraham, first prophet of the male deity Yahweh. Archaeologists had traced the worship of the Goddess back to the Neolithic communities of about 7000 BC, some to the Upper Paleolithic cultures of about 25,000 BC. From the time of its Neolithic origins, its existence was repeatedly attested to until well into Roman times. Yet Bible scholars agreed that it was as late as somewhere between 1800 and 1550 BC that Abraham had lived in Canaan (Palestine).

Who was this Goddess? Why had a female, rather than a male, been designated as the supreme deity? How influential and significant was Her worship, and when had it actually begun? As I asked myself these questions, I began to probe even deeper into Neolithic and Paleolithic times. Though Goddesses have been worshiped in all areas of the world, I focused on the religion as it evolved in the Near and Middle East, since these were the lands where both Judaism, Christianity, and Islam were born. I found that the development of the religion of the female deity in this area was intertwined with the earliest beginnings of religion so far discovered anywhere on earth.

DAWN IN THE GRAVETTIAN GARDEN OF EDEN

The Upper Paleolithic period, though most of its sites have been found in Europe, is the conjectural foundation of the religion of the Goddess as it emerged in the later Neolithic Age of the Near East. Since it precedes the time of written records and does not directly lead into an historical period that might have helped to explain it, the information on the Paleolithic existence of Goddess worship must at this time remain speculative. Theories on the origins of the Goddess in this period are founded on the juxtaposition of mother-kinship customs to ancestor worship. They are based upon three separate lines of evidence.

The first relies on anthropological analogy to explain the initial development of matrilineal (mother-kinship) societies. Studies of "primitive" tribes over the last few centuries have led to the realization that some isolated "primitive" peoples, even in our own century, did not yet possess the conscious understanding of the relationship of sex to conception. The analogy is then drawn that Paleolithic people may have been at a similar level of biological awareness.

Jacquetta Hawkes wrote in 1963 that "Australian and a few other primitive peoples did not understand biological paternity or accept a necessary connection between sexual intercourse and conception." In that same year, S. G. F. Brandon, Professor of Comparative Religion at the University of Manchester in England, observed, "How the infant came to be in the womb was undoubtedly a mystery to primitive man . . . in view of the period that separates impregnation from birth, it seems probable that the significance of gestation and birth was appreciated long before it was realized that these phenomena were the result of conception following coition."

"James Frazer, Margaret Mead, and other anthropologists," writes Leonard Cottrell, "have established that in the very early stages of man's development, before the secret of human fecundity was understood, before coitus was associated with childbirth, the female was revered as the giver of life. Only women could produce their own kind, and man's part in this process was not as yet recognized."

According to these authors, as well as many authorities who have written on this subject, in the most ancient human societies people probably did not yet possess the conscious understanding of the relationship of sex to reproduction. Thus the concepts of paternity and fatherhood would not yet have been understood. Though probably accompanied by various mythical explanations, babies were simply born from women.

If this was the case, then the mother would have been seen as the singular parent of her family, the lone producer of the next generation. For this reason, it would be natural for children to take the name of their mother's tribe or clan. Accounts of descent in the family would be kept through the female line, going from mother to daughter, rather than from father to son, as is the custom practiced in western societies today. Such a social structure is generally referred to as *matrilineal;* that is, based upon mother-kinship. In such cultures (known among many "primitive" peoples even today, as well as in historically attested societies at the time of classical Greece) not only the names but titles, possessions, and territorial rights are passed along through the female line, so that they may be retained within the family clan.

Hawkes points out that in Australia, in areas where the concept of paternity had not yet been understood, "there is much to show that matrilineal descent and matrilocal marriage [the husband moving to the wife's family home or village] were general and the status of women much higher." She writes that these customs still prevail in parts of Africa and among the Dravidians of India, and relics of them in Melanesia, Micronesia, and Indonesia.

The second line of evidence concerns the beginnings of religious beliefs and rituals and their connection with matrilineal descent. There have been numerous studies of Paleolithic cultures, explorations of sites occupied by these people and the apparent rites connected with the disposal of their dead. These suggest that, as the earliest concepts of religion developed, they probably took the form of ancestor worship. Again an analogy is drawn between the Paleolithic people and the religious concepts and rituals observed among many of the "primitive" tribes studied by anthropologists over the last two centuries. Ancestor worship occurs among tribal people the world over. Maringer states that even at the time of his writing, 1956, certain tribes in Asia were still making small statues known as *dzuli.* Explaining these, he says, "The idols are female and represent the human origins of the whole tribe."

Thus as the religious concepts of the earliest *homo sapiens** were developing, the quest for the ultimate source of life (perhaps the core of all theological thought) may have begun. In these Upper Paleolithic societies—in which the mother may have been regarded as the sole parent of the family, ancestor worship was apparently the basis of

---

* The term *homo sapiens* (literally "knowing or knowledgeable *man*") illustrates once again the scholarly assumption of the prime importance of the male, in this case to the point of the total negation of the female population of the species so defined. If all *"homo sapiens"* had literally been just that, no sooner than the species had developed would it have died out for lack of the capability to reproduce its own kind.

sacred ritual, and accounts of ancestry were probably reckoned only through the matriline—the concept of the creator of all human life may have been formulated by the clan's image of the woman who had been their most ancient, their primal ancestor and that image thereby deified and revered as Divine Ancestress.

The third line of evidence, and the most tangible, derives from the numerous sculptures of women found in the Gravettian-Aurignacian cultures of the Upper Paleolithic Age. Some of these date back as far as 25,000 BC. These small female figurines, made of stone and bone and clay and often referred to as *Venus figures,* have been found in areas where small settled communities once lived. They were often discovered lying close to the remains of the sunken walls of what were probably the earliest human-made dwellings on earth. Maringer claims that niches or depressions had been made in the walls to hold the figures. These statues of women, some seemingly pregnant, have been found throughout the widespread Gravettian-Aurignacian sites in areas as far apart as Spain, France, Germany, Austria, Czechoslovakia, and Russia. These sites and figures appear to span a period of at least ten thousand years.

"It appears highly probable then," says Maringer, "that the female figurines were idols of a 'great mother' cult, practiced by the nonnomadic Aurignacian mammoth hunters who inhabited the immense Eurasian territories that extended from Southern France to Lake Baikal in Siberia." (Incidentally, it is from this Lake Baikal area in Siberia that the tribes which migrated to North America, supposedly about this same period [there developing into the American Indians], are believed to have originated.)

Russian paleontologist Z. A. Abramova, quoted in Alexander Marshak's recent book *Roots of Civilization,* offers a slightly different interpretation, writing that in the Paleolithic religion, "The image of the Woman-Mother . . . was a complex one, and it included diverse ideas related to the special significance of the women in early clan society. She was neither a god, an idol, nor the mother of a god; she was the Clan Mother. . . . The ideology of the hunting tribes in this period of the matriarchal clan was reflected in the female figurines."

THE NEOLITHIC MORNING

The connections between the Paleolithic female figurines and the later emergence of the Goddess-worshiping societies in the Neolithic periods of the Near and Middle East are not definitive but are suggested by many authorities. At the Gravettian site of Vestonice, Czechoslovakia, where Venus figures were not only formed but hardened in an oven, the carefully arranged grave of a woman was found. She was about forty years old. She had been supplied with tools, covered with mammoth shoulder blade bones and strewn with red ochre. In a proto-Neolithic site at Shanidar, on the northern stretches of the Tigris River, another grave was found, this one dating from about 9000 BC. It was the burial of a slightly younger woman, once again strewn with red ochre.

One of the most significant links between the two periods are the female figurines, understood in Neolithic societies, through their emergence into the historic period of written records to represent the Goddess. The sculptures of the Paleolithic cultures and those of the Neolithic periods are remarkably similar in materials, size, and, most astonishing, in style. Hawkes commented on the relationship between the two periods, noting that the Paleolithic female figures "are extraordinarily like the Mother or Earth Goddesses of the agricultural peoples of Eurasia in the Neolithic Age and must be directly ancestral to them." E. O. James also remarks on the similarity, saying of the Neolithic statues, "Many of them are quite clearly allied to the Gravettian-Paleolithic prototypes." But perhaps most significant is the fact that Aurignacian sites have now been discovered near Antalya, about sixty miles from the Neolithic Goddess-worshiping community of Hacilar in Anatolia (Turkey), and at Musa Dag in northern Syria (once a part of Canaan).

James Mellaart, formerly the assistant director of the British Institute of Archaeology at Ankara, now teaching at the Institute of Archaeology in London, describes the proto-Neolithic cultures of the Near East, dating them at about 9000 to 7000 BC. He writes that during that time, "Art makes its appearance in the form of animal carvings and statuettes of the supreme deity, the Mother Goddess."

These Neolithic communities emerge with the earliest evidences of agricultural development (which is what defines them as Neolithic). They appear in areas later known as Canaan (Palestine [Israel], Lebanon, and Syria); in Anatolia (Turkey); and along the northern reaches of the Tigris and Euphrates rivers (Iraq and Syria). It may be significant that all these cultures possessed obsidian, which was probably acquired from the closest site of availability—Anatolia. One of these sites, near Lake Van, would be directly on the route from the Russian steppes into the Near East.

At the site that is now known as Jericho (in Canaan), by 7000 BC people were living in plastered brick houses, some with clay ovens with chimneys and even sockets for doorposts. Rectangular plaster shrines had already appeared. Sybelle von Cles-Reden writes of Jericho, "Various finds point to an active religious life. Female clay figures with their hands raised to their breast resemble idols of the mother goddess which were later so widely disseminated in the Near East." Mellaart too writes of Jericho: "They carefully made small clay figures of the mother-goddess type."

Another Neolithic community was centered in Jarmo in northern Iraq from about 6800 BC. H. W. F. Saggs, Professor of Semitic Languages, tells us that in Jarmo, "There were figurines in clay of animals as well as of a mother goddess: The mother goddess represented by such figurines seems to have been the central figure in Neolithic religion."

Hacilar, some sixty miles from the Aurignacian site of Antalya, was inhabited at about 6000 BC. Here, too, figures of the Goddess have been found. And at the excavations at Catal Hüyük, close to the Cilician plans of Anatolia, near present day Konya, Mellaart discovered no less than forty shrines, dating from 6500 BC onward. The culture of Catal Hüyük existed for nearly one thousand years. Mellaart reveals, "The statues allow us to recognize the main deities worshiped by Neolithic people at Catal Hüyük. The principal deity was a goddess, who is shown in her three aspects, as a young woman, a mother giving birth or as an old woman." Mellaart suggests that there may have been a majority of women at Catal Hüyük, as evidenced by the number of female burials. At Catal Hüyük, too, red ochre was strewn on the bodies; nearly all of the red ochre burials were of women. He also suggests that the religion was primarily associated with the role of women in the initial development of agriculture, and adds, "It seems extremely likely that the cult of the goddess was administered mainly by women."

By about 5500 BC, houses had been built with groups of rooms around a central courtyard, a style used by many architects even today. These were found in sites along the northern reaches of the Tigris River, in communities that represent what is known as the Hassuna period. There, as in other Neolithic communities, archaeologists found agricultural tools such as the hoe and sickle, storage jars for corn, and clay ovens. And once again, Professor Saggs reports, "The religious ideas of the Hassuna period are reflected in clay figurines of the mother goddess."

One of the most sophisticated prehistoric cultures of the ancient Near and Middle East was situated along the banks of the northern Tigris and westward as far as the Habur River. It is known as the Halaf culture and appeared in various places by 5000 BC. At these Halaf sites, small towns with cobbled streets have been discovered. Metal was in use, which would place the Halaf cultures into a period labeled by archaeologists as Chalcolithic.

Saggs writes that, judging from a picture on a ceramic vase, "It is probably from the Halaf period that the invention of wheeled vehicles date." Goddess figurines have been found at all Halaf sites, but at the Halafian town of Arpachiyah these figures were associated with serpents, double axes, and doves, all symbols connected with Goddess worship as it was known in historical periods. Along with the intricately designed polychromed ceramic ware, at Arpachiyah buildings known as *tholoi* appeared. These were circular shaped rooms up to thirty-three feet in diameter with well-engineered vaulted ceilings. The round structures were connected to long rectangular corridors up to sixty-three feet in length. Since it was close to these *tholoi* that most of the Goddess figurines were discovered, it is likely that they were used as shrines.

By 4000 BC, Goddess figures appeared at Ur and Uruk, both situated on the southern end of the Euphrates River, not far from the Persian Gulf. At about this same period, the Neolithic Badarian and Amratian cultures of Egypt first appeared. It is at these sites that agriculture first emerged in Egypt. And, once again, in these Neolithic communities of Egypt Goddess figurines were discovered.

From this point on, with the invention of writing, history emerged in both Sumer (southern Iraq) and Egypt—about 3000 BC. In every area of the Near and Middle East, the Goddess was known in historic times. Though many centuries of transformation had undoubtedly changed the religion in various ways, the worship of the female deity survived into the classical periods of Greece and Rome. It was not totally suppressed until the time of the Christian emperors of Rome and Byzantium, who closed down the last Goddess temples in about 500 AD.

RECONSTRUCTING
TRADITION

THE spectrum of writing on herstory, despite its fine gradations, can be divided into two camps. Some herstorians are reformists attempting to reinterpret and transform tradition from within, while others are revolutionaries searching for new forms of female religious expression. This distinction also applies to constructive feminist work in religion. In doing theology and creating rituals from the perspective of women's experience, feminist thinkers must choose a context in which to work—Judaism, Christianity, an alternate tradition, or women's experience alone.

The articles in this section represent reformist approaches to theology and ritual. Their authors are feminists who are committed personally and politically to one of the major traditions of the West. They recognize that Judaism and Christianity are patriarchal religions, but they deny that patriarchy is what these religions are about. They find in tradition a valuable core that has proved liberating to them personally and that, they believe, can liberate tradition itself from its patriarchal bias. Some women discover this core in themes dealing explicitly with liberation—the exodus from Egypt, the prophetic plea for justice, or Jesus' concern for the poor and oppressed. Others find it in the idea of a God who transcends all limitations, including the sexuality, in feminine images such as Mary or the Shechinah, or even in the notion of tradition. But wherever this core is located, it is taken as the "true" tradition, as a more fundamental statement of the nature of Judaism or Christianity than sexist images or institutional structures.

Obviously, there are continuities, even overlaps, between this section and the first two. Trible's, Fiorenza's, and McLaughlin's search for a usable past clearly is rooted in their reformist commitment to the continued viability of Christian tradition. The first three essays in this volume by Saiving, Ruether, and Daly are also reformist: they criticize and challenge Christian theology not to jettison it, but to transform it. The articles in this section are different from the others, however, in that they assume the feminist criticism of religion and the insights of herstory and use them as starting points to defend or delineate new forms of Christianity and Judaism.

Elisabeth Fiorenza's "Feminist Spirituality, Christian Identity and Catholic Vision" provides a clear rationale for the reformist position. Fiorenza takes seriously Daly's radical critique of Christianity as "inherently and essentially sexist," but her own *experience* of Catholic tradition tells her that Daly is mistaken. Since she began to question female cultural roles precisely because of her Christian faith, Fiorenza discusses those aspects of Catholicism that supported her growth. The God whom Jesus preached, she claims, is not—as Daly insists—an authoritarian "other" but is, for her, the same creator and nurturer of life central to feminist spirituality. While this God was imaged in increasingly patriarchal ways, the compensatory figure of Mary allowed Catholics to experience the divine also as female. Moreover, the call to sainthood, which is no respecter of persons, has provided Christian women with opportunities to choose vocations other than wife and mother. Fiorenza never claims that these liberating insights prove the church free of sexism. But she finds them sufficient grounds to hope and work for the church's repentance, rather than abandoning it for its sins.

Sheila Collins' "Theology in the Politics of Appalachian Women," brings together two different and extremely significant directions in feminist constructive work: story theology and liberation theology. Writing for the concrete setting of a conference on Appalachian women, Collins envisions the empowering of poor and defeated women as part of a continuing struggle toward shaping the "commonwealth" of God on earth. As women give voice to their own oppression—as women, as Appalachian, as poor, as black—they become part of an ongoing biblical history. Articulating their own experiences, their own stories, becomes the basis both for the appropriation of biblical themes of bondage and liberation *and* for strong and united political action. This feminist reclaiming of biblical history is critical and careful: it rejects distortion of biblical language and intentionality by the powerful and by the emerging coalition on the right. But it does so in the name of the "true" biblical history, which tells of the liberation of the oppressed. The groaning of the Israelites in slavery, the longing for the promised land, and Jesus' preaching to the poor are fundamental themes in a feminist theology that is shaped by the pain and struggles of all women, but most especially of poor women.

Although feminist theologians find liberating themes in Christian tradition, their appropriation of these themes is not always easy and unambiguous. As Nelle Morton points out in her article, feminist celebration—and, we would add, theology—faces a dilemma. When so many Christian symbols seem to negate the personhood of women, where can women find a language free of sexism with which to affirm their life experience? Morton's gropings toward an answer place her on the boundary between reformist and revolutionary. Sometimes scripture seems to express the mysteries of life and death so central to women's experience; at other times, it does not. It may be necessary, Morton suggests, to go beyond biblical language to earlier myths in which the Bible is grounded. It will take a period of experimentation and ripening, she believes, before authentic forms of celebration can emerge from women's painful struggle for self-creation. Just how traditional these new forms will be remains to be seen.

The problem Morton raises of how women can find ritual forms expressive of their own experience seems particularly important for Jewish women. Since Judaism is a religion of ritual, law, and study, rather than theology, creed, and doctrine, Jewish feminists have devoted their efforts not so much to defining and overcoming the patriarchal structures of Jewish *thought* as to criticizing specific attitudes toward women and to working for the full incorporation of women into Jewish religious life. Feminist contributions to the reconstruction of tradition most often focus on creation of new rituals. (Hence the absence of a Jewish article in the last section.) Even those Jewish thinkers who are most theoretical frequently express a practical concern.

Rita Gross' argument for female God language, a plea for expanding religious imagination relevant to all women, is firmly rooted in Jewish worship. Female God language is *possible,* Gross argues, because God is absolutely transcendent and therefore is as much—and as little—female as male. Female God language is *necessary* because the notion of a personal (and therefore anthropomorphic) God is fundamental to Jewish prayer. If liturgy is not to make an idol out of maleness, it must speak of God in both male and female terms. The Sabbath prayers by Maggie Wenig and Naomi Janowitz can be read as a concrete response to Gross' call for female God language in liturgy. Although expressing themes relevant to all women, they too are firmly rooted in a Jewish context. Used by a women's congregation at Brown University these prayers both address God as female *and* image Her in terms that grow out of women's experience. Thus not only the sex but also the attributes of God begin to be transformed.

Judith Plaskow's ceremony celebrating the birth of a Jewish daughter redresses an inequity in life cycle rituals for Jewish boys and girls. While boys are circumcised at birth and then welcomed into the adult community with *bar mitzvah* at thirteen, the only life cycle celebration in girls' lives is marriage. Assuming that God's covenant with Israel is with the *whole* people, Plaskow creates a ritual formally to initiate girls into the covenant community of Israel. Cantor's Haggadah, or Passover service, uses the occasion of the Jewish festival of freedom to celebrate the participation of women in Jewish liberation struggles. Disturbed by the complete absence of women in the traditional Passover text, Cantor searches for a way to acknowledge the continued oppression of women within Judaism while remaining faithful to the spirit of joy and unity characteristic of the holiday.

The rituals created by Jewish feminist reformists presuppose loyalty to Jewish tradition, while focusing on themes within tradition that allow for growth and change. The transcendence of God, the notion of covenant, the idea of liberation are interpreted more inclusively, but within the context of commitment to Jewish religious life.

The a priori commitment to tradition, shared by Jewish and Christian reformists, poses a problem. As Nelle Morton asks in the most radical essay in this section: Can symbols deeply rooted in patriarchy be expected to function adequately in the new—and in many ways conflicting—context of feminist ritual and thought? Deciding in advance that the new feminist language will reverberate with certain traditional themes runs the risk of muting the insights found in women's new stories and experiences. The seriousness of this danger depends to some degree on the malleability of tradition. The articles in this section testify to the continued strength and vitality women can find in their religious pasts and also suggest that traditional stories need not be fixed and stagnant but can become new with reinterpreting. It may well be, moreover, that women deceive themselves in thinking they can be done with history and begin anew. By reappropriating tradition critically and consciously, feminist reformists at least guard against its sneaking up on them from behind.

Feminist Spirituality, Christian Identity, and Catholic Vision

ELISABETH SCHÜSSLER FIORENZA

. . . As a biblical scholar, I have long ceased to think of theology in "confessional" terms. My experience of feminist liturgies and theological dialogue, moreover, has taught me that feminist theology is truly *ecumenical,* since the Christian as well as the Jewish religious tradition and symbols share in the same patriarchal culture and language. If I therefore refer here to the Catholic vision, I do not intend to imply that this vision is not shared by other Christian churches and other religions, but only to say that my approach to the topic is strongly colored by my experience as a Catholic woman and theologian. As a teacher of women's courses in theology at a Catholic university, moreover, I am challenged again and again to explore the relationship between feminism, Christian faith, and the Catholic community and tradition.

When our daughter Christina was baptized, one of my college students asked me: "How can you with your feminist consciousness baptize a girl child into such a patriarchal and sexist community as the Roman Catholic Church appears to be?" The former Roman Catholic

This essay originally appeared in *National Institute for Campus Ministries Journal* (Fall 1978), and is reprinted by permission of the journal.

theologian Mary Daly spells out this question in the most radical way when she insists that the myth and symbols of Christianity are *inherently and essentially* sexist. "Since 'God' is male, the male is God. God the Father legitimates all earthly God-fathers" and "the idea of a unique divine incarnation in a male, the God man of the 'hypostatic union' is inherently sexist and oppressive. Christolatry is idolatry."[1] The assertion of some theologians that Christ was male and, therefore, that women cannot be ordained as priests and represent Christ before the community appears to substantiate Dr. Daly's contention.

Yet if maleness is the essence of God, and maleness but not humanness the goal of incarnation, how could women have been saved and made in baptism full members of the people of God?

FEMINIST SPIRITUALITY

It is, however, not so much theology but my own experience as a woman having grown up in the Catholic tradition that leads me to question that maleness is the essence of Christian faith and theology. Despite all masculine terminology of prayers, catechism, and liturgy, despite blatant patriarchal male spiritual guidance, my commitment to Christian faith and love first led me to question the feminine cultural role which parents, school and church had taught me to accept and to internalize. My vision of Christian life-style, responsibility, and community brought me to reject the culturally imposed role of women and not vice versa. What was this liberating vision that came through to me despite all patriarchal packaging and sexist theological systematization? What was the driving force or spirituality that led me to question and to reject the cultural myth of femininity?

A comparison between radical feminist spirituality and the Christian spirituality which understands the Spirit, not in a platonic sense but in the biblical sense of the divine power and dynamic enabling us to live as Christians, can show that both are inspired by the same vision, even though radical feminist spirituality is often formulated over and against a patriarchal theology and sexist praxis of the Christian churches. Feminist spirituality proclaims wholeness, healing love, and spiritual power not as hierarchical, as *power over,* but as *power for* as enabling power. It proclaims *the Goddess* as the source of this power, as the enabling context of human lives and of a nonhierarchical, nonauthoritarian, noncompetitive community. The Goddess is the giver and nurturer of life, the dispenser of love and happiness. Woman as her image is therefore not "the other" of the divine. She is not body and carnality in opposition to spirit and soul, not the perpetuator of evil and rebellion. Being a woman, living in sisterhood under the aegis of the Goddess, brings us in touch with the creative, healing, life-giving power at the heart of the world.

In my opinion, the Goddess of radical feminist spirituality is not so very different from the God whom Jesus preached and whom he called "Father." In ever new images of life, love, light, compassion, mercy, care, peace, service, and community, the New Testament writings attempt to speak of the God of Jesus Christ, and of this God's life-giving power, the Holy Spirit. All the New Testament authors agree that Christian faith has to be lived in the very concrete praxis of agape. In various ways, they spell out that Jesus rejected all hierarchical forms and power in his community of followers and explicitly warned that Christian leadership should not be exercised in the "power to lord over others" but in serving. The Second Vatican Council follows this New Testament spirituality when it attempts to speak of the Church in terms of enabling love, inclusive community, and service for all humankind.

The traditions about the Goddess and those of the New Testament are conflated in the Catholic community's cult of Mary. The more the Christian understanding of God was patriarchalized—the more God became the majestic ruler and the stern judge, the more people turned to the figure and cult of Mary. The more Jesus Christ became divinized, the more it became necessary to have a mediator between the majestic-transcendent God or his Son and the Christian community. One could almost say that through the dynamics of this development of the gradual patriarchalization of the God image, Mary became the "other face," the Christian "face," of God. All the New Testament images and attributes which characterize God as loving, life giving, compassionate and caring, as being with the people of God are now transferred to the "mother of God," who is as accessible as was the nonpatriarchal God whom Jesus preached. Even though any Catholic school child can explain on an *intellectual-theological* level the difference between the worship of God and Christ and the veneration of Mary, on an *emotional, imaginative, experiential* level the Catholic child experiences the love of God in the figure of a woman. Since in later piety Jesus Christ becomes so transcendentalized and divinized that his incarnation and humanity are almost totally absorbed into his divinity, the "human face" of God is almost solely experienced in the image of a woman. The cult of Mary thus grew in proportion to the gradual repatriarchalization of the Christian God and of Jesus Christ. The Catholic tradition gives us thus the opportunity to *experience* the divine reality in the figure of a woman.

The Catholic cult of Mary also provides us with a tradition of *female language* and imagery to speak of the divine. Christian theology has always maintained that we can speak of God only in an "analogical way" and has never identified any human concept or image of God with the divine reality. God transcends all our human perceptions and language expressions. Yet the Jewish and Christian traditions have spoken of God predominantly in patriarchal language and imagery. We all are used to hearing: "God the Father loves you, and if you join the brotherhood and fellowship of all Christians you will become sons of God and brothers of Christ, who died for all men." Such masculinized God language has communicated for centuries to women that they are nonentities, subspecies of men, subordinated and inferior to men not only on a cultural but also on a religious plane. The combination of male language for God with the stress on the sovereignty and absolute authority of the patriarchal God has sanctioned men's drive for power and domination in the church as well as in society.

If Christianity preaches a God of love who liberates every person for new possibilities and for discipleship, then we have to speak of this God in nonpatriarchal, nonsexist terms. Language about God, if it is rooted in a living faith and a living community, can and does change. The cult of Mary in the Catholic church provides us with a tradition of theological language which speaks of the divine reality in female terms and symbols. This tradition encompasses the myth and symbols of the Goddess religion and demonstrates that female language and symbols have a transparency towards God. Only if we speak of God in male and female terms will our language about God truly become "analogical."

Yet this female-matriarchal language ought not to be absolutized if we do not want to fall prey to a reverse sexist understanding of God. The Christian language about God has to transcend patriarchal as well as matriarchal language and symbols, while at the same time employing a variety of human expressions to reflect a pluriformity of human experiences. The truly Christian God language has to affirm mutuality, fulfillment, maturity, and human potentiality not only in terms of gender but also in terms of class, culture, race, and religion if it is to be truly catholic and universal. Christian faith would then enable all kinds of people to affirm themselves as whole human persons, chosen and loved by God, and partaking in the divine reality. Moreover, such a truly Christian and Catholic spirituality would empower all of us to take on responsibilities for eliminating discrimination, oppression and the sin of sexism and for building a new community of mutuality and pluriformity which would mirror the universality of God's redeeming presence and let us experience her power of life and love.

CHRISTIAN IDENTITY

The other liberating experience which the Catholic tradition provided for me as a woman is the assertion that everyone is called to *sainthood*. Even the vocation to the priesthood is superseded by the call to become a saint. Any Catholic girl who grows up reading the "lives of the saints" might internalize all kinds of sexual hangups, but she would not think that her only vocation and her genuine Christian call consists in becoming married and in having children. Granted, from a theological and hagiographical point of view the life choices of the women saints were often limited and conformed to male stereotypes. Yet they still contradicted the middle-class cultural message that women's Christian vocation demands the sacrifice of one's life for the career of a husband and the total devotion of one's time to diapering babies or decorating one's living room. The biographies of the saints are indeed different from the "total woman" propagated by the feminine mystique.

The "lives of the saints" provide a variety of role models for Christian women. What is more important is that they teach that women, like men, have to follow their vocation from God even if this means that they have to go frontally against the ingrained cultural mores and images of women. Women, as well as men, are not defined by their biology and reproductive capabilities but by the call to discipleship and sainthood. The early Christians considered themselves as those who were called and elected by God, the saints of God. This call broke through all limitations of religion, class, race, and gender. The gospels affirm in various ways that Jesus' call to discipleship has precedence over all other obligations, religious duties and family ties.

Jesus did not respect the patriarchal family and its claims but replaced it with the new community of disciples. When his mother and brothers asked for him, he replied, according to Mark,

Who is my mother? Who are my brothers? And looking round at those who were sitting in the circle about him he said: 'Here are my mother and my brothers. Whoever does the will of God is my brother, my sister, my mother'. (Mk 3:31–35)

This theological self-understanding of the Christian community is best expressed in the baptismal formula of Gal. 3:27–29. In reciting this confession, the newly initiated Christians proclaimed their vision of discipleship and inclusive community. Over and against the cultural-religious patterns shared by Jews and Hellenists alike, the Christians affirmed at their baptism that the Christian call eliminates all distinctions of religion, race, class, and caste and leads into a truly universal and catholic community of disciples.

This definition of Christian self-identity was derived by the early Christians from the call to become disciples of Jesus and members of the Christian community. Unfortunately, this early Christian self-understanding did not inform the definitions of Christian self-identity and Christian community proposed by later theology. Instead, theology derived the understanding of Christian identity from cultural anthropology and gleaned the structures of the Christian community from patriarchal societal orders. Instead of formulating a new Christian anthropology in accordance with the call to discipleship and sainthood, it spelled out Christian vocation and discipleship in terms of a cultural anthropology embedded in patriarchy.

DUALISTIC ANTHROPOLOGY

Catholic theology and anthropology has operated for a long time with the concept of the "two natures" of humanity, according to which women and men are by nature and essence different from each other. This attempt to see human nature and Christian discipleship expressed in two essentially different modes of being human led in tradition and theology to the denigration of women and to the glorification and mythologization of the feminine.

Women are not only different from men but also inferior to them. Traditional theology combined this male–female dualism with the body–spirit dualism. Women then represented sexuality, carnality, and evil. Whereas this tradition defines man by his mind and reason, it sees woman as determined by her "nature" and sexuality. Motherhood, therefore, is the true Christian vocation of every woman, regardless of whether or not she becomes a natural mother. However, in the ascetic Christian tradition nature and body have to be subordinated to mind and spirit, so woman because of her nature has to be subordinated to man. This subordination of woman is sanctioned by scripture. The official stance of the Roman Catholic Church on birth control is, moreover, based on this dualism. Women are not allowed through effective means of control to integrate their reproductive capabilities into a life plan of discipleship and vocation, but they have to remain subject to "natural" biological reproductive processes.

Catholic women have either to fulfill their nature and Christian calling in motherhood and procreation, or they have to renounce their nature and sexuality in virginity. Consequently, this traditional theology has a place for women in the Christian community only as mother or virgin. Since "the genuine" Christian and human vocation consists in transcending one's biological limitations, the ideal Christian woman's vocation is represented by the actual biological virgin who lives in concrete ecclesial commitment. The Roman Catholic sisterhood is not open to all women but is based on sexual stratification and on patriarchal anthropology. The most pressing issue within the church today is therefore, in my opinion, to create a new, inclusive sisterhood based on the Christian commitment to discipleship and call to sainthood.

The more contemporary theological aspect of the "two natures" concept of humanity is the assertion that women and men are equal but different. This "dual nature" concept emphasizes the polarity and complementarity of women and men. Only women and men together achieve human wholeness. This concept is often wrongly derived from Gn. 1:27, insofar as this Old Testament passage is taken as an explicative, dogmatic statement and not as an etiological explanation.

This theological anthropology corresponds with Jungian depth psychology, according to which the masculine and the feminine represent archetypes or principles embedded in a collective unconscious. In the opinion of Jungian theologians, the archetypes express not only the given structure of human reality, but also the structure of divine reality. The term *archetype* expresses the presence of a divine force within the human soul which manifests itself in all the typically human patterns of thought, feeling, imagery and behavior. . . . So, when we say women are stuck in archetypal feminine roles, we must recognize that these roles are not simply human creations but that they also express an aspect of the divine.[2]

Many Christian feminists have found in the Jungian myth a "feminine religious identity." The thrust of this form of Christian feminism leads to a glorification of the so-called feminine qualities associated with the emotions, the body, the unconscious, the tribal-communal, and magic. It leads also to the rejection of the predominant cultural so-called masculine principle, associated generally with rationality, intellect, linear and hierarchical thinking, technology, and competitiveness. Whereas in traditional theological anthropology woman represented evil and temptation, in this new version of the "dual nature" concept of humanity, woman is the source of wholeness, life, and salvation. Consequently, the Father God of patriarchal religion has to be replaced with the Mother Goddess of matriarchy. In my opinion, this form of feminist theology is in danger of reintroducing into Christian faith and self-understanding a kind of gnostic dualism that maintains two ultimate principles and creative powers.

The "two natures" concept of humanity, in its negative as well as in its positive forms, reflects the myth of female power. Both the fear and demonization of women and the mythic exaltation and praise of feminine qualities presuppose the myth of the magic life power of the female. This myth has decisively influenced the Catholic understanding of the sacraments and the priesthood of the ordained.

THE MYTH OF FEMALE POWER

In cultures and periods when the mother was the only known parent and her pregnancy was easily attributed to the wind or to ancestral spirits, the power of women to create life must have been awesome indeed. In his study *The Masks of God,* J. Campbell suggests that the power of the female to create life was understood as a magical force which gave to women prodigious powers. In the very earliest forms of art, like the Venus of Willendorf, the swollen breasts, bellies, and huge buttocks of the female are stressed. Campbell believes that these earliest examples of the "graven image" were the first objects of worship and religion. In recent times, anthropologists have, moreover, found numerous primitive peoples who are unaware that the male seed is as necessary to procreation as the female ovum and womb.

This awe for the magical female power to give life is not only a characteristic of primitive people but is deeply ingrained into the psyche of the modern person. A few weeks after having given birth to Christina, we had a faculty retreat, at which I had to make a presentation on the relationship of Lonergan's method in theology to the historical-critical method of biblical scholarship. To my great surprise, the chairman summed up my accomplishments: "Elisabeth did something that none of you men could have done. She gave birth to a child, while at the same time working at theological methodology." My ability to give birth had nothing to do with my intellectual ability to present a theological argument.

Scholars of religion suggest that the myth of female power may have led to the celebration of religious rituals and to the existence of religion as such. They interpret initiation ceremonies, at which one of the elders of the tribe confers adult status on the boys, as efforts by men to act out the rite of birth which nature denies them. Though women give birth to children in the ordinary course of events, by enacting the sacred rites of passage men turn these unfinished creatures into adult human beings. In token of this rebirth, the initiates often take on new names and are granted new privileges and dignities. The ceremonial religious act becomes as significant for the process of human maturation as pregnancy and birth.

In the light of cultural anthropology, it appears to be no accident that those churches which have a sacramental priesthood resist most strongly the ordination of women to the priesthood. The Christian sacraments are all rites which convey life. Baptism is a rebirth to a new everlasting life, the eucharist is the "bread of life," catechesis and proclamation are compared to "mothermilk and solid food." The sacrament of reconciliation restores life to its fullness. The sacrament of marriage protects and sanctifies the source of natural life. The sacraments, as rituals of birthing and nurturing, appear to imitate the female power of giving birth and of nurturing the growth of life. One would think that, therefore, women would be the ideal administrators of the sacrament.

Yet there appears to exist a deep fear in men that women's powers would become so overwhelming if they were admitted to the priesthood and the sacramental ritual, that men would be relegated to insignificance. The demand of women to be admitted to the sacramental priesthood is, therefore, often not perceived as a genuine desire of women to live their Christian vocation and to serve the people of God, but as an attempt completely to "overtake" the church. What men are often afraid of is that the change in role and position will not mean a mere shift in the relationship between men and women but a complete destruction of any relationship or a fatal reversal of the patriarchal relationship.

As long as the theology of church and ministry is based on a Christian anthropology rooted in the myth of female power, women will not be accepted into the sacramental ordained priesthood. On the other hand, as long as women are not accepted as ordained priests, the sacraments will not completely lose their magical character in the eyes of many people. As long as the sacraments and the priesthood are understood in magical terms, they are not nurturing, enabling and serving institutions, but they represent the male power over the spiritual life of Christians. The male–female dualism of traditional Christian anthropology thus engenders the clergy–lay dualism of Catholic ecclesiology. This dualism is, however, not inherent in Christian theology, but was only gradually introduced into theology and church.

THE PILGRIM CHURCH

To affirm that Christian faith and theology are not inherently patriarchal and sexist and, at the same time, to maintain that Christian theology and the Christian churches are guilty of the sin of sexism is the task of feminist theology. Christian feminists respond to the ideology and praxis of sexism in the church basically in two different ways. We do not differ so much in our analyses and critique of the cultural and theological establishment as in our spirituality and strategies. Those who advocate an exodus from all institutions of Christianity and religion for the sake of the Gospel and the genuine experience of transcendence point as justification to the history of Christianity and to their own personal histories to prove that the submission of women is absolutely essential to the churches' functioning. In the present Christian structures and theologies, women can never be more than marginal beings.

Christian feminists who hope for the repentance and radical change

of the Christian churches and religion affirm our own prophetic roles
and critical mission within organized Christianity. We attempt to bring
our feminist analysis and critique to bear upon theology and the
Christian church in order to set free the traditions of emancipation,
equality, and genuine human community which we have experienced
in our Christian heritage. We do not overlook or cover up the
oppression and sin which we have suffered because of Christian
institutions and traditions, but we point them out in order to change
them.

We Christian feminists who still identify with the Catholic tradition
and remain within the institutional structures of the Church can do so
because we take seriously the Church's self-understanding expressed in
Vatican II. The constitution on Divine Revelation, for instance, asserts
that only those statements of the Bible are the revealed Word of God
which pertain to "our salvation." Cultural and anthropological frameworks are not the content of divine revelation, just as scientific and
cosmological statements are only expressions of the human perception
and knowledge of the sacred authors. The Council takes seriously the
principle of incarnation when it asserts that divine revelation is only
given in human, cultural, and societally conditioned language. This
principle of incarnation is also employed by various documents of the
Council which describe the reality of the Church.

> Until there is a new heaven and a new earth where justice dwells (2 Peter
> 3:13), the Pilgrim Church in her sacraments and institutions which pertain to
> this present time takes on the appearance of this passing world. (*Lumen
> Gentium* 48)

This incarnational principle demands a feminist hermeneutic understanding that is not just directed toward the actualizing continuation
and perceptive understanding of Christian tradition and church, but
rather toward a critique of Bible, tradition, and church to the extent
that they contribute to the oppression and domination of women in a
patriarchal and sexist culture and religion. Feminist spirituality has to
grow out of a feminist theology as a critical theology of liberation. The
task of such a theology is to uncover Christian theological traditions
and myths that perpetuate sexist ideologies, violence, and alienation. A
Christian feminist spirituality thus has as its theological presupposition
our own and the Christian community's constant need for renewal and

conversion. Christian existence, church, and theology are caught in the middle of history and, therefore, are in constant need of prophetic critique.

A positive formulation of a feminist Christian spirituality and identity can, in my opinion, never prescind from theological and cultural critique and demand of women that they forget their own anger and hurt and overlook the violence done to their sisters. In Christian terms, no cheap grace is possible. At the beginning of the Christian life and discipleship stands *metanoia,* a new orientation in the life power of the Spirit. Christian theology and the Christian community will only be able to speak in an authentic way to the quest for feminist spirituality and for the religious identity of women when the whole church, as well as its individual members, has renounced all forms of sexist ideology and praxis which are exhibited in our church structures, theologies and liturgies. The Church has publicly to confess that it has wronged women. As the Christian community has officially rejected national and racial exploitation and publicly repented of its tradition of anti-Semitic theology, so it is still called to abandon all forms of sexism.

An analysis of Christian tradition and history, however, indicates that Church and theology will transcend their own sexist ideologies only when women are granted full spiritual, theological, and ecclesial equality. The Christian churches will only overcome their oppressive patriarchal traditions and their present sexist theologies and praxis if the very basis of these theologies and praxis is changed. If women were admitted to the full leadership in church and theology, the need would no longer exist to affirm theologically the maleness of God and Christ and to suppress the Spirit who moves women to full participation in the Christian church and ministry. Church leaders and theologians who do not respect the Spirit of liberty and responsibility among Christian women deny the church and theology its full catholicity. Only if we, women and men, are able to live in nonsexist Christian communities, to celebrate nonsexist Christian liturgies, and to think in nonsexist theological terms and imagery will we be able to formulate a genuine Christian feminist spirituality.

NOTES

1. M. Daly, "The Qualitative Leap Beyond Patriarchal Religion," *Quest* (Women and Spirituality) I (1974), p. 21.

2. R. M. Stein, "Liberating the Feminine," in R. Tiffany Barnhouse and U. T. Holmes, III, (eds.), *Male and Female: Christian Approaches to Sexuality,* New York: Seabury Press, 1976, p. 77.

Theology in the Politics
of Appalachian Women

SHEILA COLLINS

The theme of this conference, "Appalachian Women: Our Theology and Politics," is an unusual one. By bringing theology and politics together—by seeing their relationship—women expose the tacit agreement between the state and organized religion to keep women from defining their role in either sphere, an agreement that maintains a status quo characterized by sexual, racial, and class oppression.

Discrimination against women and denial of power to them in the public political sphere has long been reinforced by organized religion, not only through the church's promulgation of the familiar ideology that women are the "natural" nurturers and sustainers of the "private" sphere exclusively, but through the church's offering women a reduced and compensatory way of working on worldly matters through "doing good." Women in churches have served as a form of cheap domestic labor for the larger political economy, reclaiming the social landscape for the community after it has been stripped of its protective covering. Women in churches have provided the nurturance and emotional release for their families and community that the workplace could not provide. They have been used to mop up the wounds created by the cruelties of industrial capitalism—for example, in making bandages

This essay was originally delivered as a speech at "Appalachian Women: Our Theology and Politics," a conference held in New Market, Tennessee, October 14–16, 1977.

during wartime, sending mittens and canned goods to Peru after American companies have stripped that country of its ability to support its own people; and giving Thanksgiving baskets to the local poor because, in the richest country in the world, we are unable to provide meaningful employment for all our people.

Even as the church has reinforced women's domesticated role vis-à-vis the public sphere, it has contained their ability to shape the private, religious sphere as well (through exclusion from the clergy, policy-making positions, and theology), thus serving to prevent women from offering an alternative religious world view that might threaten the cozy relationship between organized religion and the state. (This relationship has operated under the guise of the official doctrine of "separation between church and state.") Male clerics, serving the function of "wives" to the larger political-economic order (businessmen often convey to clergymen that they are incapable of handling business or financial matters), have been too willing to keep women one step beneath them in order to justify the contradictory, feminized role they must play for the rest of society.

We might seize this time to redefine our role as women in the religious sphere, remembering that there is a deep connection between religion and politics. There is no such thing as neutral or apolitical religion. The political right wing understands this and is currently using religious language, institutions, and religious motivation to promote its own political ends. What we do, or fail to do, about our theology and religious practice will have implications for what we do in our political work, our economic activity, and our community organizing.

I want to talk about an understanding of theology that I did not learn in seminary, although, thanks to the agitation of blacks, Latin Americans, and feminists, it is slowly beginning to sneak into the curricula of some seminaries. I will set my remarks against the background of the faith tradition out of which we come, for the biblical tradition of Christianity, for better or for worse, is as integral to the cultural fabric and self-understanding of Appalachian people as Mormonism is to Utah. Liston Pope, in his classic sociological study of the efforts to organize the Loray mill workers in Gastonia, North Carolina, in 1929 concluded that the factor that more than any other alienated the majority of workers from the union leadership was the "indifference and occasional open contempt of the organizers for religion."[1] Religious folkways are key to an understanding of the politics of Appalachia, just as a correct understanding of our own political situation is key to the revitalization or renewal of our religious heritage.

When I attended seminary, theology began deductively, with abstract syllogisms composed by men, who usually had German names— men who had never had to change and wash dirty diapers, sit for six hours in the welfare office, stay up all night with a sick child, pick cotton in a dusty field, sell their bodies for a living, or work all day in the mills and then come home to do the dinner, the laundry, and the dishes. Such men had wives and secretaries to take care of their bodily needs. Their sons and daughters went to Harvard and Oberlin (or their German equivalents) not to Pleiku or the Scotia mine pits. They were paid handsomely to spin out beautiful theories that only their peers could understand. They claimed that their theories were derived from the Bible, although it took them hundreds of pages to explain why. I believe it took them hundreds of pages because their process was inherently unbiblical!

If theology is to be meaningful for us, it must not start with abstractions, but with *our stories*—just as the early Hebrews and Christians of the Bible began with theirs. Somehow, our churches got the order reversed. How many of us were taught as children to memorize Bible stories and verses before we ever understood or had a chance to articulate our own story? We cannot appreciate the meaning of another's experience—especially if that experience occurred two and three thousand years ago—until we have asked the right questions of our own.

I want to talk about the Bible, not as a set of facts or propositions to which we must twist our experience to fit, but as a guide or primer to participating in the creation of our own biblical history. The mistake (or perhaps the deliberate tactic) of the official Christian church was to make us believe that biblical history stopped at the end of the first century A.D., just as our schools have taught us that American history began with Columbus or the Mayflower. To the extent that those of us who call ourselves Christian still find important the cluster of meanings surrounding the Exodus, the entry into the Promised Land, and the ministry, death, and resurrection of Jesus, we participate in shaping the continuation of that story, just as surely as did Moses and Miriam, Peter, Priscilla, Paul.

Theology begins with our stories: what we do with our time; how we feel about our families, our friends, our coworkers, our bosses; how we feel about money and who gets it; what we do when we get up in the morning; how we make it through the day; what pains us, enrages us, saddens and humiliates us; what makes us laugh; what enlightens and empowers us; what keeps us holding on in moments of despair; where we find separation and alienation; where we find true community and trust.

Nothing that is of us can be alien to our theology. Where did we ever get the idea that to admit to anger and rage—even in the face of injustice—is unchristian? Certainly not from Jesus, who threw the money changers out of the temple and who called the corporate lawyers and establishment preachers of his day "broods of vipers" and "tombs with a coat of whitewash." Where did we get the idea that to talk about who controls the money in our community and how economic decisions are made in the family is not the proper subject for a "religious" discussion? Certainly not from the Bible, which seems to be "obsessed with riches and poverty, wages and coins, the overriding questions of subsistence and survival." [2]

In one sense, when I talk about theology starting with our stories I am not saying anything new. Testifying is a cherished tradition in the churches of Appalachia, and telling our stories to one another is what women have always done—over the garden fence, at the food co-op, down at the pump. Yes, the tradition is the same; only the structure and significance we give to it are different.

Testifying in church usually signifies you've already been saved. One isn't supposed to talk about troubles unless one's already found Jesus and arrived in the Promised Land. But if you're still in the Wilderness, it's pretty hard to see your way through. And if you're still in bondage back in Egypt, you might not even know there is a liberator who has just been found among the bullrushes. Yet if the Hebrews had not preserved the stories as they went along—stories of groaning and complaining, stories of despair—if they had had no rich oral tradition to preserve the sting of the lash, the memory of having sown while another reaped, how would they have known what the taste of liberation was all about? How would they have recognized it when it came?

Our churches, promulgating a pietism that is false to the continuous reversals of our experience and to the experience of those in the Bible, have not offered us women a place to speak our bitterness. And if we have not been able to name our pain, to see the collective parameters of our oppression, how shall we be able to name the Kingdom (or, as I prefer to say, Commonwealth) that lies past our suffering—except in the abstract and fanciful rhetoric that has always clothed such visions in the religion of Appalachia—except as a series of "mansions in the sky," as that "Jubilee Land" to which we return beyond the veil of death.

By telling our stories, we must force our churches to hear what we have suffered and the ways in which we have gotten through. We must pull them away from their domesticity and otherworldly preoccupations and force them to deal with the nitty gritty of bread and justice. But we cannot tell our stories as we women have done in the past—as an endless litany of individual disasters and unimportant gossip. We must come together in a new way—consciously, politically. Our stories are of individuals, but only as they are told collectively do they move us forward. In the process of telling our stories as a conscious, political act, we begin to define ourselves and our reality. We cease, thenceforth, to be defined by the men who run our churches, by the corporations who project our images, or by the men in Washington who seek to control our destinies.

The Hebrews told their stories as a conscious political act in order to define themselves over against the other cultures of their day. The early Christians who preserved the stories of Jesus paid for these political acts with their lives. They told the story of Jesus in such a way as to set him over against the imperial, emperor-worshipping cult of Rome. The story was so powerful that Rome had finally to coopt it by establishing Christianity as a state religion under the emperor Constantine. Women were part of the power of that early story. Perhaps that is why it was so subversive of both established religion and the state. Women were the first to tell the world of the events of the resurrection. They were preachers and teachers of the new message, who refused to play the tradition-bound roles of breeder and domestic.

Subversive language, however, must be constantly reinvented, because it is continually being coopted by the powerful. We can no longer afford to use some of this language: for example, the royal male language for God, nor the language of the "blood of the lamb" or the "suffering servant" for Jesus. And supernatural resurrection does not convey the deep longing for the reforestation of Appalachia and the reinvigoration of its people with life, health, and hope in their own future. Cut off from the sociopolitical context that charged original Christian language with its significance, that language, in the hands of a male-dominated clergy, used by a church that reinforces powerful business interests and allies itself with the state, has become a weapon of cultural imperialism. Notice how the emerging coalition of the right—composed of John Birchers, the Ku Klux Klan, large insurance companies and frightened housewives—is using the language and institutions of Christianity against everything that Jesus stood for: against the implicit faithfulness found among the pariahs of his time (in our age, the gays); against the strength, courage, and independence of women; against the rights of the poor and oppressed; against communities of new families, formed for the purpose of sustaining one another even though they may not be related by blood.

So much of the old language has been corrupted beyond recognition that we must write our own dictionary from the words that express best our own experience and the experience of the as yet unarticulated lives of our sisters past and present. This does not mean that we throw out the Christian tradition. On the contrary, what we must do is learn to reappropriate that faith history in a new way. Some language will have to be discarded; other language turned inside out. But we cannot find the handles of reappropriation until we have gone through the process of collective, politicized storytelling and the collection of language for a new dictionary.

In the process of collective storytelling, we begin to see patterns: networks of oppression connecting women in Harlan, Kentucky, with women in Altoona, Pennsylvania, and upstate New York. If we go far enough, we unravel the skein that leads us back to our great-grandmothers, across the country to women in Chicago and on the Cheyenne Indian reservation in Wyoming, to women in the Bantustans of South Africa and women in the countrysides of Puerto Rico and Chile. We begin to ask ourselves: Why these patterns of defeat? Why, after a century of struggle, is our land more devastated than ever; why after the advent of birth control and women's liberation are more thirteen-, fourteen-, and fifteen-year-olds having babies than ever before, and why are women in Puerto Rico, New York, on Indian reservations, and in Appalachia being sterilized in large numbers? Why are women, as a group, losing ground according to every socioeconomic indicator available? Recognizing that our oppression is so widespread, our defeats so redundant, relativizes our suffering. We no longer feel ashamed of our failure to live up to the individualized standards set by the men in Washington or Madison Avenue, knowing that our oppression is a small part of the systematized repression of the majority of the earth's people.

Such knowledge is powerful. We begin to identify not with the privileged, whom we have always been taught to emulate, but with the common people of the earth. It was such identification Jesus talked about in his Sermon on the Mount. A colonialist church has never been able to understand how the first could be last and the meek inherit the earth. Such knowledge is the beginning of Wisdom, who is personified in the Old Testament as a woman, wild and unladylike, shouting aloud in the streets for bread and justice because no one in the synagogues, the courts or the legislature would listen.

As we collect our stories, they begin to shape themselves into a body of experience—a kind of litany—that can no longer be denied. They become the means for a collective self-expression that feeds and strengthens those who are able to hear, just as the stories of the Hebrews in bondage in Egypt, in flight and in temporary restitution, repeated generation after generation, have strengthened the diaspora. Just as the stories of Jesus, told and retold, sustained the early Christian community through persecution.

Through the telling and retelling of our stories, the inessentials are gradually sloughed off, until only the veins, the life-bearing vessels, remain. It is then that we begin to see the patterns of triumph, steadfastness, of salvation and liberation inherent in them. Just as the early Hebrews and early Christians looked back over their lives and discovered these patterns, so we discover what it was in women's experience that has kept women going through tragedy and devastation, through the daily rituals of feeding and caring. We discover the secret that keeps hope more alive in the oppressed who are conscious of the source of their oppression than in those who do the oppressing. Only then can we name that which has brought us through as the God of *our* experience—not the God of an alien and imposed culture. Only then can we distinguish with any clarity the true prophets from the false.

The process of discovering and naming that God is the process of our own liberation or salvation. It is the commonwealth of God Jesus spoke about as being like a mustard seed in our midst. Salvation for us is dynamic, *this*-worldly. It is not a static, blissful realm beyond the cares of this earth. We were never promised a life free from fear and struggle. We were offered the hope that by committing ourselves to the struggle for a righteous society in solidarity with the wretched of the earth we would discover the secret of life. Remember what Jesus said to his disciples?

Nation will rise against nation, and kingdom against kingdom; there will be great earthquakes and in various places famines and pestilences; and there will be terrors and great signs from heaven. But before all this they will lay their hands on you and persecute you, delivering you up to the synagogues and prisons, and you will be brought before kings and governors for my name's sake. This will be a time for you to bear testimony. Settle it therefore in your minds not to meditate beforehand how to answer; for I will give you a mouth and wisdom which none of your adversaries will be able to withstand or contradict. You will be delivered up even by parents and brothers and kinsmen and friends, and some of you they will put to death; you will be hated by all for my name's sake. But not a hair of your head will perish. By your endurance you will gain your lives. (Luke 21:9–19).

"By your endurance you will gain your lives." Jesus didn't mean by that that we would gain individual wealth and prosperity as so many pseudo-Christian evangelists would like us to believe. Rather, it is in the midst of the struggle against debased and deformed human existence with its demands for moral sensitivity, self-discipline, solidarity, and the constant resetting of one's sights upon the vision of liberation that one is closest to the pulse of the universe, to the secret of human life. Rosemary Ruether, a feminist theologian, has pointed out that "such a struggle, even in its outward failure and disappointment, is recollected as a time of fellowship, commitment and ecstatic hopefulness as the highest point of living."[3]

Only as we redefine ourselves through the telling of our stories, discover the sources and patterns of our oppression and name the God of *our* salvation, can we then begin to reappropriate the Christian tradition and the special Appalachian folkways in which it was transmitted in a way which is truly empowering and liberating.

Perhaps when Appalachian women begin to share the stories of how their sons were dragged off to a war in Southeast Asia, fought to propitiate the American male God of power, they can identify with that Sarah of ancient times who watched in the same immobilized way as her husband, Abraham, took the son of her old age to the mountains as an offering, in the mistaken notion that God demands the sacrifice of the innocents for the sins of the guilty.

Perhaps when black women share stories of how their sons and husbands were taken from them through slavery, hunger, dope, war, and the criminal justice system, they can gain strength through remembering Hagar, Abraham's concubine, who, through the jealousy of Sarah, was banished to the wilderness with her infant son but because of her faithfulness was promised by God that her son would live to establish a nation.

Perhaps when Appalachian women begin to share stories of their aunts, who, driven from the farms to the cities during the depression, ended up as prostitutes—the only job they could get that would pay them enough to send some back home—only then perhaps will we truly identify with the woman of ill repute, who bathes Jesus' feet with her tears and whose implicit faithfulness has become a part of the record of salvation.

Perhaps when the day comes that black and white women, poor and middle-class women are able to share their stories—and through that sharing to discover the painful contradictions of women's existence in a patriarchal, competitive, and profit-oriented society—then, perhaps, there can be a reconciliation between Sarah the wife and Hagar the concubine.

When we have brought to consciousness, articulated, and honed to the essentials the stories of our bondage and liberation, then we can reconnect with the buried traditions in our own folk history. No people is ever willingly, or without resistance, colonized. We must learn to look for those remnants of resistance that are often disguised as passivity, stubbornness, hostility, and superstition. For instance, we can recover the themes of salvation through struggle that are inherent in the early religious music of the Appalachian mountains—before they were overlaid with the theme of salvation through personal conversion, which was the message of the colonizing church and the Nashville recording industry. We can use that wonderful democratic tradition of "testifying" in church to talk about how the coal and textile companies, the family planning experts, and the welfare officials are keeping women down, and how, by participating in that sit-in at the welfare office, we were able to get food in our stomachs and spirit for our souls. We can take all those marvelous hymns that give us the shivers when we sing them and change the words around: changing the

"I's" to "we's," the male pronouns to generic ones, the "blood of the Savior" to the blood of our sisters and brothers killed in the mines and the floods, and those mansions in the sky by-and-by to the green, rolling hills of West Virginia. We can rediscover the forgotten heroines embedded in our history and name them in our services when it comes time for a recollection of the saints.

A past, a tradition, is important for people who are living in bondage. But it must be their own tradition, their consciously claimed heritage, not a tradition imposed by their captors. In thinking about my own faith tradition, I prefer to think of Jesus the Liberator, Jesus the representative of the common people. The term "Son of Man," it seems to me, originally signified something like "Son of the People." I prefer to remember that throughout the Gospels it was women who held fast to the essentials, as one by one Jesus' male followers betrayed him, disowned him, and finally disbelieved the evidence of his ultimate victory over death and defeat. This is the kind of faith remembrance that gives me strength.

The preceding has been a series of notes toward a new way of doing theology. What the content of a theology drawn from the lives of Appalachian women would look like is yours to discover. What form you will give to the ancient themes of bondage, the Promised Land (or Kingdom of God), to crucifixion and resurrection, to the idea of apostasy, to sin and salvation—how you will name God—will be yours to work out as you engage in the process.

NOTES

1. Liston Pope, *Millhands & Preachers* (New Haven, Conn.: Yale University Press, 1942), p. 262.
2. John Pairman Brown, "Techniques of Imperial Control: The Background of the Gospel Event," *The Bible and Liberation: A Radical Religion Reader,* edited by The Radical Religion Collective (Berkeley: Community for Religious Research and Education, 1976), p. 79.
3. Rosemary Ruether, *The Radical Kingdom,* (New York: Harper & Row, 1970), p. 288.

The Dilemma of Celebration

NELLE MORTON

Women appear at an impasse in celebration. Traditional symbols root too deeply in a patriarchal culture to function adequately in their new context, and new symbols have not yet emerged.[1]

The search for symbols seems to take the form of a "no-saying" and a "yes-saying" in which we see both the no and the yes as positive. We are not saying no to the whole created order of things—our traditions and ourselves included—we are saying no to those images, symbols, structures, and practices which cripple us and keep us from claiming our rightful personhood. We are saying no to a system that legitimates these images through cosmic myths, language, and daily dramas of etiquette.

We began our "no" by substituting feminine words of liturgy for those masculine words that exclude women. But soon we found that word change was not enough. The masculine words had conjured up images that continued to persist in the community psyche to proclaim gender instead of humanness. But the change provided affirmation of ourselves as persons and enabled us to hear that life is for us—directly, wholly, and lovingly. I remember once when some of us were experi-

Nelle Morton, an Associate Professor Emerita from Drew Theological School, Drew University, attended New York Theological School, the University of Geneva, and L'Institat de Rousseau, Geneva, Switzerland. She has been active in the women's movement, especially in its theological dimensions, and has published many articles on feminism and religion. This essay appeared originally in *Women in a Strange Land,* edited by Claire Benedicks Fisher, *et. al.,* copyright © 1975 by Fortress Press, and is reprinted by permission of Fortress Press.

menting with feminine terminology several heard, some for the first time, a word of unconditional acceptance.[2] We were not forced to make the usual transfer from the familiar masculine words to the feminine.

Our search led beyond the sexist imagery of the biblical text to the wholeness embedded deep within, beyond biblical history to earlier myths yielding insights that did not survive patriarchy. Anne Bennett has already shown how *Elohim* is not subject to gender reduction.[3] Elizabeth Gould Davis traces *Yahweh* to a Sumerian goddess,[4] while Gerhard von Rad claims any sexuality in "Jahweh" alien to Israel.[5] Others have probed the feminine in wisdom, presence, dove, spirit, and Torah.[6]

Robert Graves's newest work describes patriarchal rejection of woman as contributing to the decline of man,[7] and Robert Bly inserts in his recent volume of poems a prose chapter on the Great Mother.[8] He cites a quatrain from Job which, because of disunity of images, should read:

> I came out of the Mother naked,
> and I will be naked when I return.
> The Mother gave, and the Mother takes away,
> I love the Mother.

(The Job ending: The Lord gave, and the Lord takes away, blessed be the name of the Lord.)

It takes little imagination to restore the creation story in Genesis 2 to its original. The rib was womb. The patriarch's abhorrence of blood led the Creator to allow Adam a great sleep while fashioning a "helper fit for him." The chapter ends with the man leaving his family and cleaving to his wife, thus clearly matriarchal.

A comparison of John 1:1-4 with Proverbs 8:1-31 shows Word (*logos,* masculine) a substitute for wisdom (*sophia,* feminine).

Since the Judeo-Christian tradition had only a patriarchal language in which to record its salvation history, and only a hierarchical perception of the universe out of which to fashion its ecclesiology, it might prove fruitful to examine some scholars' views of prepatriarchal culture. A lifetime of research has assured J. J. Bachofen that "the mythical tradition may be taken as a faithful reflection of the life of those times in which historical antiquity is rooted. It is a manifestation of primordial thinking and immediate historical revelation and consequently a highly reliable historical source."[9] His findings of days when the "human race has not yet . . . departed from its harmony with creation and the transcendent Creator,"[10] reveal certain similarities to today's woman experience. Primary, perhaps, is the nature of language itself, which appeared mythopoetical in character. As language became controlled, utilitarian, and linear in patriarchal culture, metaphoric speech became reduced. In time, literal interpretations became inevitable, since myth tends to literalize metaphor.

Many claim the multidimensional speech of women is closer to the metaphorical than that of men.[11] If this is true, one may attribute it partly to the fact that women are more in touch with their bodies and nature in general, and also more intimately present to the symbolic of children's first speech.

Speaking organically moves near the metaphorical. Metaphor witnesses to unity between person and cosmos. Organic reflects unity between body and mind. Organic speech, then, would mean speech before the body and the spirit were split. Organic designates at-homeness in the body—the mind dipping into, and interrelated with, all the senses at their moment of sensing. The organic opens itself to mystery and wonder and awe in common aspects of life. Therefore, moments of communal ritual in prepatriarchal culture seemed to be triggered more by occasions that made the common appear of momentous import—as a birth, eating a meal, sowing seed, gathering grain, or a death. Out of physical happenings, the symbolic took shape.

The ordinary word *mother* came to symbolic proportions in *Mother Earth* and then again in *Mother God*.[12] Origin from a common womb was regarded the closest possible bond and originally the only true form of kinship. When the womb came to mean the Great Womb of the Creator, the term *stranger* was not known. To injure any human being or animal was a special crime.[13] Love arising from such a bond died with the development of paternity. Mystery, the true essence of ritual, was rooted in the nature of woman and her close alliance between nature and spirit. It was thought to spring from her intimacy with death in nature and in her own body (menstruation and bleeding at childbrith). It was this mystery that evoked empathy, comfort, and raised up hope through pain.[14] The two central symbols in the cultic life of the prepatriarchal people appeared as birth and death. Birth, never completely separated from physical birth, became transparent for the whole mystery of the cosmos and creation itself. It was so with death—never bereft of its pain and its grief—but death, as birth, moved people close to the mystery of the universe.

When the knowledge of paternity, which women must have discovered first, became known to men, the men tried to usurp women's part in the birthing process. They established themselves as sole parents, reducing women to nurturing "their seed"—"their miniscule babies"—which they planted in wombs. Birth was separated from physical birth, first as an initiation rite into manhood, then sacralized into spiritual birth with men performing the functions of women.

In their ego ascendency, men contrived to beat death. They would do the naming. They would have sons, and their sons' sons would have sons and thus pass on their names forever. They would amass property to pass into the hands of their sons, and their sons would add property until their ever-greater lands would compete in the whole earth. "Their seed would inherit the earth." Their tombs would be built near the hearths of their homes and their bodies moved as the sons moved, and thus they would be revered for generations and so outwit death.[15] Note how few liturgies to this day allow for grief to come full circle as a necessary part of the human experience. Modern religious structures function, as did the patriarchal, to evade death.

It is not surprising that the symbolism of birth and death from prepatriarchy became overshadowed by sexist images. In time, the sexist imagery acquired a life all its own as it spun itself out in liturgy, theology, and ecclesiastical structures until the control group became unable to perceive the distortions in the life of the community.

The patriarchal effort to suppress the feminine in Judeo-Christian history was never completely accomplished. In times of greatest harmony and peace, of hope and vision, the feminine surfaced to approximate a mutuality and balance in the community. Even though the covenant community excluded women in their primary membership, women were never entirely silenced.

Perhaps modern women experience birth and death similarly to the prepatriarchal rites. The following excerpts from accounts of a birth and a death support such a theory.

The persons present at the birth (including several seminary graduates) had, at one time or another, lived together under one roof, sharing food and work, pain and joy, strengthening one another's days, and hearing one another's anger. By right of having lived together in this fashion, they considered themselves a family, and, as family, belonged to be present at the advent of the new member, who was loved before she was born.

Susie gave birth to Leila . . . but many helped. I suppose there were twenty-five present . . . mostly women. Two children wandered in and out among us . . . Three-year-old Blake said, "She popped out." Safra, Leila's sister asked, "Is she my baby?" Soon after she said she was Leila's mommy. . . .

Three women nurses or midwives were there. . . . One helped lift Leila out when the time came. . . . The doctor, like God, walked in and out with his suit and tie; his knowledge and his authority. He affirmed that Susie was in transition. He did not know any of us. He walked out again. I was glad he did not stay. . . .

At a low time, when we thought Susie might have to leave her friends for the hospital, Mariette felt she wanted to pray. But she said she fought that off because she knew we have to find inside ourselves how to get through.

Joe breathed with Susie through her contractions . . . he stayed by her side most of those eighteen hours. . . . Some women knelt on either side rubbing her feet and legs or forehead . . . watching for any place she began to tense . . . getting her ice . . . talking with her between contractions. In general, people were quiet. . . . We weren't trying to speak. . . . It was just a time of great emotion.

Someone made chicken soup, which Susie had requested. All were relaxed until the pushing began and we knew the baby was coming. When Susie began pushing, her face strained . . . got red . . . everyone held their breaths and pushed with her. The pushing felt good. It was exciting because the baby was finally going to come. Even though in great pain, Susie's face was smiling. . . . Susie pushed. . . . We all pushed for about three to five minutes . . . then the baby's head showed. . . .

Leila did almost pop out. She cried immediately. . . . At first she was white . . . then turned pink slowly. . . . She smelled good. When Leila cried everyone in the room cried too. . . . We hugged and kissed one another. Someone laid Leila across Susie's breasts. She nursed. A nurse helped get the placenta out . . . Joe cut the cord. Leila cried some more. In an hour or so Susie got up and sat in a rocker in the sunshine with Leila. . . . Friends went out and cooked the biggest dinner of all that night. . . . It seemed that Leila had come to all of us. Later we talked of the overwhelming awe. The birth was life-giving.[16]

In the death account, the father, mother, and sister sat in a front pew during the service for their four-year-old, who had been killed by a driver under the influence of drugs. One minister provided traditional prayers and structure. Another told stories out of the life of the little girl, now dead. Still another, a woman, assigned to read the Scripture, began:

How could a service such as this have begun with a hymn of praise? How could we sing together out of the strange happening in our midst?

Long ago a psalmist (Ps.22) struggled with similar questions. "O God, Our God, why have you forsaken us? Why are you so far from hearing us, so far from the world of our anguish and our anger? We cry out by day but you do not answer. We cry out in the night but find no rest." . . . After his anger the psalmist cried, "O Lord, be not longer so far off. You are our help. Hasten to our aid." He ended with a paean of praise introduced by the telling phrase, "In the midst of the congregation we can praise."

Here emerged a clue to the answer of our questions. . . . In the midst of the human community of faith, singing is possible . . . before the anguish is over. Praise is possible before the fact . . . before the joy and meaning are fully known.

In the midst of this congregation gathered, with so much love, to support and sustain you, Joyce, and Debbie, and Bob . . . grace may communicate itself to you even while it is yet dark. No . . . because it is dark.

Matthew (18:1–4), too, speaks of a congregation . . . the nucleus of the church-to-be. The disciples had been vying with one another as to which of them would be most important in the ecclesiastical hierarchy, so they brought their question to Jesus. And Jesus called a little child, like Susan, and put the child in the midst of them. Then he said to the men, "Unless you turn and become like a child you will never enter the kingdom of heaven. . . . Whoever can become like this child, that one is greatest."

If this be true, then children belong as congregation . . . not as objects to be ministered to or potential adults to be indoctrinated . . . but as persons in their own right to minister to us all. And if this be true, Susan's so short life was ministry indeed.[17]

There was recognition throughout the days of mourning that grief belongs at such a time. Friends and family affirmed the living. They allowed for the joy before it became a reality. But they could not predate the celebration, for it had already begun to take place.

In the light of our tradition, our experiences as women provide a clue to the structure of a new symbol. We do not look up and out for our story as we have been conditioned to do all our lives. We touch the pain in our own lives to find it derives from false images imposed upon us.

Once we took the painful journey to the core of our lives, we found that we were sustained. In the awful loneliness, we were not alone. Something shaped our cry—brought forth our speech, fragmentary as it was. We had been told all our lives that the word created, that the word came first—even in the beginning, before the beginning. Now we know a priority to the word—a hearing that brought forth the word.

We literally heard one another down to a word that was *our* word, and that word was ourselves.

Hearing, as we have come to experience it, proceeds not from a collective ear that would suggest an aggregate, but from a great ear at the heart of the universe hearing persons to humanness. And the humanness is marked by wholeness (the whole word, and not just the masculine word). In the morphology—down, then up from down under—we have experienced birth, not rebirth, not new birth, or rite of passage or entry, but birth of ourselves for the first time. We have experienced creation, not re-creation, or new creation, but a primordial creation of ourselves. In the new shape of our experience, we have confronted death, but not death of the self, or death to self. We have experienced the death of the stereotyped images, the breaking of them from within so that self can be affirmed and potentialized. No one can take this journey of women but the women themselves who are involved. To put it on "Jesus," or the priest, or the therapist is to perpetuate the same dependency we are now seeking to throw off.

One can only speculate on what celebration could be were mutuality (love) possible in the community of faith; were the oppressed of the earth trusted to become a valid part of that community.

It may be that the most authentic celebration is not that which can be structured from above—not that as considered by the control group proper for the oppressed, nor as some would have us believe—Dionysian (induced). Maybe the most authentic celebration begins with rejoicing in that which is breaking up from down under.

NOTES

1. Cf. Amos N. Wilder, "Theology and Theopoetic I"; "Theology and Theopoetic II"; "Theology and Theopoetic III"; *The Christian Century,* 23 May 1973; 5 December 1973; 13 March 1974.
2. Conference on "Women Exploring Theology," Grailville, Ohio, 1972, when 2 Cor. 5:17 was read "for *she* is a new creation."
3. Anne McGrew Bennett, "Women in the New Society," *Journal of Current Social Issues,* Winter 1972-73.
4. Elizabeth Gould Davis, *The First Sex* (Baltimore: G. P. Putnam's Sons, 1971), p. 67.
5. Gerhard von Rad, *Old Testament Theology* (New York: Harper & Row, 1957), p. 146.

6. See Theodor Reik, *Pagan Rites in Judaism* (New York: Farrar, Straus and Co., 1964), pp. 75–76; Erich Neumann, *The Great Mother,* Bollingen Series 47 (Princeton: Princeton University Press, 1955); Erminie Huntress Lantero, *Feminine Aspects of Divinity,* Pendle Hill Pamphlet 191 (Wallingford, Pa., 1973).

7. Robert Graves, *Difficult Questions, Easy Answers* (New York: Doubleday & Co., 1974).

8. Robert Bly, *Sleepers Joining Hands* (New York: Harper & Row, 1973), p. 31.

9. J. J. Bachofen, *Myth, Religion, and Mother Right* (Princeton: Princeton University Press, 1967), p. 73.

10. Ibid., p. 16.

11. Anne Schaef, psychologist, presented this view at the annual meeting of the Society for the Advancement of Continuing Education for Ministry, Denver, Colorado, June 1972; see also Helen Lynd, *On Shame and the Search for Identity* (New York: Harcourt, Brace, and Co., 1958), esp. "New Ways in Language", pp. 171–81.

12. Bachofen, *Myth, Religion, and Mother Right,* p. 80.

13. Davis, *The First Sex,* p. 65.

14. Bachofen, *Myth, Religion, and Mother Right,* p. 87.

15. See Fustel de Coulanges, *The Ancient City* (Boston: Lee and Shepherd, 1925).

16. Condensed from a long account by Judy Davis (staff member of the Institute for Policy Studies, Washington, D.C.). Used by permission.

17. Book on the death of Susan Clark (1973), daughter of the Rev. and Mrs. Robert Clark, Madison, N.J., now in the process of being written.

Female God Language
in a Jewish Context

RITA M. GROSS

The most profound, intriguing, and inviting of all Jewish theologies, the Kabbalah, teaches us that *galut*, "exile," is the fundamental reality and pain of present existence. It teaches that one of the causes of *galut* is the alienation of the masculine from the feminine in God, the alienation of God and the Shechinah. But it also teaches, especially in its Lurianic phases, that each of us can effect the turning of *galut* by dedicating all our efforts to the reunification of God and the Shechinah. Now that the masculine and feminine have been torn asunder and the feminine dismembered and banished, both from the discourse about divinity and from the human community, such a *tikkun*, "reparation," is obligatory *(a mitzvah)*. When the masculine and feminine aspect of God have been reunited and the female half of humanity has been returned from exile, we will begin to have our *tikkun*. The world will be repaired.

I can no longer remember the first time I imagined a *b'rachah* ("blessing") in the female grammatical form. I do remember the first

Rita M. Gross received her Ph.D. from the University of Chicago and teaches at the University of Wisconsin, Eau Claire. She is active in the American Academy of Religion and Naropa Institute, is editor of *Beyond Androcentrism,* and has published articles on women and religion in *Journal of the American Academy of Religion* and *Anima.* An earlier version of this essay appeared in *Davka Magazine,* (17), © 1976, and is published by permission of the Los Angeles Hillel Council, 900 Hilgard Avenue, Los Angeles, Ca. 90024.

time I heard it voiced aloud communally, years after having first experienced participation in my own right in the Jewish ritual covenant community. It was as appropriate and natural as any Jewish expression—and less problematic and alienating than many. In fact, the potential for meaning and identification inherent in the act of saying "God—She" convinced me that it must be so. Since then, I have been using female pronouns of God relatively frequently in various contexts—teaching, reflection, private religious expressions. As the linguistic forms and the sound of the words become less exotic, it no longer seems daring or unconventional to speak of God in such a manner. Instead, it seems appropriate, natural, what one would expect, the way things would be except for a massive skewing and programming of religious consciousness.

Therefore, it is time to move beyond God the Father. However I propose to move beyond God the Father, not to the "Verb of Verbs," to the nonpersonal God concept, which Mary Daly opts for, but to an imagery of bisexual androgynous deity by reintroducing the image of God as female to complement the image of God as male. I wish to argue for this option because I am convinced that Judaism is theistic through and through and that theism—the view that the absolute can be imaged as a person entering into relationships of love and responsibility with humans—requires anthropomorphism. But I am equally convinced that images of God as a male person without complementing images of God as a female person are both a mirror and a legitimation of the oppression and eclipsing of women.

Let me say immediately that I am quite aware that God is not really either female or male or anything in between. I only wish the people who argue to retain solely male imagery were as aware that God is not really male as I am that God is not really female. I am talking about the only thing we can talk about—*images* of God, not God. And I am talking about female *images* of God. Those images, it seems to me, should not be daring, degrading, or alien. If it is daring, degrading or alienating to speak of God using female pronouns and imagery, that perhaps indicates something about the way women and the feminine are valued. Therefore, we might say that the ultimate symbol of our degradation is our inability to say "God-She."

To understand *why people currently use exclusively* masculine God language and *why we should attempt to create* female God language, we must *first* explain the *nature of God language* and its limitations.

We must then *describe the process* by which God languages are created and changed.

To speak of God is among the most difficult and audacious things that humans do. To address God is even more difficult. Yet religious people attempt both as a matter of course. The essential difficulty of God language is that it proposes to talk about that which is absolutely transcendent—that which is not encompassed by or contained within any of the categories that point to it. The paradox, the linguistic impossibility, of words such as *absolute, transcendent,* or *infinite,* combined with their linguistic necessity, is the embarrassment of all religious language.

All the words used in the religious enterprise are, in the long run, analogous and metaphorical. Every statement contains a bracketed "as if" or "as it were." Statements about God cannot be taken literally. They do not exhaust the possibilities at all. Rather, they are the best that can be done at present by means of an imperfect medium. They have no inherent finality, no ultimate truth, no unalterable relevance. They are tools—linguistic conventions. Such are the inherent limitations of language about God and such is the inevitable logic bound up in the use of the word *God* in any meaningful fashion, a logic that is well known in the theological tradition of the *via negativa.*

Although it is often ignored, this attitudinal "as if," or "as it were," is fundamental to the religious enterprise. If the "as if" changes to "it is," if what is focused on is the metaphor, instead of what it points to, religion becomes idolatry. Although it is usually an empty category in contemporary religious discourse, the category of idolatry, reinvested with this meaning, would prove useful in current religious reflection and discourse. For a poverty of religious imagination, characteristic of the contemporary milieu, makes many people idolaters today. They simply block out of their consciousness the metaphorical nature of religious language and become addicted to the linguistic conventions, the signs and tools of religious discourse.

Although these considerations apply in general to all elements of God language, they are especially applicable to the exclusively masculine pronouns and imagery of God language. However, it has never been sufficiently articulated that the *via negativa,* the process of negation, should also be applied to the exclusively masculine pronouns and imagery of God language. Philosophers often criticize anthropomorphic language, the attributing of *human* characteristics to God, but even critiques of theism—the absolute as person—never specifically focus on the maleness of the personal images and those who defend the theistic option always do so with masculine pronouns. Yet the designation "He" is subject to all the difficulties found in any other positive attribute of God and does not really tell us anything about God.

Why, then, are masculine imagery and pronouns so universal? Why has this single designation escaped unscathed even in a theological tradition that tries to question all positive and therefore inaccurate God language? Shouldn't "He" and all variants of it be as circumscribed as any other positive attribute of God—or more circumscribed, since they are more misleading?

If theological reflection teaches the limitations of God language, cross-cultural, historical study of religion indicates how specific elements of a positive God language came into existence. A God language does not really tell us about God, but it does tell us a considerable amount about those who use the God language. Analogies and metaphors have a base. The model from which our religious expressions are built up is necessarily our own experience. There is no other source for expressions by means of which one may communicate the essentially ineffable religious experience. This insight is central and crucial, but it must be precisely and carefully understood. Reductionists, whether they be social scientists or religious conservatives, falsely contend that the religious enterprise is futile if religious language is not literally true and/or unchangeable. What is futile is not the religious enterprise but the temptation to regard any specific religious expression as anything but a metaphor that tells us more about its users than about God. This insight into the nature of religious language is not antithetical to being religious and in fact promotes much more subtle and adequate religious experiences than dogmas that ignore the basic nature and process of religious language.

What conclusions, then, may be drawn from the fact that, despite its theological inconsistency, the use of exclusively masculine pronouns and imagery has not been criticized? From the fact that the language of "God-He" is so automatic that it is not questioned even by the nonreligious who deny *"His"* existence altogether? From the fact that most people respond to "God-She" with hilarity or hostility, even though they know that God is not a male? Why does everyone cling to the masculine imagery and pronouns even though they are a mere linguistic device that has never meant that God is a male? *If we do not mean that God is male when we use masculine pronouns and imagery, then why should there be any objections to using female imagery and pronouns as well?*

The minimal and most abstract answer is that the androcentric model of humanity prohibits most people from seeing through this theological mistake. The exclusively male God language tells us nothing about God, but it does tell us much about society and religion. So long as the prevailing male-centered definition and model of humanity seems adequate and accurate, such linguistic conventions did not raise questions, despite their theologically questionable nature. God language has been blind to the inadequacies of that particular linguistic convention because the male monopoly on the central aspects of Jewish life and thought seemed appropriate, adequate, even normative. That is another way of saying that Judaism has been blind, either to its own androcentrism or to the inadequacy of androcentrism, and therefore, *automatically,* unreflectingly, used male pronouns and imagery of God.

It takes courageous honesty to recognize all the links between exclusively male God language and the androcentric model of humanity, with its consequent eclipsing of women. It also requires a thorough consciousness of the subtle ways in which linguistic conventions shape and limit world view and reality constructs. Because they are so automatic, even in highly reflective people, linguistic conventionalities are among the most potent factors in shaping people's perceptions and then limiting them to that socially constructed reality—as if it were inevitably the way things are. Thus we see that the conventions of theology are not so innocent or arbitrary as they seem. Therefore, they must be reimagined, not so much because they are theologically inadequate, although that too is true, but because they are socially destructive, and Judaism demands that socially destructive forms be reversed.

It is one thing to understand the inadequacy of exclusively male God language and another to offer a feasible corrective. Although, theoretically, two correctives might offer themselves—that of an impersonal, neuter, and abstract God language on the one hand, and that of an androgynous, bisexual God language on the other—I have already stated that at present and given the concerns of this essay, only the option of reintroducing female God language into the language of Jewish prayer and devotion will do. There are several reasons for this.

First of all, female God language compels us to overcome the idolatrous equation of God with androcentric notions of humanity in a way that no other linguistic device can. Some who argue for an impersonal God language do so because, while they recognize the limitations of "God-He," they find "God-She" too degrading and unnatural to consider. Deliberately saying "God-She" makes it impossible to mask or hide one's unconscious sexism behind abstract language.

Secondly, female God language is especially important in the Jewish context because so much of the Jewish religious enterprise involves talking, not about God, but *to* God. In Jewish God language, forms of address, language in the second person, are more important than language in the third person. That is where an impersonal, abstract God language breaks down in the Jewish context. It not only breaks down; it also covertly reintroduces all the problems of exclusively male God language by slipping into the masculine forms of the pronouns of address. Anthropomorphism can be exorcised from theology to some degree; but it is the inevitable concommitant of theism and prayer. If we want theism and prayer (and the Jewish enterprise becomes unrecognizable without them), the best we can do is to attempt to keep our anthropomorphisms from being idolatrous and oppressive. The only way that we can simultaneously retain the language of address, and overcome the problems of exclusive male God language, is by adopting female forms of address *in addition to* male forms.

There are also significant reasons at the sociological level for making such a linguistic reform. Beginning to address God as "She" in addition to "He" is a powerful reflection and indication of the "becoming of women" in the Jewish context. The ultimate symbol of our degradation, of our essential non-Jewishness—which finds expression in all forms of Jewish life—is our *inability* to say "God-She" or to create female imagery of God. As women *become* Jews, persons, humans in the Jewish context, "God-She" *becomes* a compelling and appropriate metaphor. These two events occur simultaneously, as is always the case in the *process* by which God language is formulated. The ability to say "God-She" is the sign of Jewish women's authentic entrance in their own right into the ritual covenant community of Israel, as well as the unexpected resource for Jewish self-understanding that comes with that entrance. However, at present, both in terms of theological language and in terms of their entrance into full Jewishness, Jewish women experience "becoming," but not yet "being." That is why we cannot yet fully delineate the forms that the language will take or offer a plan for female God language.

However, we can delineate several positive implications of adding "God-She" to our religious vocabulary. "God-She" is not some new construct added onto the present resource of Jewish God language, but distinct and separate from it. Instead, "God-She" applies to all elements of Jewish God language. In other words, the familiar *ha-kadosh baruch hu* ("the Holy One, blessed be He") is also *ha-k'dosha barucha he* ("the holy One, blessed be She") and *always has been*. Only the poverty of our religious imagination and the repressiveness of our social forms prevented that realization. Everything that has ever been said or that we still want to say of *ha-kadosh baruch hu* can also be said of *ha-k'dosha baruch he* and, conversely, "God-She" is appropriately used in every context in which any reference to God occurs. That is to say, whenever the symbol, or metaphor, or construct "God" is still relevant in any way, then we must imagine "God-She" and speak to her.

Beyond the use of female pronouns in addition to male pronouns, in the already familiar contexts, what more will we say to and about God? Imagery is more significant than language. When God-She becomes less abstract and more independent of God-He, how will She look and what will She do? What would the reintroduction of directly female imagery into our repertoire of theological images and metaphors do to it? What new shapes and tones would it take on? It seems to me that is the question I cannot answer for others, although for myself many suggestions have presented themselves. Minimally, we can say that the whole matter is analogous to the innovations and reform in ritual practices. What seemed preposterous ten years ago now has to be considered by everyone. Less than ten years ago, it was rare for women even to be counted in a *minyan* (quorum for prayer), and many who wished to make *aliyot* (be called to the Torah) or to *daven* (pray) in *tallit* (prayer shawl) and *t'fillin* (phlacteries) simply encountered incredulous stares. Today, even in relatively remote sections of the Jewish world, such practices are beginning to be accepted. At the same time, we are starting to comprehend that *mere participation in male rituals to a male deity* is only *be'reshit,* "the beginning," of our becoming. Once enough of us *daven* (pray) long enough, the question cannot·be suppressed. We do not yet know the potential and gift that comes with the entrance of Jewish women into Judaism. We do not fully know the lineaments of God-She. But we do know that She is inevitable and insuppressible.

Sabbath Prayers for Women

NAOMI JANOWITZ and MAGGIE WENIG

The authors of rabbinic midrashim (homiletical interpretations) expressed their world view in the form of commentary on Jewish texts. We too express our world view in the form of a "commentary" on and translation of traditional texts. But our commentary is not only to be read and studied—it is to be prayed, for we have entered the process of the creation of liturgy. Our liturgy is, like those that precede ours, a product of the experiences of its authors—in this case the experience of contemporary Jewish women.

Our prayers, then, are not a critique of the classical liturgy from a feminist perspective, but an affirmation of our choice to remain within the tradition and to sanctify our everyday lives as women. Our prayers are not a treatise on the rights of Jewish women. They do, however, have social implications. Through our prayers, we define ourselves as women in terms of our relationship with God. In addition, our liturgy assumes the inclusion of women in the *minyan* and their full participation in the Torah service. It assumes that women will serve as

Naomi Janowitz received her B.A. from Brown University and her M.A. from the University of Chicago Divinity School, where she is now a doctoral student. While at Brown she was a member of the women's minyan.

Maggie Wenig received her B.A. from Brown University. Currently a rabbinical student at Hebrew Union College—Jewish Institute of Religion, an article of hers appeared in *Lilith*. Wenig and Janowitz are coauthors of *Siddur Nashim: A Sabbath Prayer Book for Women* (© 1976 by Janowitz and Wenig), from which this material is taken. Excerpts of these prayers also appeared in *Lilith*, the independent Jewish women's magazine, published at 250 West 57th Street, New York, NY 10019. © Lilith Publications, Inc. 1978.

"messenger of the congregation" and that they will recite the mourners' *Kaddish*. It acknowleges women's participation in these rituals by using women's own words in the prayers and blessings they are to recite.

In writing prayers, we struggle with the meaning of our relationship with God. Our metaphors and ideas come initially out of a wrestling with the liturgy—trying to make it embrace our experience—rather than out of an effort to develop a systematic theology. In the process, we have arrived at concepts and interpretation in which we can believe and through which we can pray, ideas that have the power to shape our world view and give meaning to our experiences.

Some of our prayers are radical in their ideas; most are traditional in their form. These forms of liturgy have been sustained by the Jewish people for generations. We retained them for their conciseness and strength and for the legitimation of our expression that we gain through them.

With these prayers, we offer encouragement to women, as they look around and inside themselves for God, to write prayers, to pray together and to renew the meaning of all that has been passed down to us. We have found that, when women are reminded that they too are created in the image of God, they can bring forth what they carry inside—the beauty, wisdom, and strength gained as the bearers of 4,000 years of tradition.

KADDISH D'RABBANAN (Rabbi's Prayer)

Magnified and sanctified is the great Name of G-d* throughout the world that She created according to Her will. May She establish Her dominion in the days of your life and in the life of all the house of Israel, speedily and soon, and say Amen.

Let Her great Name be blessed for ever and ever and to all eternity.

Blessed and glorified, exalted and honored, magnified and praised is the Name of the Holy One, blessed is She, whose glory transcends all praises, songs, and blessings that can be rendered unto Her, and say Amen.

May Israel, our teachers, their students and their students' students, and all who are involved in the study of Torah, here and everywhere,

---

* Many Jews, especially the Orthodox, do not write out the holy name (Ed.)

find great peace, lovingkindness, mercy, long life, and salvation from
our Mother who is in heaven, and say Amen.

Let there be unending peace from heaven, and a good life, for us and
for all Israel, and say Amen.

May She who creates peace in the heavens create, in Her mercy,
peace for us and for all Israel, and say Amen.

BARUCH-SHE-AMAR (Blessed is he who spoke)

Blessed is She who spoke and the world became. Blessed is She.
Blessed is She who in the beginning, gave birth.
Blessed is She who says and performs.
Blessed is She who declares and fulfills.
Blessed is She whose womb covers the earth.
Blessed is She whose womb protects all creatures.
Blessed is She who nourished those who are in awe of Her.
Blessed is She who lives forever, and exists eternally.
Blessed is She who redeems and saves. Blessed is Her Name.

Blessed are You, Lord our G-d, Ruler of the universe, G-d and
Mother of the womb. Exalted in the mouth of Her people, praised and
glorified by the tongue of Her pious ones and servants. With the songs
of David and Miriam, your servants we will praise You. Lord our G-d
with psalms and songs we will exalt, extol, and glorify You. We will
call upon Your Name and proclaim You our Ruler, our G-d, the only
One, the life of all worlds. Ruler, lauded and praised, Your great
Name will be forever and ever. Blessed are You Adonai, Ruler extolled
with psalms of praise.

AZ YASHIR (And then he sang)*:

That day the Lord saved Israel from the hand of the Egyptians.
Israel saw the great power that the Lord used against them, and the
people feared the Lord. Miriam the prophetess took up her tambourine
and all the women followed her, dancing to the sound of tambourines,
and Miriam led them with this song:[1]

I will sing my praise to the Lord,
To Her alone I will sing praise.

---

* Moses' song, Exodus 15:1–18, is traditionally said at this point in the Preliminary
Morning Service. We have replaced it with our version of Miriam's song.

The Lord is my Mother, my Strength.
I will exalt Her all my days.

For She subdued the waves with Her might
And softened the sands with Her touch.
Her arm rescued the enslaved,
And Her voice comforted our people in their despair.

Women, gather timbrels, cymbals, and flutes.
Make heard the glory of the Lord.
Wear your colors, ribbons, bells, and gold
To honor the victory of our G-d.
Come barefooted, dance on the shore.
Send forth a song, Sing Hallelujah.

Sing praise to the Lord.
To Her alone sing your praise.

For the horizons cannot restrain Her power,
Nor the heavens contain Her radiance.
Her children cannot tire Her understanding,
And Her womb is deep and broad.

Sing, daughters of Israel, sing aloud,
For I still hear the crash of the waves
And the wailing of the Egyptian women,
And my voice trembles
I can only whisper before the wonder of my G-d.

So sing now, sing Her praise,
Praise Her in the sight of Her power,
Praise Her for Her mighty acts,
Praise Her for Her overwhelming greatness,
Praise Her with the blast of the horn,
Praise Her with the timbrels and dance,
Praise Her with strings and the pipe,
Praise Her with the clear-toned cymbals,
Praise Her with the loud-sounding cymbals,
Let all that has breath praise the Lord.[2]

For She will bring us in
And plant us on Her own mountain, the place where She dwells.[3]
She will reveal Herself to us in a cloud of glory
She will reveal Herself to speak to us.[4]

Sing now, my sisters,
Sing of our salvation;
For once in G-d's presence
We will be silent and still,
For what is our song
To the voice of the Lord?

NOTES

1. Exodus 15:19–21.
2. Psalm 150.
3. Exodus 15:17.
4. From the first line of the *Shoforoth* blessings in the Rosh Hashana Musaph service (a part of the High Holiday Service).

Bringing a Daughter into the Covenant

JUDITH PLASKOW

Boys have traditionally been welcomed into the Jewish community with far more pomp and ceremony than have girls. At eight days, they are initiated into the covenant of Abraham in the dramatic *brit milah* (covenant of circumcision) ritual. Firstborn sons are symbolically redeemed from the necessity of Temple service with a *Pidyon ha-Ben* (redemption of the firstborn). And often the grandparents of boys will throw a party (*Ben Zachar*) celebrating their arrival. Girls, on the other hand, are named in the synagogue in the course of a regular Sabbath service. The father is called to the Torah, generally in the absence of mother and child, and little marks the event as a unique and joyous occasion.

In the past few years, many Jewish parents, myself included, have tried to rectify this inequality in life cycle rituals by creating distinctive ceremonies for the birth of a daughter paralleling the *brit milah*.[1] In my case, as I awaited the birth of my child (who turned out to be a son!), I knew I wanted to celebrate the birth of a daughter, but I felt

Judith Plaskow received her Ph.D. from Yale University and now teaches at Wichita State University. A past cochair of the Women and Religion Section of the American Academy of Religion, she is active in the women's movement and in Jewish feminist organizations, and is coeditor of *Women and Religion* (Scholars Press). Her articles on feminism and religion have appeared in *Signs, The Jewish Woman,* and *Response.* She wrote this ritual in 1977 during her last month of pregnancy.

stymied in my attempt to find a central ritual symbol or act, equivalent to circumcision, which could carry the weight of initiating a girl into the covenant. Finally, after much thought and with some misgivings, I gave up on finding a physical symbol and decided to focus my ceremony on women's experiences within the Jewish tradition that were important to me and that I hoped would be important to my daughter. Since—despite its patriarchal content and framework—the covenant between God and Israel is not a covenant with men but with the whole community, it seemed appropriate to look at some moments at which women, named and unnamed, brought their bodies, their talents, and their sense of themselves to the life of the Jewish people.

My misgivings about this ceremony center on its transitional character. In insisting that girl children are also the heirs and guarantors of tradition, it reminds us that—just as they are excluded from *brit milah*—they have in fact been excluded from much of Jewish religious life. I hope there will come a time when the exclusion of women, and therefore insistence on their inclusion, will be an anachronism. Since for me, full participation of women in the Jewish community is indissolubly connected with our willingness to speak of God as male and female, I use female God language in the ritual. It, like the ceremony as a whole, is deliberately compensatory.

THE CEREMONY

The mother says: We begin with the song of Hannah on the birth of Samuel.

> My heart exults in my God;
> my strength is exalted in God.
> My mouth derides my enemies,
> because I rejoice in thy salvation.
>
> There is none holy like God,
> There is none besides thee;
> There is no rock like our God.
> Talk no more so very proudly,
> let not arrogance come from your mouth;
> for God is a God of knowledge,
> and by Her actions are weighed.
> The bows of the mighty are broken,
> but the feeble gird on strength.

> Those who were full have hired themselves out for bread,
> but those who were hungry have ceased to hunger.
> The barren has borne seven,
> But she who has many children is forlorn.
> God creates and destroys;
> She brings down to Sheol and raises up.
> God makes poor and makes rich;
> She brings low and also exalts.
> She raises up the poor from the dust;
> She lifts the needy from the ash heap,
> to make them sit with royalty
> and inherit a seat of honor.
> For the pillars of the earth are God's,
> and on them She has set the world. (1 Samuel 2:2–8)[2]

The father continues:

> When Israel stood to receive the Torah, the Holy One,
> Praised be She, said to them: "I am giving you my Torah.
> Present me good guarantees that you will guard it, and
> I shall give it to you."

> They said: "Our ancestors are our guarantors."

> The Holy One said to them: "Your ancestors are not
> sufficient guarantors. Bring me guarantors, and
> I shall give you the Torah."

> They said: "Ruler of the universe, our prophets are
> our guarantors."

> God said to them: "The prophets are not sufficient
> guarantors. Yet bring me good guarantors, and I shall
> give you the Torah."

> They said: "Here, our children are our guarantors."

> The Holy One, Praised be She, said: "They are certainly
> good guarantors. For their sake I give the Torah to
> you."[3]

It is not only our sons who are our guarantors, but also our daughters, for the laughter of Sarah is part of the history of our people. (A friend reads:)

[And the three men said to Abraham,] "Where is Sarah your wife?" And he said, "She is in the tent." And God said, "I will surely return to you in the spring, and Sarah your wife shall have a son." And Sarah was listening at the tent door behind him. Now Abraham and Sarah were old, advanced in age; and it had ceased to be with Sarah after the manner of women. So Sarah laughed to herself, saying, "After I have grown old, and my husband is old, shall I have pleasure?" The Lord said to Abraham, "Why did Sarah laugh and say, 'Shall I indeed bear a child, now that I am old?' Is anything too hard for your God? At the appointed time I shall return to you, in the spring, and Sarah shall have a son." But Sarah denied, saying, "I did not laugh"; for she was afraid. God said, "No, but you did laugh." (Genèsis 18:9-15)

And the song of Miriam is part of the history of our people. (A friend reads:)

Then Miriam, the prophetess, the sister of Aaron, took a timbrel in her hand; and all the women went out after her with timbrels and dancing. And Miriam sang to them. "Sing to our God, for She has triumphed gloriously; the horse and his rider She has thrown into the sea." (Exodus 15:20-21)

And the judgeship of Deborah is part of the hisory of our people. (A friend reads:)

Now Deborah, a prophetess, the wife of Lappidoth, was judging Israel at that time. She used to sit under the palm of Deborah . . . and the people of Israel came up to her for judgment. She sent and summoned Barak . . . and said to him, "The God of Israel commands you, 'Go gather your men at Mount Tabor, taking ten thousand from the tribe of Naphtali and the tribe of Zebulun. And I will draw out Sisera, the general of Jabin's army to meet you by the river Kishon with his chariots and his troops; and I will give him into your hand.' " Barak said to her, "If you will go with me, I will go; but if you will not go with me, I will not go." And she said, "I will surely go with you; nevertheless, the road on which you are going will not lead to your glory, for God will sell Sisera into the hand of a woman." Then Deborah arose, and went with Barak to Kedesh. (Judges 4:4-9)

And the prophecy of Huldah is part of the history of our people. (A friend reads:)

And when Josiah heard the words of the book of the law, he rent his clothes. And the king commanded [his servants] saying, "Go inquire of God for me, and for the people, and for all Judah, concerning the words of this book that has been found. . . ."
So [they] went to Huldah the prophetess, the wife of Shallum the son of Tikvah, son of Harhas, keeper of the wardrobe (now she dwelt in Jerusalem in the Second Quarter); and they talked with her. And she said to them, "Thus says the God of Israel, 'Tell the man who sent you to me, Thus says our God, Behold, I will bring evil upon this place and upon its inhab tants, all the words

of the book which the king of Judah has read. . . .'" And they brought back word to the king. (2 Kings 22: 11–13a, 14–16, 20b)

And the unnamed thousands of women, they too are part of the history of our people. (A friend reads:)

When Adam had lived a hundred and thirty years, he became the father of a son in his own likeness, after his image, and named him Seth. . . . When Seth had lived a hundred and five years, he became the father of Enosh. . . . When Enosh had lived ninety years, he became the father of Kenan. . . . When Kenan had lived seventy years, he became the father of Jared. . . . When Jared had lived a hundred and sixty-two years, he became the father of Enoch. (Genesis 5:3, 9, 12, 15, 8)

Noah and his sons, Shem and Ham and Japheth, and Noah's wife and the three wives of his sons with them entered the ark. (Genesis 7:13)

And there was a certain man of Zorah . . . whose name was Manoah; and his wife was barren and had no children. And an angel of God appeared to the woman and said to her, "Behold, you are barren and have no children; but you shall conceive and bear a son." (Judges 13:2–3)

When Ahijah heard the sound of her feet, as she came in at the door, he said, "Come in, wife of Jeroboam." (1 Kings 14:6)

When Enoch had lived sixty-five years, he became the father of Methuselah. . . . When Methuselah had lived a hundred and eighty-seven years, he became the father of Lamech. . . . When Lamech had lived a hundred and eighty-two years, he became the father of a son, and called his name Noah. (Genesis 5:21, 25, 28–29)

The parents say: "Praised are you our God, Ruler of the universe, who sanctified us with your commandments and commanded us to bring our daughters into the covenant of the people of Israel." And they continue:

Our God, God of our fathers and mothers, preserve this child to her father and mother, and let her name be called in Israel _____, the daughter of _____ and _____. Let the father rejoice in his offspring and the mother be glad in the fruit of her body; as it is written, let thy father and thy mother rejoice, and let her that bare thee be glad. And it is said, God remembers Her covenant forever, the word which She commanded for a thousand generations. O give thanks to God, for She is good; Her lovingkindness endures forever. This little child _____, may she be great. Even as she enters into the covenant, so may she enter into the Torah, the marriage canopy, and good deeds.[4]

The parents conclude: "May She who blessed our mothers Sarah, Rebecca, Rachel, and Leah, Miriam the prophetess, Hannah the barren one, Deborah the judge, bless also this little child. May She bless you and keep you. May She be with and be gracious to you. May She show kindness to you and give you peace.

NOTES

1. See, for example, Toby Fishbein Reifman, *Blessing the Birth of a Daughter: Jewish Naming Ceremonies for Girls,* New York: Ezrat Nashim, 1976.
2. All biblical references are to the Revised Standard Version, with pronouns changed.
3. This midrash is taken from Sandy Sasso's "Brit B'not Yisrael: Covenant for the Daughters of Israel," in *Blessing the Birth of a Daughter,* pp. 9–10.
4. This is taken from the traditional *brit milah* ceremony.

Jewish Women's Haggadah

AVIVA CANTOR

Several years ago, a group of young Jews in New York constituted themselves the Jewish Liberation Project. We came from a variety of backgrounds—old and New Left, Zionist, religious, Yiddishist—and in time we came to define ourselves as Socialist-Zionists. We became involved in a variety of work within the American Jewish community and on the left. We talked a lot about "alternative politics" and "alternative life-styles."

A family feeling definitely existed among us in those early years. When Pesah came around, we wanted to be able to hold a Seder that reflected both our politics and our feeling of community. Thus the Jewish Liberation Seder was born. It was written by three people: Itzhak Epstein, Yaakov (then Jerry) Kirschen, and myself. I wrote the basic draft, drawing on much research and on long discussions with my two collaborators; they helped me cut, refine, and polish it. Kirschen did all the art.

What we wrote was a ceremony that was both Jewish and radical in values and concepts, traditional in ritual, and modern in its pace and language. We tried to tie in the struggle for Jewish liberation today

Aviva Cantor is a Socialist Zionist and feminist primarily involved in writing and lecturing on the Jewish woman. One of the founders of *Lilith* magazine, she currently works as its acquisitions editor. She is active in Jewish communal life, the women's movement, and animal welfare and environmental protection organizations. She is author of *The Jewish Liberation Haggadah,* and her articles have appeared in *Lilith, Jewish Liberation Journal, Israel Horizons,* and *Response.* This essay first appeared in expanded form in *Sistercelebrations,* edited by Arlene Swidler, copyright © 1974 by Fortress Press, and is reprinted by permission of Fortress Press.

with struggles of our people in the past and to draw on Jewish experience and Jewish sources to speak to what we ourselves were going through.

We began at the obvious point: we cut a lot of what we considered excess verbiage that related to medieval scholastic debates—but added a lot of our own verbiage! We added material on the Holocaust, Israel, and Soviet Jewry. One of the main things we did was to infuse old rituals with new content and meaning. For example, while retaining the four cups of wine that must be drunk at the Seder, we attached new meaning to each one, making each stand for a particular struggle against oppression.

A couple of years later, while wandering through a bookstore, I picked up Beverly Jones's and Judith Brown's paper, "Toward a Female Liberation Movement." On reading it, I experienced a flash of recognition and identification and promptly became a feminist. More reading and thinking followed. Later I began to do research on the Jewish woman; I lectured on the subject and taught a course on it at the Jewish Free High School.

About two years after that, as more women were also trying to synthesize their new Jewish consciousness and their feminist consciousness, one woman sent out a circular to all her friends and acquaintances, calling them to a meeting to discuss how we feel and think as Jewish women. Several large meetings followed. A core group of five women eventually became my Jewish women's consciousness-raising group, which met for over two years. In our weekly meetings, we tried to understand how our Jewish background made us what we are and explored what it meant to be a Jewish woman.

The first year, having become close and loving friends, we decided that we wanted to hold a Jewish Women's Seder. We felt that we were a family and that we could use this most Jewish of ceremonies to bring us and other Jewish women closer to each other and to our history and values. What follows are excerpts from the Seder I put together for this occasion. . . .

I did not write the Haggadah from scratch. I took the Jewish Liberation Haggadah, used it as a basic framework, cut some material, and then added feminist material. My first shock came in rereading the Jewish Liberation Haggadah. First, I was bothered by the obvious things: the four sons, the "he" all over the place not followed by "and she." But even more disturbing—especially since I was the main author of the Haggadah—was the almost complete absence of women, our invisibility. Except for one poem, there was very little to indicate that Jewish women had been active participants in Jewish life and struggles.

So I rewrote the Haggadah, first taking care of the minor changes: making God "ruler of the universe" instead of "king," adding the names of Jacob's wives to the Exodus narrative, and changing "four sons" to "four daughters." The major change was to utilize the four-cups ritual and to dedicate each cup of wine to the struggle of Jewish women in a particular period. The Haggadah's aim was to provide connecting links between Jewish women of the past and us here in the present. A great deal of material came from Jewish legends and historical sources, some only recently discovered. Although the Seder proved enjoyable to us and our friends, I still feel quite dissatisfied with it and in no way regard it as complete.

The first and most obvious problem is the fact that this Seder is based on another Seder and is therefore not really "original." Although beautiful in many respects, it represents an almost verbatim takeover of its "predecessor's" account of the Exodus. Then, too, changing "four sons" to "four daughters" while leaving the rest of the segment (written by Itzhak Epstein) largely intact makes that excerpt less relevant than it might be if it were completely rewritten.

However, there is a more fundamental problem involved in writing a Seder for Jewish women and that is the tension between the very nature of the Seder and the needs of the participants. I think this tension cannot be fully resolved, and whoever writes such a Seder should be aware of it.

On the one hand, the Seder is a Jewish celebration. It marks a *specific*—national—liberation from a *specific*—national—oppression. The Jewish woman, however, cannot celebrate this liberation with a whole heart because she knows that her oppression continues. This might lead us to want to incorporate into the Haggadah a whole lot of material on the oppression of women in Jewish life, and indeed my first draft did just that. But that would bring us into conflict with the essential nature of the Seder, which is joyous and emphasizes those things that unite Jews rather than divide them (for example, at a Seder we do not stress the class struggle).

Thus the women's Seder is in danger of becoming irrelevant to the needs of its participants. The only solution I could see was to draw on

Jewish history, extracting material about the participation of Jewish
women in the struggles for Jewish liberation (which is the theme of the
Seder). Emphasizing our participation in Jewish struggles, however,
creates two problems: (1) It makes it seem as if the Haggadah is our
"entrance card" to Jewish society, as if through it we were saying,
"Look, we're *real Jews* after all." (2) It makes it seem as if Jewish
women have never had any problem at all in Jewish society, as if they
have always been allowed to participate as equals, and, this, of course,
is untrue. So the question remains: how to deal with the oppression of
the Jewish woman *within the context of the Seder as a ceremony
marking Jewish national liberation.* As yet I have no answer to this
question; perhaps women can find the solution together.

My final reservation about the Jewish Women's Haggadah is even
more basic. As much as I loved a Seder with my sisters, what gnawed
at me was my memory of the Seders I had at home, in my parents'
house, Seders of men and women of several generations, with children
running underfoot and spilling the wine. The Seder has always been a
family celebration and, for me, a Seder just for women seems incom-
plete.

What I would like to see—and for me it has not yet crystallized—is
a Seder that focuses on the oppression of Jews and on Jewish
liberation *from a Jewish feminist viewpoint.* Such a Haggadah would
deal honestly with the oppression of women while keeping the main
focus on Jewish liberation. It would be a Seder for families of all kinds,
whether by blood or by choice. In such a Seder, women would be as
"visible" as men, but neither men nor women would be the entire focus
of the Seder. This is the kind of Seder I would like to take my children
to—if and when I ever have children. I would also, of course, invite my
dear friend Nadia Borochov Ovsey who celebrated her ninety-second
birthday in October of 1975, the woman of valor to whom I dedicated
this Haggadah.

JEWISH WOMEN'S HAGGADAH

Haverot, shalom.

We have gathered here tonight to celebrate Pesah, the festival of the
liberation of the Jewish people. Pesah is the night when all the families
of Israel gather to celebrate and to strengthen their ties—to each other
and to all Jews. We too are a family, a growing family. We too have

ties we hope to strengthen. For, while we are not related by blood, we are related by something perhaps even stronger: sisterhood.

Then follows the blessing on the wine, the dipping of the greens in salt water, the breaking of the middle matzah, the four questions, and the core of the Seder—the telling of the story of the Jew's struggle for liberation from slavery in Egypt. As the first cup of wine—dedicated to the first uprising of the Jews against oppression and the first liberation—is lifted, the following is said:

As we hold this cup of wine, we remember our sisters in the land of Egypt who fearlessly stood up to the Pharaoh.

Our legends tell us that Pharaoh, in the time-honored pattern of oppressors, tried to get Jews to collaborate in murdering their own people. He summoned the top two Jewish midwives, Shifra and Puah—some legends say one of them was Yocheved, who was also Moshe's mother—and commanded them to kill newborn Jewish males at birth and to report the birth of Jewish females so that they could be raised to become prostitutes. Pharaoh tried at first to win over the midwives by making sexual advances to them. When they repulsed these, he threatened them with death by fire. The midwives did not carry out Pharaoh's command. Instead of murdering the male infants, they took special care of them. If a mother was poor, they went around to the other women, collecting food for her and her child. When Pharaoh asked the midwives to account for all the living children, they made up the excuse that Jewish women gave birth so fast that they did not summon midwives in time.

Like our Jewish sisters through the ages, those in Egypt were strong and courageous in the face of oppression. Our sages recognized this when they said: "The Jews were liberated from Egypt because of the righteousness of the women."

The parable of the four sons is here retold as "The Four Daughters," in language reflecting our struggle to find ourselves as Jewish women. The nature of oppression is also defined and the Holocaust described in "Go and Learn":

Go and learn how the enemies of the Jews have tried so many times and in so many places to destroy us. We survived because of our spiritual resistance and our inner strength. Throughout the ages, Jewish women have provided much of this strength, courage, and loyalty. During very desperate times, Jewish women were allowed to show their strength openly. Yocheved, Miriam, Deborah, Yael, Judith, Esther—who was called a "redeemer"—how few are the names of the heroic Jewish women which have come down to us! How many more were there whose names we will never know?

We speak of rebellion as the only way to overthrow oppression. The Ten Plagues are mentioned one by one. Then we raise and dedicate the second cup of wine to the ghetto fighters.

We drink this second of four cups of wine to honor the glorious memory of the Jewish fighters in the ghettos, concentration camps, and forests of Nazi Europe. They fought and died with honor and avenged the murder of our people. Their courage and hope in the face of unutterable brutality and despair inspires us.

As we hold this cup of wine, we remember our glorious and brave sisters who fought so courageously against the Nazi monsters. We remember Hannah Senesh and Haviva Reik, who parachuted behind enemy lines in Hungary and Slovakia to organize resistance and rescue Jews. We remember Vladka Meed, and Chaika and Frumka Plotnitski, who served as couriers and smuggled arms for the ghetto fighters. We remember Rosa Robota who organized the smuggling of dynamite to blow up a crematorium in Auschwitz. Chaika Grossman, Gusta Drenger, Zivia Lubetkin, Gisi Fleischman, Tosia Altman, Zofia Yamaika, Niuta Teitelboim—these are but a few of the names we know. Their willingness to sacrifice their lives for their people shines through the words of Hannah Senesh, written shortly before her execution (Nov. 7, 1944):

> Blessed is the match that is consumed
> in kindling the flame
> Blessed is the flame that burns
> in the secret fastness of the heart
> Blessed is the heart strong enough to
> stop beating in dignity
> Blessed is the match that is consumed
> in kindling the flame.

We sing the traditional Dayeynu, *eat* matzah *and the bitter herbs and discuss their symbolism, and then talk of liberation and the importance of the Jewish homeland.*

In every century, Jews longed to return to Zion. In our own day, many Soviet Jews are struggling for their right to settle in Israel. Ruth Alexandrovitch, Raiza Palatnik, and Sylva Zalmanson were imprisoned for their part in this struggle.

When the Prophet Jeremiah watched the Jews being led away into Babylonian captivity, he saw a vision of our Matriarch Rachel, a symbol of this tragedy and of the yearning to return to Eretz Yisrael:

> .A voice is heard on high
> A keening, mournful wail.
> Rachel is crying for her children
> Refusing to be consoled
> For their loss.
>
> The Lord Says:
> Hold back the cries in your throat
> And the tears in your eyes
> For there is a future of hope for you:
> Your children shall return
> To their own land. (Jer. 31:15-18)

The third cup of wine is blessed.

We drink the third cup of wine to honor the Jews of our own time who fought and died to establish Israel.

As we lift this cup of wine, we also bring to mind our many sisters in Israel who started the "first wave" of feminism there. We remember the *halutzot,* the women pioneers who won their struggle to work in the fields and as laborers in the cities—as equals in the upbuilding of Israel.

We remember our sisters Manya Schochat, Sarah Malchin, Yael Gordon, Techia Lieberson, Hannah Meisel, and so many others, who set up women's collectives and women's agricultural training farms and organized the working women's movement in Eretz Yisrael. We remember two of these organizers, Sarah Chisick and Dvora Drachler, who fell in the defense of Tel-Hai with Yosef Trumpeldor. We remember our many sisters who fought in the underground and in the army during the War of Independence.

In Passover of 1911, the first meeting of working women in Eretz Yisrael was held. Ada Maimon wrote:

The girls who had the opportunity to work in the fields were few and far between and even within the pioneering, revolutionary labor movement in the Land of Israel, women were relegated to their traditional tasks—housekeeping and particularly kitchen work. . . .

The girls wanted very much to discuss ways of changing and improving the situation. A meeting of their own, they felt, was absolutely necessary, for it had become clear that women would not raise their voices at general conferences and that the male delegates would not put the special problems of women workers on the agenda.

The first meeting of the working women took place in Kvutzat Kinneret. There were seventeen participants. . . . The proceedings went on behind closed doors; no men were allowed to attend.

Emotional outpouring rather than systematic analysis of problems characterized the meeting. From this meeting, the Working Women's Movement was born.

We talk of what Jewish identity means and how assimilation is self-oppression. We bless and then drink the fourth and last cup of wine.

We drink this fourth and last cup of wine on this Seder night to honor our Jewish sisters who are struggling to find new and beautiful ways to say "I am a Jew."

We honor all our sisters in the small but growing Jewish feminist movement, here, all over North America, in Europe and Israel; our mothers and our grandmothers whom we have so often misunderstood and fought with; our daughters and granddaughters.

We are liberating ourselves from the assimilationist dream-turned-nightmare and moving toward creating Jewish life-styles, rediscovering our history and our traditions, our heritage and our values, and building on them and from them. It is possible that in struggling to free ourselves, we shall at one and the same time be instrumental in the struggle to liberate the Jewish people as well. That, too, is our goal.

Now we speak of what we've been waiting for—the food! We eat, sing, share the afikoman, *say "Grace After Meals," and sing the traditional* Had Gadya—*"One Goatling." After singing "Next Year in Jerusalem," we conclude:*

We have talked on this Pesah night about our liberation from oppression and thus we conclude the formal part of the Seder. Just as we have been privileged to join with our sisters in holding this Seder, so may we be privileged to join with them in struggling for our liberation as Jewish women. May we carry out our self-liberation soon, joyously returning to our heritage and our homeland and our people—to be redeemed and to participate in the redemption of the Jewish people.

Next Year in Jerusalem!

CREATING
NEW TRADITIONS

T HE essays in the preceding section were written by women struggling to maintain a creative tension between Judaism or Christianity and feminist experience. While the feminist reformists speak for many women in churches and synagogues throughout the country, the authors of this last section speak for other feminists who are rejecting the biblical traditions and instead grounding theology and ritual primarily in women's lives. For these revolutionary thinkers, the essential theological task is not to reconstruct tradition but to explore the religious dimensions of women's experience free from constraints imposed by loyalty to a particular past. Having learned through the women's movement that women's experience is valuable and worthy of attention, feminist theologians are taking this experience in all its variety as a source of possible insight into the ways human beings find sense and grounding for their lives. Feminist experience, traditional women's experience, women's experience past and present—all are potential starting points for theological reflection.

Revolutionary feminist theology, then—as opposed to reformist theology—places primary emphasis on women's experience. But it understands women's experience from a particular viewpoint: feminism is the lens or filter through which experience is

seen. The feminist theologian examines women's experience not
to create new images of the eternal feminine but to provide an
understanding of reality that validates femaleness and thus
makes possible female—and human—growth and change. This
common goal explains the emergence of similar themes from
different starting points. The need for holistic vision and for
getting in touch with our bodies and nature, the significance of
community with other women and of the stories and rituals that
grow out of community, the rising of female imagery and
symbolism—these are concerns that surface in this very varied
section again and again.

The first essay reprinted here, Judith Plaskow's, is a transition between this section and the last. Coming out of a series of
small group meetings at a 1972 conference on women exploring
theology, at Grailville in Loveland, Ohio, the paper, by its own
admission, is caught between a reformist and revolutionary
stance. The group which generated the article meant to bracket
tradition and explore the theological implications of consciousness raising. No sooner had it done so, however, than it felt
compelled to relate this process to traditional (Protestant) theological terms. The essay thus expresses a tension that is
epitomized by the myth with which it ends. Attempting to
dramatize the meaning of contemporary feminist experience,
"The Coming of Lilith" retells a story from the biblical-rabbinic
tradition. While this might mark the essay as reformist, the
retelling threatens to move beyond the tradition from which it
stems. Not only does it reverse the traditional image of Lilith as
the archetypal evil woman, seeing her instead as the archetype of
female freedom, but it also leaves open the question of whether
Eve and Lilith will "reconstruct" the garden or create it anew.

If Plaskow is uncertain as to whether feminism should be the
sole norm of feminist theology, Daly is not. In the excerpt from
Beyond God the Father included here, Daly insists on the
importance of God to feminists—*but only as God is understood
through feminist experience.* Ultimate transcendence acquires
meaning not through tradition but through feminism as a
movement that reveals the nature of *be-ing.* Daly views con-

sciousness raising as a modern mystical journey in the course of which women move from *nonbeing,* from encounter with the nothingness of sexist structures that define their lives, to an affirmation of *be-ing,* of the radical possibility of defining and becoming themselves for the first time. In the light of this experience, which is an experience of new be-ing, God can be understood as the endlessly unfolding be-ing in and with whom all things continuously become. This is a reinterpretation of traditional philosophical concepts of God, but Daly refuses to identify the be-ing that undergirds the women's movement with the Father and Son of Christianity. She believes the biblical symbols of divinity have supported a hierarchal patriarchal system in which women's experience of the power of be-ing has been severely restricted.

Plaskow and Daly thus both focus on women's feminist experience, but Daly more fully acknowledges feminism as the primary theological norm. The next three articles all stand with Daly in grounding theology entirely in women's experience, but they locate women's experience in different places. Naomi Goldenberg looks to women's dreams as interpreted in a feminist dream group as a source of revelation. Carol Christ sees contemporary literature written by women as reflecting a new sacred story. And Penelope Washbourn examines the spiritual dimension of the life crises associated with having a female body. Each is trying to uncover a means of access into unexamined aspects of women's experience. Bracketing the question of the relation between women's experience and tradition, each concentrates on the religious meanings that emerge from the rich texture of contemporary women's lives. They focus on experiences that might be shared by many women rather than feminists alone.

Given their interest in the broad range of women's experience and given their different starting points, it is interesting that they share certain concerns not only with each other but also with Daly and Plaskow. Christ discovers, for example, that a central feminist experience, the experience of nothingness, is shared by many modern women who begin their life journeys lacking an adequate image of self. Her notion of a spiritual quest rooted in women's experience is central to all three articles. For Goldenberg, Christ, and Washbourn, women's quest leads through encounter with despised aspects of the self in Western culture— the unconscious (Goldenberg, Christ, Washbourn), the body and nature (Washbourn), and the depth dimension of traditional women's experiences (Christ, Washbourn). When the quest is successful, it leads to self-integration and integration with the powers of the universe. Here we find reiterated Daly's notion that women's self-affirmation stems from connection with the power of be-ing and is a process of naming toward God.

The themes of spiritual quest and discovery of being emerge once more in the last essays in the section, which ground feminist theology and ritual in still another aspect of women's experience—the female-centered religions of the past. In the ancient traditions of witchcraft and Goddess worship that were suppressed by the biblical traditions, feminists have found sources of powerful female symbolism that—viewed selectively—can provide the basis for contemporary religious community in which femaleness is affirmed. The articles by Starhawk and Zsuzsanna Budapest are articulations of a grass roots spirituality movement that has emerged spontaneously around the country in the past several years. Starhawk and Budapest proudly identify themselves as "witches" in affirmation of solidarity with those women and men who—they believe—were killed for daring to challenge patriarchal spiritual norms. They carefully distinguish their own witch traditions from Satanism or devil worship, which they view as Christian heresies spawned by the witch persecutors. Others in the spirituality movement eschew the term *witch* because it is so often misunderstood, and simply call themselves participants in the "womanspirit movement." These women celebrate the Goddess without connecting her worship to particular witch traditions. The sense of female selfhood and power that emerges so slowly and painfully from dreams, literature, and contemporary body experience is here proclaimed with fierce exuberance by those who have reclaimed the Goddess symbol. Women's sexuality, the birthing power that connects women to nature and the life and death forces of the universe, and the sense of wholeness that emerges from recognizing women's connection with all waxing and waning processes are all celebrated as fundamental to the religious life. It is to enable these affirmations that women need the Goddess, Carol Christ argues in the last article. The Goddess symbol allows women to free themselves from the "patriarchal policeman" within and to proclaim their beauty and power, which have so long been denied.

There is a freedom and enthusiasm in these articles by Starhawk, Budapest, and Christ that is lacking in the other essays on women's spiritual experience and that may stem from the sense of being rooted in tradition. Theirs is not the often solitary and painful casting in the dark for sources of women's experience on which to base theological probings. They have uncovered whole religions, rich in symbolism and ceremonial forms. Of course, these ancient religions are appropriated through a feminist filter—they are "invented" as much as "remembered." But that means these authors bypass the problem of relating tradition and experience by discovering and creating new old traditions that seem to be in harmony with feminism.

The vision of a spirituality rooted in the body and nature is an important response to the dualism of body and soul, nature and spirit, that Rosemary Ruether argues is at the heart of the suppression of women in Western religion and culture. On the other hand, one might ask whether celebration of women's body experience fully transcends this dualism or simply elevates its rejected side. One might also question whether ancient traditions of the earth are wholly appropriate to the realities and problems of a modern technological culture. But whatever questions might be raised about feminist witchcraft and Goddess worship, it is clear these last three articles share and boldly express the affirmation of womanhood that is at the heart of all feminist thinking in religion.

The Coming of Lilith: Toward a Feminist Theology

JUDITH PLASKOW

The present questioning of theological language, premises, methods, and systems by women in every relation to religious life has critical and constructive sides. Women are both articulating the problems with traditional theology and struggling for ways to express their new relationships with their traditions and themselves. If the feminist theology,[1] which is just beginning to emerge from this struggle has any one distinctive characteristic, it may well be its faithfulness to those experiences that engender it; content and process are inseparable. Since the felt need for such theology arises through the consciousness-raising experience, this theology constantly needs to measure itself against and recapture the richness of feeling and insight gained through consciousness raising, finally becoming a continuation of it. Thus much feminist theology may be communal theology, for, in sharing the theological task, content and process have the chance to come together in a very real way. In this paper, I would like to share the results—fragmentary as they are—of one group's attempt to do theology[2] communally in the hopes that our questions will be taken up by other women and our process made part of an ongoing one.

It is not self-evident that theology must remain close to the experi-

---

An earlier version of this essay was published in a Church Women United packet, "Women Exploring Theology at Grailville," 1972.

ences that generate it. Experience may provide the occasion for general, abstract reflection or argument. There are reasons why, in the case of feminist theology, the close relation between content and process seems imperative. Not surprisingly, these reasons have to do with the nature of consciousness raising itself. Through consciousness raising, I come to affirm the value of my experience as a woman person, the value of my whole, not only intellectual self. I affirm my experience with and through other women in a process that is communal in essence. I cannot then write a theology that abstracts from my experience and ignores part of myself, or that abstracts from the community of which I am a part.

These considerations form the framework within which to see our group's work. Our group process reflected them, and the content of our discussions further developed them. The question with which we began was whether we could find in the women's movement a process, event, or experience that somehow expresses the essence of the movement and that might function as a central integrating symbol for a theology of liberation. Aware that such a symbol would have value only as it arises out of and remains close to the life of the movement, we proceeded to explore this question by sharing and reflecting on our experiences as women in the women's movement. We then discussed the ways in which these experiences are similar to or are religious experiences, and finally, attempted to reflect theologically on what we had done.[3]

THE WOMEN'S MOVEMENT

Becoming involved in the women's movement means moving from isolation as a woman to community. Through the telling my story, I reach out to other women. Through their hearing, which both affirms my story and makes it possible, they reach out to me. I am able to move, gradually, from defensiveness to openness, from fear of questioning, to a deep and radical questioning of the premises from which I have lived my life. I experience relief; my anger has been heard, and I am not alone. But I am also frightened; I am undermining my own foundations. The walls come tumbling down.[4] *Anger, fear, rage, joy, celebration, rejoicing, high, flying, bursting forth, pregnant with newness, pregnant with possibility, hearing, wholeness*—these were the words we began with in attempting to describe our consciousness-raising experiences. What we wanted to do was to move from these words or experiences to one central word symbol or experience that captured them all. Mary Daly's "sisterhood of man"[5] was in our minds from the start of our discussion, but it was not quite what we were looking for. We felt that sisterhood happens between women because of something else happening to them—an individual process of coming-to-wholeness within community—and we wanted to try to get at that something else.

The "Yeah, Yeah" Experience

We arrived at a term for part of our experience quite spontaneously. One of us said something, and the others responded excitedly, "Yeah, yeah." Somehow, this triggered a double recognition. We saw ourselves in the experience to which we responded, and we also recognized ourselves as women come together, recognizing our common experience with other women. We spent the next hour trying to define the "yeah, yeah experience."

The "yeah, yeah experience" is, first of all, *the process through which we come to be sisters.* It may be the experience that brings me into the movement. I read an article by another woman, defending myself against it, and all of a sudden, undeniably, a piece of my life is there before me on the page. ("Yeah, yeah.") I attend a meeting, a lecture, "just to see what it's all about," and I am "converted," turned around, the pieces of my life fall together in a new way. ("Yeah, yeah.") The "yeah, yeah experience" is all the many individual moments of recognition and illumination through which I come to a new awareness of my situation and myself.[6] I talk to other women, and one describes as her hangup something I thought was peculiar to me— and everyone else is nodding too. I read, I hear, I talk about the oppression of women, and all at once, it's *our* oppression.

Thus the affirmative, early Beatles, sound of "yeah, yeah" is not meant to suggest that the "yeah, yeah experience" is always a joyful one. It can, of course, express deep joy—joy in sharing, joy in self-recognition, joy as I increase my freedom in relation to my past. But I can also say "yeah, yeah" as I put my finger on a hidden source of bitterness, as I hear my own anger spoken, or as I articulate my rage on behalf of my sisters' past and my own. In all cases, however, I express my conviction and my openness. I move forward; I respond toward a future where anything can happen.

My response, although sometimes an affirmation of only a limited area of agreement, is a response of my whole person. When I say "yeah, yeah," I am moved, and I move. I move physically, toward the one who spoke, and I move figuratively, into the consciousness-raising process. I affirm my sister and encourage her to go on while I myself enter the dialogue.

The "yeah, yeah experience" is thus a different way of thinking from our usual "yes, but" reasoning, which is inherently nondialogical and out of touch with its own basis in experience. "Yes, but" thinking focuses on the logic of the speaker or the argument advanced, to the exclusion of the awareness of being addressed by the speaker or argument. When I say "yeah, yeah," on the other hand, I do not forget logic or the fact that genuine disagreement may be, should be part of the dialogue into which I have entered. But I commit my whole person to speak and to really hear. This true speaking and hearing is a possibility for all persons. The "yeah, yeah experience" is potentially universal.

Sisterhood

The value of my being with and for others that develops through the "yeah, yeah experience" finds its expression in sisterhood. But sisterhood is not only what evolves through the "yeah, yeah experience"; it is in some sense its presupposition. Sisterhood grows through my speaking and hearing, but were it not already partly there, I could not begin to speak and hear.

The experience of sisterhood is many-sided. It has, first of all, both a general and a specific dimension. In affirming my own womanhood— or personhood as woman—I affirm it in all women. But I also and particularly affirm those women with whom I share the experience of affirmation. (The other side of this—sisterhood as presupposition— would be that in affirming all women I affirm myself as a woman.) This does not mean that, in community, I acknowledge in myself the characteristics of the "eternal feminine" or make peace with my assigned role. On the contrary, what I proclaim is precisely my freedom as a woman over these limited stereotypes.

Thus this experience is, secondly, both deeply personal and intensely political. I affirm myself as a woman, but only as I enter into a new, and hitherto silent, community. In saying yes to myself, where I and my society had said only no, I open the possibility of seeing other women as persons and friends; I discover a source of energy for personal and social growth and change. I acquire a sense of freedom that is rooted in my new consciousness of personal integrity and wholeness; I express it by uniting with other women in the common task of creating our future. I am freed to repossess or to try to free myself from parts of my past, but I can do this effectively only as I work for interpersonal and institutional change in the present.

But sisterhood, more than an experience of community, *is* a community. It is a place where women can "get themselves together," begin to understand, and thus begin to overcome, their common oppression. It is a place where women can begin to act out their new sense of wholeness, making their own decisions for their own lives. Thus the nonhierarchically structured women's movement refuses to replace one set of authorities with another. Instead, women who have rejected the myth of their own powerlessness create in community alternatives to a stunted past.

THE WOMEN'S MOVEMENT AS A RELIGIOUS EXPERIENCE

Throughout our discussion of the women's movement, we found ourselves both repeatedly seeing our experiences in the movement as religious experiences and repeatedly questioning the value of doing so. (See Question 5 at the end of the paper.) While the words *grace, illumination, mission,* and *conversion* kept cropping up in our conversation, we recognized that women who do not think in religious categories, who would in fact reject them, share the experiences we expressed in this language. We did not wish imperialistically to insist that their experiences too are "really" religious despite their refusal to recognize the fact. Moreover, if we asked what we added to the "root" experiences by calling them *religious,* there was nothing specific we could identify. On the other hand, we did feel this was a valid way of looking at our experiences in the women's movement, a way that could enrich our understanding of both these experiences and of religious experience itself.

We began our discussion of the women's movement with the "yeah, yeah experience" rather than with sisterhood because we wanted to get more precisely at the experience of coming-to-wholeness that sisterhood presupposes. If our discussion of the "yeah, yeah experience" got at part of this process, our discussion of religious experience dealt with it from another angle. We saw the stages of consciousness raising as analogous to the stages in a religious journey, culminating in the experience of full, related, selfhood.

Again and again we came back to the word *graceful* to describe certain of our experiences with other women. At moments I can never plan or program, I am given to myself in a way I cannot account for by studying the organic progression of my past. Listening to another woman tell her story, I *concentrate* on words spoken and experienced as if our lives depended on them, and indeed they do. And yet I could not say what enables me to be really there, hearing, in a way that makes me feel that I had never really heard before—or been listened to as I am now.[7] Nor could I say why precisely at this moment I become aware of myself as a total person, why I feel myself as whole, integrated, free, fully human. Some of this feeling we hoped to convey through the "yeah, yeah experience." "Yeah, yeah" is my response to an illumination that includes the intellect but is more than intellectual. In this moment in which I transcend it, I feel sharply the limits of the taken-for-granted definition of myself and my capabilities.

This is where the experience of grace can also become the experience of conversion. Seeing myself in a new way, I am called to the transformation of myself. I must become the possibilities I already am in my moment of vision, for I am really not yet those possibilities. The call necessitates a decision, a response.

Here two factors come into play. The feeling of wholeness, which is also a call to self-transformation, is not continuous with my previous development. But this does not mean that I have skipped over a "stage" in my life. I must still decide whether and how to change myself and, having decided, work slowly through the difficulties and pain that my decision entails. My clear perception of the limits of my upbringing, of the lost opportunities and confining decisions of my past does not relieve me of a lifetime of questioning and requestioning assumptions that I reject but cannot entirely overcome. On the other hand, there is a sense in which, once I have made a decision, I am already on the other side. At least I have overcome the fear that can only express itself in defensiveness. I have defined my goals and released the source of energy to achieve them.

Once again, the importance of sisterhood as a community comes into play. I make my decision for self-transformation in the context of a community whose support is ongoing. The continuing process of questioning, growth, and change remains collective. Thus, not only is my decision reinforced, but my energies for change are pooled with the group's energies. This expresses itself in a communal sense of mission. After a certain amount of time spent on consciousness raising, a group generally feels the need to move outward, to become involved in projects that translate its goals into reality and that reach and bring in other women. Strengthened in themselves, its members feel ready and anxious to spread the good word to others.

This sense of community also expresses itself—and this is the last way in which we looked at the women's movement as a religious experience—in the formation of embryonic rituals and symbols. Telling our stories has become a ritualized way of getting into the consciousness raising experience. Calling each other "sister," feeling a new freedom to touch and hug one another are concrete expressions of the new bonds between us. We have our heretics and our infidels; we have defined the "others" in a way that conditions behavior toward them: the token woman, the pussycat, and, of course, the male chauvinist pig. We have our political symbols: the woman symbol, the clenched fist. We indulge in ritual language corrections; we call all women "Ms." We are writing our songs, and we are beginning to find and define our peculiar forms of celebration.

THEOLOGICAL PROCESS

With regard to this list of rituals, the first task we envisaged for theology in relation to the women's movement was a critical one. We needed a critical principle to act as a bulwark against the tendency to absolutize either particular issues in the movement or the movement itself. We needed to move beyond defining "others" and, instead, to find those others in ourselves. We saw the need to regard every center, every feminist goal, as only provisional. Beyond each of our "ultimate" perspectives is a still broader one from which ours is judged limited. (See Question 4.)

With reference to our main, constructive task, we found it easier to discuss the women's movement and religious experience than to reflect theologically on either. (See Question 1.) What is theology? What does it mean to apply a theological process? Is feminist theology the expression of a new religion? How can we relate ourselves to the old without destroying our new experiences through the attempt to understand them in terms of old forms? These were crucial questions we felt we had to, but could not, answer. There were times we found ourselves getting into some rather traditional discussions—the ambiguity of grace that is both fulfilled and "not yet" fulfilled; the question of which comes first, sisterhood or the "yeah, yeah experience," grace or the experience of grace. Many of the things we talked about set off old associations. There is a clear relation, for example, between the true speaking and hearing of the "yeah, yeah experience" and the I-Thou relation in Martin Buber. We considered what it would mean to write a systematic theology that affirmed the experiences we had been discussing—choosing a philosophical framework, our texts, our rabbis, or our saints. But we were worried about the disappearance of the four of us sitting there, our coming together, behind the framework we would create. We clearly needed a form that would grow out of the content and process of our time together.

OUR STORY: THE COMING OF LILITH

It was here that we realized that, although we had failed to come up with a single event or symbol that captured all of feminist experience, there had emerged out of our discussion many of the central elements of a myth. We had a journey to go on, an enemy (or enemies) to vanquish, salvation to be achieved both for ourselves and for humanity. If we found ourselves with a myth, moreover, this was particularly appropriate to our experience, for we had come together to do theology by beginning with our stories. It was no coincidence, then, that we arrived back at the story form.

We recognized the difficulties of "inventing" a myth, however, and so we wanted to tell a story that seemed to grow naturally out of our present history. We also felt the need for using older materials that would carry their own reverberations and significance, even if we departed freely from them. We chose, therefore, to begin with the story of Lilith, demon of the night, who, according to rabbinic legend was Adam's first wife. Created equal to him, for some unexplained reason she found that she could not live with him, and flew away. Through her story, we could express not only our new image of ourselves, but our relation to certain of the elements of our religious traditions. Since stories are the heart of tradition, we could question and create tradition by telling a new story within the framework of an old one. (See Question 3.) We took Lilith for our heroine, and yet, most important, not Lilith alone. We try to express through our myth the process of our coming to do theology together. Lilith by herself is in exile and can do nothing. The real heroine of our story is sisterhood, and sisterhood is powerful.

In the beginning, the Lord God formed Adam and Lilith from the dust of the ground and breathed into their nostrils the breath of life. Created from the same source, both having been formed from the ground, they were equal in all ways. Adam, being a man, didn't like this situation, and he looked for ways to change it. He said, "I'll have my figs now, Lilith," ordering her to wait on him, and he tried to leave to her the daily tasks of life in the garden. But Lilith wasn't one to take any nonsense; she picked herself up, uttered God's holy name, and flew away. "Well now, Lord," complained Adam, "that uppity woman you sent me has gone and deserted me." The Lord, inclined to be sympathetic, sent his messengers after Lilith, telling her to shape up and return to Adam or face dire punishment. She, however, preferring anything to living with Adam, decided to stay where she was. And so God, after more careful consideration this time, caused a deep sleep to fall on Adam and out of one of his ribs created for him a second companion, Eve.

For a time, Eve and Adam had a good thing going. Adam was happy now, and Eve, though she occasionally sensed capacities within herself that remained undeveloped, was basically satisfied with the role of Adam's wife and helper. The only thing that really disturbed her was the excluding closeness of the relationship between Adam and God. Adam and God just seemed to have more in common, both being men, and Adam came to identify with God more and more. After a while, that made God a bit uncomfortable too, and he started going over in his mind whether he may not have made a mistake letting Adam talk him into banishing Lilith and creating Eve, seeing the power that gave Adam.

Meanwhile Lilith, all alone, attempted from time to time to rejoin the human community in the garden. After her first fruitless attempt to breach its walls, Adam worked hard to build them stronger, even getting Eve to help him. He told her fearsome stories of the demon Lilith who threatens women in childbirth and steals children from their cradles in the middle of the night. The second time Lilith came, she stormed the garden's main gate, and a great battle ensued between her and Adam in which she was finally defeated. This time, however, before Lilith got away, Eve got a glimpse of her and saw she was a woman like herself.

After this encounter, seeds of curiosity and doubt began to grow in Eve's mind. Was Lilith indeed just another woman? Adam had said she was a demon. Another woman! The very idea attracted Eve. She had never seen another creature like herself before. And how beautiful and strong Lilith looked! How bravely she had fought! Slowly, slowly, Eve began to think about the limits of her own life within the garden.

One day, after many months of strange and disturbing thoughts, Eve, wandering around the edge of the garden, noticed a young apple tree she and Adam had planted, and saw that one of its branches stretched over the garden wall. Spontaneously, she tried to climb it, and struggling to the top, swung herself over the wall.

She did not wander long on the other side before she met the one she had come to find, for Lilith was waiting. At first sight of her, Eve remembered the tales of Adam and was frightened, but Lilith understood and greeted her kindly. "Who are you?" they asked each other, "What is your story?" And they sat and spoke together, of the past and then of the future. They talked for many hours, not once, but many times. They taught each other many things, and told each other stories, and laughed together, and cried, over and over, till the bond of sisterhood grew between them.

Meanwhile, back in the garden, Adam was puzzled by Eve's comings and goings, and disturbed by what he sensed to be her new attitude toward him. He talked to God about it, and God, having his own problems with Adam and a somewhat broader perspective, was able to help out a little—but he was confused, too. Something had failed to go according to plan. As in the days of Abraham, he needed counsel from his children. "I am who I am," thought God, "but I must become who I will become."

And God and Adam were expectant and afraid the day Eve and Lilith returned to the garden, bursting with possibilities, ready to rebuild it together.

QUESTIONS

1. Was the group's basic approach—beginning with the women's movement, then discussing religious experience, then reflecting theologically on the two—fundamentally misguided? Did we begin by assuming overly traditional notions of religion and theology, notions that would make it difficult to do anything really new? Had we understood theology as, say "the religious self-interpretation of [a] community," [8] we might have seen ourselves as theologizing already in discussing our experiences, and thus been able to enrich our understanding both of our experiences and theology. We could certainly have written our myth anyway, but we would not have seen it as an alternative to "doing theology."

2. There is a fundamental ambiguity in the term *feminist theology* that we never resolved. Is the expression "feminist theology" of the same sort as "Christian theology" or "Jewish theology" or are we always to understand it to mean "feminist (Jewish or Christian) theology"? Are we trying to create a new religion, reflecting on the experiences

of a totally new community? Or are we trying to think in a new way within the boundaries of commitment to our own traditions?

3. If we do understand "feminist theology" to mean "feminist (Jewish or Christian) theology," what will be our relation to tradition? Critical? Will we see tradition as having fallen away from a truth to which the women's movement can return it? Will we attempt to extend or reinterpret tradition? (As our myth may be seen as doing.) Is our primary purpose to introduce a new style of theologizing, to replace, so to speak, the "yes, but" with the "yeah, yeah experience?"

4. Can the women's movement, in fact, function on its own as a religious community? It is certainly "a group of people who share a common vocabulary of images, concepts, gestures, who identify themselves with a common past and common hopes for the future," but does it have a sense of a "transcendent reality" by which it "believes itself constituted"?[9] Are these valid criteria of a religious community? Does the women's movement lack criteria for self-judgment? Must these be imposed from without? Would it then need to be seen in a broader framework? What framework? A religious framework cut loose from any particular tradition? What does that mean?

5. Is our discussion of the women's movement as a religious experience in fact a discussion of the movement as a Christian religious experience? Grace, the call to self-transformation, being given to myself, the idea that decision puts me on "the other side"—these are all Christian conceptions. What we have charted is really the experience of individuals coming together to form a new church. Are there other religious frameworks that can be used to interpret feminist experience? Were we trapped in one model by our theological educations?

6. Certain of the experiences a feminist theology would want to affirm, for example, the importance of "total" as opposed to "head" thinking, are experiences that stereotypically have been assigned to women. This paper has dealt with the positive aspects of certain of these experiences. Clearly there are problems with them as well. The "yeah, yeah experience," for example, can be coercive, can lead to fuzzy thinking, and is simply inappropriate or impossible in certain situations. What would a feminist theology have to learn from reflecting on "women's experience" as a whole? What in

women's experience do we want to adopt, reintegrate, affirm? What do we want to reject and why?

NOTES

1. For discussion of the term *feminist theology,* see Question 2 at the end of this paper.
2. At the Conference of Women Exploring Theology at Grailville, Loveland, Ohio, June 18-25, 1972. The other women in the group were Karen Bloomquist, Sister Margaret Early, and Elizabeth Farians.
3. See Question 1 at the end of this paper for a consideration of this process.
4. For further reflection on the effects of consciousness raising on women, see Nelle Morton, "The Rising Woman Consciousness in a Male Language Structure," *Andover Newton Quarterly,* 1972, *12* (4), 179.
5. Mary Daly, "The Spiritual Revolution: Women's Liberation as Theological Re-Education," *Andover Newton Quarterly,* 1972, *12* (4), 163-76.
6. The "click" is part of this experience. See Jane O'Reilly, "The Housewife's Moment of Truth," *Ms.,* Spring 1972, pp. 54-55, 57-59.
7. Morton, p. 180.
8. Stephen Crites, "Five Philosophical Points on the Nonphilosophical Truth of Theology," *Soundings,* 1970S *LIII* (2), 191.
9. Crites, pp. 192, 198.

Why Speak About God?

MARY DALY

It might seem that the women's revolution should just go about its business of generating a new consciousness, without worrying about God. I suggest that the fallacy involved in this would be an overlooking of a basic question that is implied in human existence and that the pitfall in such an oversight is cutting off the radical potential of the movement itself.

It is reasonable to take the position that sustained effort toward self-transcendence requires keeping alive in one's consciousness the question of ultimate transcendence, that is, of God. It implies recognition of the fact that we have no power *over* the ultimately real, and that whatever authentic power we have is derived from *participation in* ultimate reality. This awareness, always hard to sustain, makes it possible to be free of idolatry even in regard to one's own cause, since it tells us that all presently envisaged goals, life-styles, symbols, and societal structures may be transitory. This is the meaning that the question of God should have for liberation, sustaining a concern that is really open to the future, in other words, that is really ultimate. Such a concern will not become fixated upon limited objectives. Feminists in the past have in a way been idolatrous about such objectives as the

This selection originally appeared in *Beyond God the Father,* © 1973 by Mary Daly, and is reprinted by permission of Beacon Press. Daly notes, "Since the publication of *Beyond God the Father* in 1973, I have changed my position on the word *God*. When speaking anthropomorphically, I now use gynomorphic imagery. That is, I use the term *Goddess* rather than the hopelessly male identified term *God*. This is explained in my book *Gyn/Ecology: The Metaethics of Radical Feminism* (Boston: Beacon Press, 1978)."

right to vote. Indeed, this right is due to women in justice, and it is entirely understandable that feminists' energies were drained by the efforts needed to achieve even such a modicum of justice. But from the experience of such struggles we are in a position now to distrust token victories within a societal and structural framework that renders them almost meaningless. The new wave of feminism desperately needs to be not only many-faceted but cosmic and ultimately religious in its vision. This means reaching outward and inward toward the God beyond and beneath the gods who have stolen our identity.

The idea that human beings are "to the image of God" is an intuition whose implications could hardly be worked through under patriarchal conditions. If it is true that human beings have projected "God" in their own image, it is also true that we can evolve beyond the projections of earlier stages of consciousness. It is the creative potential itself in human beings that is the image of God.[1] As the essential victims of the archaic God projections, women can bring this process of creativity into a new phase. This involves iconoclasm—the breaking of idols. Even—and perhaps especially—through the activity of its most militantly atheistic and areligious members, the movement is smashing images that obstruct the becoming of the image of God. The basic idol breaking will be done on the level of internalized images of male superiority, on the plane of exorcising them from consciousness and from the cultural institutions that breed them.

WOMEN'S LIBERATION AS SPIRITUAL REVOLUTION

I have indicated that, because the becoming of women involves a radical encounter with nothingness, it bears with it a new surge of ontological hope. This hope is essentially active. The passive hope that has been so prevalent in the history of religious attitudes corresponds to the objectified God from whom one may anticipate favors. Within that frame of reference, human beings have tried to relate to ultimate reality as an object to be known, cajoled, manipulated. The tables are turned, however, for the objectified "God" has a way of reducing his producers to objects who lack capacity for autonomous action. In contrast to this, the God who is power of being acts as a moral power summoning women and men to act out of our deepest hope and to become who we can be. I am therefore in agreement with Johannes Metz that authentic hope will be active and creative.[2] The difference is that I see the specific experiential basis for this as an ontological experience. This experience in its first phase is one of nonbeing. In its second phase it is an intuition of being which, as Jacques Maritain described it, is a *dynamic* intuition.[3] Clearly, from what has preceded in this chapter, I see this ontological basis of hope to be particularly available to women at this point in history because of the marginal situation of females in an androcentric world.

This hope is communal rather than merely individualistic, because it is grounded in the two-edged courage to be. That is, it is hope coming from the experience of individuation *and* participation. It drives beyond the objectified God that is imagined as limited in benevolence, bestowing blessings upon "his" favorites. The power of being is that in which all finite beings participate, but not on a "one-to-one" basis, since this power is in all while transcending all. Communal hope involves in some manner a profound interrelationship with other finite beings, human and nonhuman. Ontological communal hope, then, is cosmic. Its essential dynamic is directed to the universal community.

Finally, ontological hope is revolutionary. Since the insight in which it is grounded is the double-edged intuition of nonbeing and of being, it extends beyond the superstitious fixations of technical reason. The latter, as Tillich has shown, when it is cut off from the intuitive knowledge of ontological reason, cannot get beyond superstition.[4] The rising consciousness that women are experiencing of our dehumanized situation has the power to turn attention around from the projections of our culture to the radically threatened human condition. Insofar as women are true to this consciousness, we have to be the most radical of revolutionaries, since the superstition revealed to us is omnipresent and plagues even the other major revolutionary movements of our time. Knowing that a black or white, Marxist or capitalist, countercultural or bourgeois male chauvinist deity (human or divine) will not differ essentially from his opposite, women will be forced in a dramatic way to confront the most haunting of human questions, the question of God. This confrontation may not find its major locus within the theological academy or the institutional churches, and it may not always express itself in recognizable theological or philosophical language. However, there is a dynamism in the ontological affirmation of self that reaches out toward the nameless God.[5] In hearing and naming ourselves out of the depths, women are naming *toward* God, which is what theology always should have been about. Unfortunately it tended to stop at fixing names *upon* God, which deafened us to our own potential for self-naming.

THE UNFOLDING OF GOD

It has sometimes been argued that anthropomorphic symbols for "God" are important and even necessary because the fundamental powers of the cosmos otherwise are seen as impersonal. One of the insights characteristic of the rising woman consciousness is that this kind of dichotomizing between cosmic power and the personal need not be. That is, it is not necessary to anthropomorphize or to reify transcendence in order to relate to this personally. In fact, the process is demonic in some of its consequences.[6] The dichotomizing-reifying-projecting syndrome has been characteristic of patriarchal consciousness, making "the Other" the repository of the contents of the lost self. Since women are now beginning to recognize in ourselves the victims of such dichotomizing processes, the insight extends to other manifestations of the pathological splitting off of reality into falsely conceived opposites. Why indeed must "God" be a noun? Why not a verb—the most active and dynamic of all? Hasn't the naming of "God" as a noun been an act of murdering that dynamic Verb? And isn't the Verb infinitely more personal than a mere static noun? The anthropomorphic symbols for God may be intended to convey personality, but they fail to convey that God is Be-ing. Women now who are experiencing the shock of nonbeing and the surge of self-affirmation against this are inclined to perceive transcendence as the Verb in which we participate—live, move, and have our being.

This Verb—the Verb of Verbs—is intransitive.[7] It need not be conceived as having an object that limits its dynamism.[8] That which it is over against is nonbeing. Women in the process of liberation are enabled to perceive this because our liberation consists in refusing to be "the Other" and asserting instead "I am"—without making another "the Other." Unlike Sartre's "us versus a third" (the closest approximation to love possible in his world) the new sisterhood is saying "us versus nonbeing." When Sartre wrote that "man [sic] fundamentally *is* the desire to be God," he was saying that the most radical passion of human life is to be a God who does not and cannot exist. The ontological hope of which I am speaking is neither this self-deification nor the simplistic reified images often lurking behind such terms as

"Creator," "Lord," "Judge," that Sartre rightly rejects.[9] It transcends these because its experiential basis is courageous *participation* in being. This ontological hope also has little in common with the self-enclosed "ontological arguments" of Anselm or Descartes. It enables us to break out of this prison of subjectivity because it implies commitment together.

The idea that breakthrough to awareness of transcendence comes through some sort of commitment is not new, of course. It has not been absent from existential philosophy. Karl Jaspers, for example, writing of the problem of getting beyond the subject-object split (which, of itself, without awareness of the Encompassing, yields nothing but dead husks of words), affirms that this happens when people live in commitment, but it is not too clear what sort of commitment he had in mind—a not uncommon unclarity among existentialist philosophers.[10] The commitment of which I am speaking has a locus. It is a "mysticism of sorority." I hasten to put this phrase in quotes even though it is my own, since it is a rebaptism of Metz's "mysticism of fraternity"—a correction I deem necessary since—as by now is obvious—a basic thesis of this book is that creative eschatology must come by way of the disenfranchised sex.[11]

What I am proposing is that the emergence of the communal vocational self-awareness of women is a *creative political ontophany*. It is a manifestation of the sacred (*hierophany*) precisely because it is an experience of participation in being, and therefore a manifestation of being (*ontophany*). A historian of religions such as Eliade insists that there was a sort of qualitative leap made by the biblical religions in the realm of hierophany.[12] Whether or not this is historically true is not my concern at this point. What I do suggest is that the potential for *ontological* hierophany that is already beginning to be realized in the participatory vocational self-consciousness of women does involve a leap, bridging the apparent gap between being and history. In other words, women conscious of the vocation to raise up this half of humanity to the stature of acting subjects in history constitute an ontological locus of history. In the very process of becoming actual persons, of confronting the nonbeing of our situation, women are bearers of history.

In his analysis of history-bearing groups, Tillich saw vocational consciousness as a decisive element.[13] He did not believe that humanity as a whole can become the bearer of history instead of particular groups. There is a particular *eros* or sense of belonging which provides the identity of a group to the exclusion of others.[14] This much is true of the women's movement as existing essentially in polarity with the predominantly androcentric society and its institutions. However, there is an essential way in which the women's movement does *not* meet Tillich's specifications for a history-bearing group. I am suggesting that this "nonqualification" arises precisely from the fact that our transformation is so deeply rooted in being. Tillich insists that a history-bearing group's ability to act in a centered way requires that the group have a "central, law-giving, administering, and enforcing authority."[15] In contrast to this, our movement is *not* centrally administered—although it includes organizations such as NOW and WEAL[16]—and many (perhaps most) radicalized women resist attempts to bring this about because their outlook is nonhierarchical and multidimensional.

I am suggesting that the women's movement is *more than* a group governed by central authority in conflict with other such hierarchical groups. If it were only this it would be only one more subgroup within the all-embracing patriarchal "family." What we are about is the human becoming of that half of the human race that has been excluded from humanity by sexual definition. This phenomenon, which is mushrooming "up from under" (to use Nelle Morton's phrase) in women from various "classes," races, and geographical areas, can hardly be described as a group. What is at stake is a real leap in human evolution, initiated by women. The ground of its creative hope is an intuition of being which, as Janice Raymond has suggested, *is* an intuition of human integrity or of androgynous being.[17]

When this kind of sororal community-consciousness is present—this "us versus nonbeing"—there are clues and intimations of the God who is without an over-against—who is Be-ing. The unfolding of the woman consciousness is an intimation of the endless unfolding of God. The route to be followed by theoreticians of the women's revolution, then, need not be contiguous with that followed by Marxist theoreticians such as Roger Garaudy and Ernst Bloch, even though we share their concern to maintain an absolutely open future and even though in some sense we must share also in their insistence upon atheism. We agree with their atheism insofar as this means rejection of hypostatized God projections and the use of these to justify exploitation and oppression.[18] However, there is a difference which I believe arises from the fact that Marxism does not fully confront patriarchy itself. Roger Garoudy wrote:

> If we reject the very name of God, it is because the name implies a presence, a reality, whereas it is only an exigency which we live, a never-satisfied exigency of totality and absoluteness, of omnipotence as to nature and of perfect loving reciprocity of consciousness.[19]

In effect, Garoudy distinguishes his position from that of even the most progressive Christian theologians by asserting that the exigency of the Christian for the infinite is experienced and/or expressed as presence, whereas for him it is absence. What I am suggesting is that women who are confronting the nothingness which emerges when one turns one's back upon the pseudo-reality offered by patriarchy are by that very act saying "I am," that is, confronting our own depth of *being*. What we are experiencing, therefore, is not *only* the sense of absence of the old Gods—a sense which we fully share with Garoudy and Bloch. Our exclusion from identity within patriarchy has had a totality about it which, when faced, calls forth an ontological self-affirmation. Beyond the absence, therefore, women are in a situation to experience *presence*. This is not the presence of a superreified Something, but of a power of being which both is, and is not yet.

One could hasten to point out that various theories of a developing God have been expounded in modern philosophy. Some women might find it helpful to relate their perception of the spiritual dynamics of feminism to ideas developed by such a thinker as William James, who offers the possibility of seeing the perfecting of God as achieved through our active belief, which can be understood as an enrichment of the divine being itself.[20] Others might find it helpful to correlate this experience with Alfred North Whitehead's functional approach to the problem of God, who is seen as a factor implicated in the world and philosophically relevant.[21] Other helpful insights on the problem of the developing God can be found in the work of such thinkers as Max Scheler, Samuel Alexander, E. S. Brightman, and Charles Hartshorne. In my opinion, it would not be the most fruitful expenditure of energy at this point to attempt to fit our thoughts concerning the spiritual implications of radical feminism into theories that might appear tempting as prefabricated molds. Rather, it seems to me far more important to listen to women's experiences to discover the spiritual dynamics of this revolution and to speak these dynamics in our own lives and words.

NOTES

1. Unfortunately, in the Christian theological tradition this "image" was recognized as existing unambiguously only in the male. While Augustine saw the male as being to the image of God, he conceded that woman is restored to the image only where there is no sex, that is, in the spirit (*De Trinitate*, XII, 7). Aquinas was a little more generous, granting that the image of God is in both man and woman, but adding that in a special sense it is only in the male, who is "the beginning and end of woman, as God is the beginning and end of every creature" (*Summa theologiae* I, 93, 4 ad 1).

2. Johannes Metz, "Creative Hope," *New Theology No. 5*, edited by Martin E. Marty and Dean G. Peerman (New York: Macmillan, 1968), pp. 130–41. See also Metz, *Theology of the World*, translated by William Glen-Doepel (New York: Herder and Herder, 1969).

3. Jacques Maritain, *Existence and the Existent*, translated by Lewis Galantiere and Gerald B. Phelan (New York: Doubleday-Image Books, 1956). Although he was hardly a feminist or social revolutionary, Maritain had an exceedingly fine sensitivity to the power of this intuition, which if it were carried through to social consciousness, would challenge the world. See also *Distinguish to Unite: The Degrees of Knowledge*, translated from the fourth French edition under the supervision of G. B. Phelan (New York: Charles Scribner's Sons, 1959).

4. Paul Tillich, *Systematic Theology* I (Chicago: University of Chicago Press, 1951), p. 74: "Whenever technical reason dominates, religion is superstition and is either foolishly supported by reason or rightly removed by it."

5. Maritain, in *Existence and the Existent*, p. 76, remarks: "When a man [sic] is awake to the intuition of being he is awake at the same time to the intuition of subjectivity. . . . The force of such a perception may be so great as to sweep him [sic] along to that heroic asceticism of the void and of annihilation in which he will achieve ecstasy in the substantial existence of the *self* and the 'presence of immensity' of the divine Self at one and the same time. . . ."

6. Max Weber, in *The Sociology of Religion*, p. 25, points out that "a power conceived by analogy to living persons may be coerced into the service of man." This means that whoever has the requisite charisma "is stronger even than the god." He also indicates that such a god can conveniently be blamed when things go wrong (p. 32).

7. Conversation with Linda Barufaldi, Boston, August 1972. Buckminster Fuller has referred to God as a verb.

8. It is clear that from such an experiential context there is not likely to come much rapport with language about God as "ultimate Limit" or Limiter.

9. Some of Sartre's thinking consequent to this rejection is in Jean Paul Sartre, *Being and Nothingness: An Essay on Phenomenological Ontology*, translated by Hazel E. Barnes (New York: Philosophical Library, 1956).

10. Karl Jaspers and Rudolf Bultmann, *Myth and Christianity* (New York: Noonday Press, 1958), p. 14.

11. Johannes Metz, *Theology of the World*, p. 104.

12. See Mircea Eliade, *Patterns in Comparative Religion*, translated by Rosemary

Sheed (New York: Sheed and Ward, 1958). See Jay J. Kim, "Hierophany and History," *Journal of the American Academy of Religion,* September 1972, pp. 334–348.

13. Paul Tillich, *Systematic Theology* III (Chicago: University of Chicago Press, 1963), p. 310.

14. *Ibid.,* pp. 309–310.

15. *Ibid.,* pp. 308–309.

16. The *National Organization for Women,* the *Women's Equity Action League,* and the *Saint Joan's International Alliance* (Catholic feminists) are organizations with dues-paying members. While these have important functions, the movement as I use the term is not reducible to membership in these organizations. It is far more widespread, complex, and immeasurable than the concept of organizational membership can encompass.

17. Janice Raymond, "Beyond Male Morality," a paper delivered at the International Congress of Learned Societies in the Field of Religion, Los Angeles, September 1–5, 1972. Published by the American Academy of Religion (University of Montana) in *Proceedings of the Working Group on Women and Religion, 1972,* edited by Judith Plaskow Goldenberg, pp. 83–93.

18. Leslie Dewart made the point that relative atheism is probably more indicative of an open consciousness than absolute theism. See *The Future of Belief* (New York: Herder and Herder, 1966), pp. 52–76.

19. Roger Garoudy, *From Anathema to Dialogue,* translated by L. O'Neill (New York: Herder and Herder, 1966), p. 94.

20. See William James, *The Will to Believe* (New York: Dover Publications reprint, 1956). See also *A Pluralistic Universe* (New York: Longmans Green, 1909).

21. See Alfred North Whitehead, *Process and Reality* (New York: Macmillan, 1929).

Dreams and Fantasies as Sources of Revelation: Feminist Appropriation of Jung

NAOMI R. GOLDENBERG

Having already criticized Jung's models of anima and animus and the feminine for sexism and a tendency to reinforce stereotypes about men and women,[1] I would now like to begin the more constructive task of articulating aspects of Jungian theory that might prove inspirational for feminist work in religion. Jung can help in answering a basic question that many feminists are asking: "If a woman comes to the conclusion that the patriarchal religions of Western culture do not help her in her life and, in fact, may very well hinder her sense of wellbeing, what can she do?" It would seem that she has two options—one is to withdraw all energy from spiritual concerns and turn her attention to other matters. A second is to devote a good deal of energy to formulate

Naomi R. Goldenberg received her Ph.D. from Yale University and now teaches at the University of Ottawa. She is active in the Women and Religion Section of the American Academy of Religion, and her articles on psychology, religion, and feminism have appeared in *Signs, Spring,* and *International Journal of Women's Studies.* The material in this essay appears in slightly different form in her book *The Changing of the Gods,* © 1979 by Naomi R. Goldenberg, and is reprinted by permission of Beacon Press.

spiritual concepts that allow her to maintain a religious view of life apart from the oppressive forms prescribed by traditional religions.

Jung's ideas about religious innovation are expressed throughout the *Collected Works* and the published *Letters*. In his autobiography, *Memories, Dreams, Reflections,* Jung describes how he was motivated to free himself from biblical "creeds" and how he developed a religious outlook utilizing visions, fantasies, and dreams. Jung says that he began to understand the importance of cultivating personal forms of religious expression at age twelve. This perception, he tells us, was triggered by his famous vision of excrement falling on a cathedral.[2] Jung states that he fought against this vision for days even though the experience began quite innocently:

> Here comes a great hole in my thoughts, and a choking sensation. I felt numbed, and knew only "Don't go on thinking now! Something terrible is coming, something I do not want to think, something I dare not even approach. Why not? Because I would be committing the most frightful of sins."[3]

After days of trying to keep back the thought, Jung gave up.

> I gathered all my courage, as though I were about to leap forthwith into hell-fire, and let the thought come. I saw before me the cathedral, the blue sky. God sits on His golden throne, high above the world—and from under the throne an enormous turd falls upon the sparkling new roof, shatters it, and breaks the walls of the cathedral asunder.[4]

Jung's comments on his feelings directly after this vision are significant in regard to the deductions he makes about "God's" attitude to "tradition," "Bible" and "Church."

> I felt an enormous, an indescribable relief. Instead of the expected damnation, grace had come upon me, and with it an unutterable bliss such as I had never known. I wept for happiness and gratitude. The wisdom and goodness of God had been revealed to me now that I had yielded to His inexorable command. It was as though I had experienced an illumination. A great many things I had not previously understood became clear to me. That was what my father had not understood, I thought; he had failed to experience the will of God, had opposed it for the best reasons and out of the deepest faith. And that was why he had never experienced the miracle of grace which heals all and makes all comprehensible. *He had taken the Bible's commandments as his guide; he believed in God as the Bible prescribed and as his forefathers had taught him. But he did not know the immediate living God who stands, omnipotent and free, above His Bible and His Church, who calls upon man to*

*partake of his freedom, and can force him to renounce his own views and
convictions in order to fulfill without reserve the command of God. In His trial
of human courage, God refuses to abide by traditions, no matter how sacred. In
His omnipotence, He will see to it that nothing really evil comes of such tests of
courage. If one fulfills the will of God one can be sure of going the right way*
[italics mine].[5]

The passage gives strong indication that from the age of twelve Jung
had decided institutional religious dogma and the "Bible" were secondary to the "immediate, living God" who appears in visions, dreams,
and fantasies. Since this decision was made on the basis of a fantasy
vision, one can understand the importance Jung put on such activities.
His stance against religious "creeds" that stifled fantasy activity in
individuals becomes clearer in light of the important information with
which fantasy activity had provided him in his early youth.

Revelation is not too strong a term to use to describe the religious
insight Jung believed dream and fantasy provide. Later he encouraged
his patients to do what he had done by letting their internal imaginal
processes reveal their own religious direction.[6] The revelation Jung
encouraged in his patients was a sort that provided them with access to
the spiritual processes at work in their own psyches independent of the
religious processes endorsed by contemporary religion.

Jung's prime method for connecting patients to this sort of revelation
lay in urging them to take dream activity very seriously. He developed
instructions for dreaming the dream onward through the method of
"active imagination." This process could be used on any product of
unconscious mental activity. The goal was to see where the dream or
fantasy was leading:

Take the unconscious in one of its handiest forms, say a spontaneous
fantasy, a dream, an irrational mood, an affect, or something of the kind, and
operate with it. Give it your special attention, concentrate on it, and observe its
alterations objectively. Spare no effort to devote yourself to this task, follow the
subsequent transformations of the spontaneous fantasy attentively and carefully. Above all, don't let anything from outside, that does not belong, get into it,
for the fantasy image has "everything it needs."[7]

Jung's emphasis on working on unconscious products such as the
dream were connected with his theory of their spiritual and thus their
therapeutic importance. Jung's first move toward ascribing a religious
function to the dream can be dated to 1914 with his paper "On

Psychological Understanding."[8] In this paper, he distinguishes two
modes of psychological understanding. One derives from the causal
standpoint that seeks to trace a symptom back to its original cause. The
other, which he holds in higher esteem, derives from the constructive
standpoint that strives to determine the goal to which the symptom is
leading:

Just as through analysis and reduction of individual events the causal
method ultimately arrives at the universal principles of human psychology, so
through the synthesis of individual trends the constructive method aims at
universal goals. The psyche is the point of intersection, hence it must be
defined under two aspects. On the one hand it gives a picture of the remnants
and traces of all that has been, and, on the other, but expressed in the same
picture, the outlines of what is to come, in so far as the psyche creates its own
future.[9]

Jung thus establishes a teleological function to the analysis of dreams.
Studying a dream from the "constructive standpoint," does, according
to Jung, indicate a future psychic outlook.

In 1914, Jung did not connect this constructive standpoint with any
spiritual or religious attitude toward the dream. It was not until 1933,
in the essay "The Meaning of Psychology for Modern Man,"[10] that
Jung spoke directly of the use of dreams to provide spiritual insight. In
this essay, Jung outlines the spiritual problem that he saw arising in
the modern age—the failure of contemporary religions to provide many
people with a religious outlook to give them a sense of meaning. Jung
suggests that a solution to the problem is provided by dreams. He
expected people to be somewhat displeased with this answer. "I
admit," he said, "that I fully understand the disappointment of my
patient and of my public when I point to dreams as a source of
information in the spiritual confusion of our modern world."[11] In the
essay, he mentions the dream as a religious entity in rather halting and
apologetic tones. He alludes to other "things besides dreams" that he
can talk about, but that he "cannot discuss":

If I spoke before chiefly of dreams, I did so because I wished to draw
attention to one of the most immediate approaches to the world of inner
experience. But there are many things besides dreams which I cannot discuss
here. The investigation of the deeper levels of the psyche brings to light much
that we, on the surface, can at most dream about. No wonder, then, that
sometimes the strongest and most original of all man's spiritual activities—the
religious activity—is also discovered from our dreams.[12]

"The Meaning of Psychology for Modern Man" probably contains Jung's strongest statements about the connection of dreams to religious activity. Jung was always aware of the sensitive nature of such a suggestion to theologians. Three months before his death in June 1961, Jung wrote a grateful letter to the Reverend John A. Sanford thanking the clergyman for sending him a sermon he had delivered in Los Angeles on the importance of dreams:

> Thank you very much for kindly sending me your sermon [on the impor-
> tance of dreams]. I have read it with interest and pleasure. It is a historical
> event, as you are—so far as my knowledge goes—the first one who has called
> the attention of the Christian congregation to the fact that the Voice of God can
> still be heard if you are only humble enough. . . .
> The understanding of dreams should indeed be taken seriously by the
> Church, since the *cura animarum* is one of its duties, which has been sadly
> neglected by the Protestants. Even if confession is a relatively poor version of
> the *cura,* the Catholic Church knows at least the function of the *directeur de
> conscience,* a highly important function which is unknown to the Protestants.
> I admire your courage and sincerely hope that you will not become too
> unpopular for mentioning a topic so heartily hated and despised by most of the
> theologians. This is so at least over here. There are only single individuals who
> risk the fight for survival. The pilgrim's way is spiked with thorns everywhere,
> even if he is a good Christian, or just therefore.[13]

This letter to Sanford shows how sensitive Jung was to offending theologians by the suggestion that dreams ought to be taken seriously by established religions. Nevertheless, we can see that he viewed dreams as the "Voice of God." Jung considered dreams a means of attuning a patient to her or his own religious processes. In his view, such processes should not be codified by religious institutions. Jung wanted "religion" to be a phenomenon that always remained open to whatever was revealed in the activities of dream and fantasy.

Jung fell short of his ideal of keeping fantasy activity open to individual variation. This point can be seen especially well in regard to Jung's conception of "the feminine." In both his idea of adding feminine imagery to religious symbology and in his theory of the operation of the anima and animus in the psyche, he codified images and rigidified them into stereotypes. Although this was done with the intention of giving women a better place in the patriarchal systems of religion and psychology, it was nevertheless limiting for women. Jung deserves some credit for trying to introduce feminine symbols into religion and psychology. Nevertheless, his good intentions should not make people ignore the faults in the work he produced.

I suggest that Jung's position on the religious nature of fantasy and dream is more important for feminists than his views on "the feminine." As a feminist, I am intrigued with Jung's use of fantasies and dreams as streams of imagery that could inspire religious reflection. The Jungian method may point to a source of religious iconography accessible to everyone and particularly appealing to those of us who are not entirely at home with orthodox creeds.

"THE AUSTRALIAN PIONEER": AN EXCURSION INTO DREAM AND FANTASY.

Over the last few months, I have been experimenting with Jungian dream theory in a feminist group. The group uses a technique of dream exploration involving two people—the dreamer and a questioner. The dreamer first describes as much of the dream as she can remember. She then closes her eyes, and the questioner asks her more about the dream in order to encourage her to explore further. The questioner may ask the dreamer to walk around the landscape of the dream, to open dream doors, or to look through dream windows. Sometimes the questioner asks the dreamer to become characters in the dream other than the one that she has identified as "I." All questions are asked for the purpose of helping the dreamer learn more about herself through the dream images. No one is forced to visualize things she prefers to leave unexplored. The group also recognizes that dream images have a certain autonomy, and although one may look at an image closely and even change it dramatically, the imagination works by its own rules and cannot be pushed into just any direction. Having one person (or several people) serve as questioners frees the dreamer from having to select avenues of inquiry and allows her to concentrate entirely on the dream picture itself.

I learned a great deal when the group guided me through a dream I had had two years ago about Australia. I still had a sense of mystery, excitement, and some fear whenever I thought about it. This was the dream text as I related it to the group:

I arrive in Australia, a place I have wanted to visit for some time. I am told that I must remain in the middle of Australia, in "Sidney" for five full days before going to any other part of the continent. This news fills me with anxiety.

Somehow the thought of being surrounded by so much space for five entire days is very disquieting. I feel it will be one of the most difficult things I have ever done. Staying on the coast would be easier, while being in the "interior" makes me tremble. I try to be calm and accept the order to stay in "Sidney."

The first thing I do is hitch a ride to a grocery store to get provisions. The driver is a friendly man who is glad for my company since the grocery store is over a hundred miles away. We set off on the highway and I look at the landscape as he drives. I feel calmer now that I seem to be coping with the "interior," but I am still very excited and quite nervous as the car goes along.

I remembered a mixed sensation of thrill and fear on first awakening from the dream. When I had asked a Jungian analyst to help me understand the images, he told me that "the dream shows you are afraid of your own depths." This interpretation seemed true enough. Nevertheless, although I was afraid of the Australian dream space, I was also intrigued by it. I always enjoyed thinking about the dream, would periodically borrow books on Australian geography, and even went so far as to check out air fares to the continent. All my thoughts and behavior connected with the dream were characterized by a sense of expectancy and excitement about new possibilities mingled with fear of the emptiness in the interior.

When I presented the dream to my group, the questioner tried to coax me to explore the terrain around Sidney. She asked me to get out of the car—but my imagination would not work in this direction. She then asked me to describe my view from the car window in greater detail. I could tell her about the soil and plant life and eventually I could describe a far-off figure who was walking about a mile away from the car. I had never known this person in the original dream. The figure was a man—very tall and sun-tanned with a lined and interesting face. I had no trouble describing him in detail even though I was viewing him from a long distance in the dream.

The questioner asked me to become the figure. I could do so easily. When I felt myself to be the man, I could watch the car with my dream self and the friendly driver speed past. I had a wonderful sensation of peace as I became him. He was a brave, clear-sighted person who was pioneering alone in Australia. I felt the strength and independence of his character. My fear of "the interior" vanished along with all other anxieties I was feeling at the moment. I felt calm and at peace with myself and with all of my surroundings. The questioner in my dream group had led me to what I describe as an experience of "grace."

"The Australian Pioneer" is a psychic figure to whom I have access whenever I feel fearful of the directions that my research, my writing or any other part of my life is taking. For the present, when I imagine the world through the pioneer's eyes I see with a sharp clarity and feel my environment charged with mystical significance.

Further work on the dream in the feminist group has enabled me to see the Australian pioneer as a woman. When I first began to imagine her, she appeared as a far-off blonde woman with a face similar to that of the man. She then approached nearer the car, which I could imagine as stopped. She came much closer than the man ever had. With her standing near, I could begin to imagine myself getting out of the car and doing my own pioneering. As I work with the female image, I have a sense of incorporating greater portions of the pioneer's sense of peace and independence into my intellectual and emotional life. The male image did not allow me to feel as close to the spiritual calm and insightful power of the pioneer. I experience this work with images as a "religious" activity that is more meaningful for me, than any institutional religious formulation has ever been.

Working with Jung's theory of "dreaming the dream onward" in a group of friends is especially satisfying. Such dream groups actually form a psychospiritual community in which the process of symbol formation is shared. For me, the success of my experiments indicates that people probably do not have to enforce a standardized set of "religious" images on everyone in order to feel a sense of community. Instead, a common ground may be developed around the activity of image making itself. In this way, the psychic creativity of individuals can be encouraged within the company of a supportive social group. Much more "pioneering" needs to be done, and I look forward to the work that excursions into the psychic "interior" are bound to produce.

NOTES

1. My original critiques are "A Feminist Critique of Jung," *Signs,* 1976, 2 (2), 443–449; "Jung After Feminism," in Rita M. Gross, ed., *Beyond Androcentrism: New Essays on Women and Religion,* (Missoula, Mont.: The American Academy of Religion and the Scholars' Press, 1977), pp. 53–66; "Feminism and Jungian Theory," *Anima,* 1977, 3 (2), 14–17. My replies to Jungian responses are "Naomi

Goldenberg Replies," *Anima,* 1977, *4,* (1), 63–64; "Reply," *Signs,* 1978, *3* (3), 724–726.

2. C. G. Jung, *Memories, Dreams, Reflections,* ed. Aniela Jaffe, trans. Richard and Clara Winston (New York: Random House, 1963), p. 36.
3. Jung, *Memories,* p. 36.
4. Jung, *Memories,* p. 39.
5. Jung, *Memories,* p. 40.
6. Jung had discussed work with patients and "individual revelation" in his correspondence with W. E. Hocking. See C. G. Jung, *Letters, Vol. 1: 1906–1950,* eds. Gerhard Adler and Aniela Jaffe, trans. R. F. C. Hull (Princeton, N.J.: Princeton University Press, 1973), p. 270.
7. Jung, *Collected Works,* Vol. 14, par. 749.
8. Jung, *Collected Works,* Vol. 3, pars. 388–424.
9. Jung, *Collected Works,* Vol. 3, par. 404.
10. Jung, *Collected Works,* Vol. 10, pars. 276–332.
11. Jung, *Collected Works,* Vol. 10, par. 313.
12. Jung, *Collected Works,* Vol. 10, par. 330.
13. C. G. Jung, *Letters, Vol. 2: 1951–1961,* eds. Gerhard Adler and Aniela Jaffe, trans. R. F. C. Hull (Princeton, N.J.: Princeton University Press, 1975), p. 630.

Spiritual Quest and Women's Experience

CAROL CHRIST

STORY AND WOMEN'S EXPERIENCE

Words spoken over two thousand years ago by a chorus of women in Euripides' *Medea* might be taken as our motto today:

> Flow backward to your sources, sacred rivers,
> And let the world's great order be reversed.
>
> . . .
>
> Story shall now turn my condition to a fair one,
> Women shall now be paid their due.
> No more shall evil-sounding fame be theirs.[1]

The current interest in feminine[2] perceptions of the ultimate stems from a widespread sensing that women's stories have not been adequately told. Women have lived in the interstices between inchoate experiences and the shapings given to experience by the stories of men. In a very real sense, women have not experienced their own experience.

Carol P. Christ received her Ph.D. from Yale University and teaches at San Jose State University. Active in the women's movement since the late 1960's, she founded the Women's Caucus—Religious Studies. She received a National Endowment for the Humanities summer stipend to complete her book, *Women's Spiritual Quest* (forthcoming from Beacon Press, 1979). Her articles on women and religion have appeared in *Signs, Journal of the American Academy of Religion,* and *Soundings.* This essay originally appeared in *Anima* (Spring, 1975), copyright © 1975 by Conococheague Associates, Inc., and is reprinted with permission of *Anima.*

There is a dialectic between story and experience. Stories shape experience; experience shapes stories. There is no primary preverbal experience utterly unshaped by stories. In a sense, without stories there is no experience. On the other hand, there is a distinction between stories and experiences which enables us to see that not all stories are adequate to our experience. Conversely we experience a shock of recognition when we find a story which articulates an as yet unarticulated part of our experience.[3]

Men have actively shaped their experiences of self and world by creating the stories they have told. Their deepest stories orient them to what they perceive as the ultimate powers and realities of the universe. We women have not told our own stories. The dialectic between experiencing and shaping experience by storytelling has not been in our own hands.

Women have discovered more and less adequate ways of circumventing this basic situation of being without their own stories. Some women have read their own lives into the stories men tell about women. They have become Eve or Mary. Others by incredible contortions have read themselves into stories about men. . . .

Still other women were unable to conform to alien stories and went mad—their speaking a gibberish to those who knew only men's stories. Others spoke in tongues (and do so today in the charismatic movements)—the nonlanguage of tongue speaking enabling them to express things untold in the available stories. Still others became mystics— perhaps recognizing an essential kinship between the silence of the mystic and the silence of culture about women's experience.[4]

In consciousness-raising groups, in conversations, and in study, women are engaged in the immensely important and exciting task of recovering and discovering the shapes and contours of our own experience. We tell each other stories which have never been told before, stories utterly unlike the stories we have all learned from the culture. Finding our speech and opening our ears to hear, we are no longer forced to speak in the tongues of madwomen, the tongues of ecstasy, the language of silence. "Since we have been a conversation and have been able to hear from one another,"[5] we have gained power to create new being.[6] Euripides knew what he was talking about when he said that "the world's great order" is "reversed" when women's stories are told.

Because women's stories have not been told, women's experiences have not shaped the spoken language of cultural myths and sacred stories. Of Mary, Luke wrote, "But Mary kept all these things, pondering them in her heart" (Luke 2:19). *Her word* never became flesh and dwelt among us. Perhaps no one ever asked her what she was thinking. Perhaps she never heard stories which could give her words for her own experience. Perhaps the man who wrote the gospel narrative simply could not imagine what it felt like to be in her position. Whatever the reason, her experience and the experiences of other women have not shaped the sacred stories of the Bible.[7]

Two hypotheses are suggested by the recognition that women's experiences have not funded the sacred stories of biblical tradition. The first is that each woman engaged in the process of recovering her own experience will experience a deepened and deepening alienation from the traditional stories. We will no longer be content to read ourselves sidewise into stories in which "the daughters do not exist." We will find that self-identification with the sons and other male images and symbols in the language of the Bible and the tradition requires us to reject our particular identities as women—the very identities we are engaged in recovering and affirming in all the other important areas of our lives. Second, as our consciousness of the shapes and contours of our own experiences deepens, we will begin to realize that the exclusion of our experience from the funding of sacred stories may point to a basic defect in the perception of ultimate power and reality provided by the traditional stories.

The articulation of a new perception of the ultimate which will arise out of the discovery and recovery of women's experience will require clarification of women's experience. At first it seems that women's experience is a simple thing. Yet as soon as one begins to study it, one realizes that it is many things. Black women, white women, rich women, poor women—all share a fundamental alienation from self, but there are many differences in their experiences. All women share certain biological processes and potentialities, but we have related to these basic facts in different ways. Feminists share many experiences with each other that we do not share, or do not yet share, with other women.

In *Beyond God the Father*, Mary Daly focuses attention on the experiences of women in the women's movement, with some attention to the experiences of outcast women of the past—witches, heretics, madwomen. The new experience of women in the women's movement is an important resource for spiritual transformation. . . .

However, upon reflection it becomes clear that women confined to so-called feminine experience (to some extent true of all of us) have preserved certain values that have been devalued by the dominant male culture. While feminine experience has not been able to transform culture in the past, it may be that women coming into power together will now be able to use the knowledge gained through more traditional feminine experiences to transform culture.

Thus it appears that women's experience must be defined broadly enough to include all the experiences of women. It is a radical act to bring the experience of any woman to articulation. After we have talked long and listened long, we may be able to decide which parts of traditional feminine experience we want to affirm, own, and transform by their incorporation into a new feminist consciousness and ethic.

But I must underline that this process takes time. The discovery and recovery of woman's experiences will not be accomplished overnight. The alienation of ourselves from our own experience is deep; the resources that can aid our journey of self-discovery are slim. To ask for definitive conclusions prematurely is to misjudge the depth of the problem. We are in a time for ripening. . . . We must discover a mode of thinking about the ultimate which can be modulated by a sense of timing, a mode which will not require the definitive word in a time when soundings are more appropriate.

Not only time, but also community is required to rediscover our experience. The consciousness raising group is communal; the best work in women's studies has been done by women working together. Many of us have known for a long time that the best work is done as part of an ongoing conversation or dialogue. But we all know that the community of scholars is more myth than reality most of the time. Women working together are living examples of a community of knowers creating new being and new ways of acting through our conversations, through telling and retelling stories. . . .

As we begin to analyze the stories that in fact shape our lives as women, we must devour literature which reflects our experience. We must seek, discover, and create the symbols, metaphors, and plots of our own experience. As a part of this process, I have been living with and teaching Doris Lessing for the past three years. When I first read *The Four-Gated City,* I dreamed about it for weeks. Whenever I have taught it, the women in the class have come alive, and the men sense that something important has happened to the women. Judith Plaskow and I worked together for a month (on separate projects) on Lessing's

The Children of Violence, of which The Four-Gated City is the final volume. The interpretations of Lessing which I will share here have grown and ripened in many and long discussions with women about the books and about our lives.

MARTHA QUEST: A CASE STUDY IN WOMEN'S EXPERIENCE

Doris Lessing is important to those who are trying to chart the religious consciousness which arises from women's experience, because Children of Violence is a Bildungsroman which charts a spiritual journey from the perspective of women's experience. Lessing was at first astonished when the women's movement claimed her as their own. She had not set out to write about women's experience, but about the experience of a generation. Yet she had, willy-nilly, written about the experience of women when she made Martha Quest the heroine of her story of the children of violence. It is therefore appropriate to look at Martha's quest as an image of the spiritual quest of women in our time and to suggest aspects of her quest which may be archetypal.[8] However, we must be clear that Martha's experience is the experience of a white middle-class woman in a particular time and place. Her experience is shaped as much by the times in which she lives as by the fact of being a woman in those times. Children of Violence charts the consciousness of a generation conceived during the first world war, and like Martha, "conceived, bred, and reared on violence."[9] What interests Lessing is the interplay between the spirit of a time and the actions and consciousness of her characters. However, it would be wrong-headed to look for "women's experience" which is not shaped by the times and places in which it is lived. Lessing's vision is useful precisely because it represents women's experience in our time.

Martha's quest begins in an experience of nothingness which stems from her inability to find a role model who can provide her with a positive self-image. She says to herself:

> She would *not* be like Mrs. Van Rensberg, a fat and earthy woman; she would *not* be bitter and nagging and dissatisfied, like her mother. But then, who was she to be like? Her mind turned to the heroines she had been offered, and discarded them.[10]

This inability to find an image of self makes women especially vulnerable to that experience of nothingness described by Michael

Novak as the experience of "the emptiness, formlessness, and chaos at the center of human consciousness."[11] Because she lacks an image of self, in the first four novels of *Children of Violence,* Martha is like a sleepwalker; she drifts, moved by forces she does not comprehend. She looks to something outside herself to establish meaning and transcendence in her life. Yet at each stage of her life she is in touch with a source of transcendence within herself which she recognizes only momentarily, then forgets.

One of the ironic features of Martha's quest is that from the beginning she has capacities which she eventually uses to gain a form of transcendence. But she does not shape her life by her experiences of transcendence, because she does not "remember" them as moments of transcendence. Lessing is fascinated by the process of knowing. What interests her is that a person can know something and yet not know it. When one has an insight, she says "But I knew that before," and yet she did not know it in a meaningful way before. The long detours in Martha's process of self-knowledge represented in the first four novels of the series reflect this mysterious quality of the process of self-knowledge. This not remembering transcendent experiences is a human problem, but it is intensified for women who not only forget their own experiences but also have no stories, models, or guides to remind them.

The Four-Gated City, the last and most complicated novel in *The Children of Violence* series, stretches from the early fifties to the late sixties, longer than the time span of the other four novels together, and has a prophetic afterword which reaches into the nineteen-nineties. There are more than twenty significant characters whose lives cross Martha's in the house on Radlett Street where she lives and works. While living in the house, Martha stops drifting and gradually learns to understand, integrate, and deepen her knowledge of herself and her times. At the beginning of the novel, Martha has just arrived in London to start a new life. At the end of the narrative, she is leaving the house on Radlett Street where she has lived for almost twenty years. She has no definite plans, yet she has a "nonpassionate feeling of inner completion."[12] The plot of the novel is constructed to provide Martha with the opportunity to take the preparatory steps which lead to her spiritual insight and to prophetic power.

At the beginning of *The Four-Gated City,* Martha, walking by the Thames in a moment of illumination, knows herself as a "soft dark empty space," a "soft dark receptive intelligence,"[13] a "quiet empty space behind which stood an observing presence."[14] She knows that this space is the location of insight. In this space the "watcher" lives, that old friend she later describes as "that part of me which watches all the time. . . . The only part of me that is real—that's permanent anyway."[15] In this space, "her whole self cleared, lightened, she became alive and light and aware." In this space, she is alone with herself. She values the experience of clarity, lucidity, knowledge, insight—the word does not matter—above all else. She wishes she could explore this region further. But she knows that she does not have the strength to get through the dark night of the soul, "what would happen when the dark deepened and one thought it would remain, being so strong."[16]

While "waiting" for something to happen, Martha takes a temporary job on Radlett Street. Then Sally-Sarah commits suicide, and Martha spends twenty years mothering the children in the house. Ironically, she who had earlier walked out on marriage and motherhood spends twenty years mothering other people's children. Yet, oddly, during the years at Radlett Street, Martha grows into a sense of herself that she had been unable to find anywhere else and which prepares her to face the darkness. Significantly Martha experiences motherhood with children not her own. Lessing implies that motherhood can provide opportunities for insight only when the mother has a sense of distance from her children that is hard to achieve when they are her own.

Because each of the twenty or so characters who live or spend time in the house at Radlett Street is marked by the chaos and violence of the times, Martha, in her position as mother, matron, and counselor—the one who holds everything together—experiences and makes her own the experiences of the other characters, which together reflect the times in which they all live. At one point, Martha describes herself as "a kind of special instrument sensitized to mood and need and state," and feels "herself (or rather the surface of herself) to be a mass of fragments, or facets, or bits of mirror reflecting qualities embodied in other people."[17] Though she experiences this time as a tremendously exhausting day-to-day struggle in which she must fight to retain her own integrity, in fact the time for Martha is one of collection and purgation. As she tunes herself to the needs of others, she integrates and assimilates unfinished business from her past, as she puts it, she "pays her debts."[18]

Martha's prophetic powers begin to develop during this time as she begins to "see" and "hear." She hears the thoughts of Mark and Paul, and she pictures Dorothy's suicide attempt a week before it happens. When she asks her psychiatrist about it, he says that she "imagined" these things,[19] and implies that she saw only what she was predisposed to see. The novel offers another explanation. Later in the book Mark writes, "what will happen is a development of what is already happening."[20] The powers Martha begins to develop are a direct result of her intense concentration on the dynamics of the relationships in the house. The powers Martha develops come from experiencing what is happening more deeply than the others experience it. Martha's whole life as mother and counselor is a process of tuning in to currents of energy in the house, which we might call the psychological dynamics of the house. That Martha takes the process a step farther than most mothers (or than most mothers recognize they have taken it) is a result of two special circumstances—her concentration on the processes of her inner life, and Lynda's presence, which enables her to talk about and recognize the processes of her inner life.

After the children are grown and no longer making constant demands, Martha enters another of her waiting periods. "I don't know what it is I'm waiting for—something."[21] Then Lynda cracks up again, and Martha is called upon to stay with her. This time with Lynda is the most crucial period in Martha's spiritual journey. All of her previous experience and especially her experience of motherhood can be seen as a preparation for the insight she gains with Lynda as her guide.

At first Martha sees her task as keeping Lynda from falling off the edge. Then she watches Lynda methodically tap and beat a path around the walls of the room with her hands and her head—until a circle of bloody marks are traced on the wall. The image of Lynda tapping and beating against the walls is one of the most powerful images in the book. It captures the fundamental dynamic of Martha's journey. Finally Martha realizes the meaning of Lynda's act. She is not, as Mark thought, trying to escape from the room.

When she pressed, assessed, gauged those walls, it was the walls of her own mind she was exploring. She was asking: Why can't I get out? What is the thing that holds me in? Why is it so strong *when I can imagine, and indeed, half remember, what is outside?* Why is it that inside this room I am half asleep, doped, poisoned, and like a person in a nightmare screaming for help but no sounds come out of a straining throat?[22]

As Martha recognizes what the "mad" woman is doing, she recognizes that "she was part of Lynda."[23] Whereas Lynda is attempting to get out of the sickness that incapacitates her, Martha wants to get out of the ordinary way of experiencing which prevents her from reaching the lit space where she understands.

Sitting in the room with Lynda, Martha plugs into the energy Lynda has concentrated for her struggle.

> She was being swept by small storms, waves of—what? It was a current that made her limbs want to jerk and dance.[24]

Martha comes to understand that there is a vast impersonal sea of energy in which all are immersed. If, instead of jerking and moving wildly, one waits, the energy will accumulate. Lynda is often tuned into this current of energy but, because she has not had a guide, she has often been overwhelmed by its power. With Lynda, Martha comes into contact with the forces that have made the century in which she lives. Her long slow experience of ordinary life gives her power to understand and differentiate these currents.

When Martha lets the energy accumulate, she begins to hear thoughts from Lynda's mind, and then she experiences a "great chaos of sound" which she calls "the sound barrier."[25] Martha is terrified by this region of sound, the source and mirror of the violence and chaos of the century. Luckily she has Lynda's experience to show her that it is possible to live through it.

While in the basement with Lynda, Martha senses that the experiences she is having are not simply the product of her own mind; they are shared by others.

> She knew . . . that if she was feeling something, in this particular way, with the same authenticity, the irresistibility, of the growing point, then she was not alone, others were feeling the same.[26]

Martha spends a month with Lynda in the basement exploring regions of nonordinary reality. This time is a rite of passage for Martha. Her earlier apprehensions of another dimension of reality are confirmed in a month's exploration of a territory she has visited only briefly before. The center of her life shifts decisively here as she clearly recognizes that this region of nonordinary reality, and the insight it offers is the goal of her quest—the four-gated city of her dreams.

Martha and Lynda are guide and teacher to each other. Lynda shares with Martha her knowledge of the nonordinary regions, based on her long experience with them. Martha shares with Lynda the strength to get through almost anything which she has learned in the long slow process of ordinary life. It is as though two separated parts of women's experience, mother and witch or madwoman, are joined. From the integration of the separated comes a new power.

Shortly after the experience with Lynda, Martha arranges to spend several months alone in a room exploring the regions she had visited with Lynda. The region of chaos and violence which Martha discovers is the current in which the twentieth century has been shaped. This current of hatred and violence lies just under the surface, and as Martha says, all a Hitler has to do is tap it, and his power is guaranteed. In confronting this region of chaos and violence within herself, Martha completes her journey of becoming a conscious member of her generation. Most are unconscious of their participation in this current. Martha's conscious appropriation of the currents of the time is the source of her power to prophesy about the time.

During this period, Martha comes into contact with the self-hater, a personal "devil" who is the inner representation of the chaos and violence of the times. Martha is not able to conquer this self-hater. She can conquer the fear which is a large part of the hater's power, and she can learn to acknowledge the hater's power without succumbing to it. But she cannot root it out of herself. The hater's power is too deeply rooted in the violence and chaos of the times of which Martha is a part. Martha's inability to root out or conquer the hater is a portent of her later prophecy of disaster.

At the conclusion of the novel, the house on Radlett Street is sold, and Martha prepares to leave it. Once again she has no definite plans, but she has learned to trust her capacity to grow and learn from any situation. She has discovered that there is no other person, no place outside herself, necessary for the process of insight which she has learned to value above all else.

> Where, What is it? How? What's next? Where is the man or woman who—she would find herself back with herself.[27]
> Where? But *where?* How? Who? No but *where,* where. . . . Then silence and the birth of a repetition: Where? Here. Here? Here, where else, you poor fool, where else has it been ever.[28]

There is no answer to the questions, or rather the questions always come back to herself and her solitude. It does not matter where she goes or what she does as long as she maintains contact with that inner core of herself which is the location of her capacity for insight. Her trust in that capacity of her self, that observing presence, accounts for what may be called her "nonpassionate feeling of inner completion."

During the period described in the appendix of the novel, Lynda and Martha develop prophetic power. The prophecy in the appendix follows two lines. One extends the negative tendencies of the century into disaster. The other extends the positive tendencies into hope for a future which transcends the disaster. The power of the prophecy resides in its connections with what went before it in the novel. The Jungian archetype of the "medium" or "medial woman" sheds light on the kind of prophetic powers Martha and Lynda develop.[29] In exploring deeper levels of her self Martha comes into contact with "the psychic atmosphere of her period,"[30] the currents of violence and hatred. Her prophetic powers "constellate what is in the atmosphere and just beginning to find expression,"[31] the vision of disaster and the vision of hope which arise from a deeper than usual understanding of the present.

A structure of a quest myth from the perspective of women's experience is suggested by Martha's journey. The spiritual quest of a modern woman begins in the experience of nothingness, the experience of being without an adequate image of self. Her drive to pursue her quest beyond the experience of nothingness without becoming trapped in a compromise with a prevailing mythology is rooted in a vision, and an experience, however fleeting, of transcendence which she identifies with the vision. She learns from motherhood to gain detachment from all of her past struggles and to broaden the range of her experience to include many of the psychic currents of the culture in which she lives. She learns from another woman. She explores a reality underlying ordinary reality and gains deeper insight into her self and the times in which she lives. Finally, perhaps, she becomes a seer, a prophet, one who knows that what will happen is a development of what is already happening.

Lessing has represented a structure of a quest myth from the perspective of women's experience which strikes a chord with many women. The extent to which the structure of the quest myth which she offers is archetypal, represents the experience of many women in this culture, can only be discovered by comparing Martha's quest to the quests of other women, both in literature and in life.

The form of spiritual consciousness which Martha develops is shaped by the experiences which make up the stages of her quest. This form of spiritual consciousness is not unique in the history of the world but it is uniquely shaped by women's experience in modern culture and represents a form of spiritual consciousness not ordinarily reached by men in modern culture.

Martha's spiritual consciousness is defined by the "watcher," that part of herself which observes, understands, becomes conscious of the deeper dimensions of her experience. Martha describes the watcher as a soft, dark, receptive intelligence, but it is not merely a passive receptacle. The watcher is an active consciousness—far from being undifferentiated passivity, it is a form of consciousness which must be developed through discipline. Waiting is the major discipline of this consciousness. Waiting is not a passive activity; Martha waits with purpose. She does not know what she is waiting for, but she recognizes it when it is given to her, and then she takes active steps to explore it further. Thus she discovers Lynda's territory in one of her waiting periods; then she takes the active step of arranging for a room in Paul's house to explore the territory further.

Martha's knowledge of self and world is always concrete, related to her experience, a deepening of it. She uses books only to verify her insights, to confirm something she knows or half knows. Her knowledge is not abstract, nor is it a knowledge unconnected to ordinary life. Nothing she knows is arbitrary, surprising, unrelated to something she had known before, but on a different level. She is conscious that her self-knowledge and knowledge of the world are intimately related.

Martha's concern to observe rather than to change stems from her sense that she is part of a larger process which she cannot control. She cannot stem the violence of the times nor root the hater out of her consciousness. When she understands the depth of the violent current, she gives up hope that individuals and groups like the left can create a new world. All she can do is refuse unconscious acquiescence in the violent current.

Martha's sense that she is part of a process which transcends her conscious control, combined with her organic relation to that process accounts for her nonpassionate sense of inner completion. Since Martha is not concerned to change the process, nor to change herself, but only to understand, she desires nothing in particular. She trusts that whatever happens, wherever she goes, the process of living will provide her with opportunities to deepen her insight.

The observing, connected, deepened consciousness is also the source of Martha's prophetic power. As she understands what is happening in her self and in the world in which she lives on its deepest level, she comes to understand what will happen as a development of what already is happening. This form of prophecy is organic, an insight into processes everyone is involved in, not revelation from an external source.

SOUNDINGS TOWARD A NEW PERCEPTION OF THE ULTIMATE

Martha Quest's story may perhaps best be seen as a new liberation myth, which like the gnostic myths, the exodus story, and the stories of Jesus have power to mediate spiritual power and insight to a group. However, in what follows, I will suggest correlations and decorrelations[32] between Martha's perception of the ultimate and that found in traditional stories and myths.

Two important stages of Martha's spiritual journey are her experiencing of motherhood as a time of purgation, collection, and integration, and her experiencing of power through Lynda's experience. The centrality of these two experiences in Martha's spiritual development suggests that a religious symbol system adequate to her experience must include, as possible models for achieving transcendence, motherhood and learning from the separated aspects of women's experience. . . .

Martha's learning from the joining of the separated aspects of women's experience—from the joining of mother and madwoman—is an important aspect of women's quest today. Martha and Lynda can be seen as representing the feminist insight that "sisterhood is powerful." They shared their stories, and when they became a conversation, they both developed new power. It is difficult to imagine how this experience could be represented in a religious symbol system where, as Johnston put it, "the daughters don't exist." But there is a myth told by Judith Plaskow[33] which grew out of the Grailville Conference of Women Theologians which represents the experience of learning from the separated aspects of women's experience. It is a new story written about some of the old characters in Genesis. In Jewish elaborations of the legends of Genesis, Lilith, the first woman created, was banished from Eden because she refused the subordinate position in intercourse.[34] Legend turned Lilith into a demoness, stating that she killed newborn children (among other things). Now, however, we can see Lilith as the archetypal outcast woman, maligned by the supporters of a system which she challenged. In the new story, Lilith and Eve meet, and as the story tells it, "They talked for many hours, not one but many times. They taught each other many things and told each other stories, and laughed together, and cried over and over, till the bond of sisterhood grew between them." Their meeting signalizes a new becoming in the world. The story concludes, "God and Adam were expectant and afraid the day Eve and Lilith returned to the garden, ready to rebuild it, together, bursting with possibilities."

The new Lilith story suggests that it might be possible to radically transform the tradition without cutting off all continuity with it. The story has been returned to its sources and told again. However, it must be pointed out that from the perspective of traditional understandings of canonical authority, rewriting the sacred stories of the tradition is proscribed. On the other hand, the traditional understanding of canonical authority might be challenged from the perspective of the history of religions. The stories which have become canonized in the Bible were redactions and retellings of stories which had been told in different ways in various cultural and religious situations. The horror with which the rewriting of traditional myths is greeted by some students of religion is based upon a naive understanding of the long history of retelling which preceded their canonization. . . .

Martha's development of the prophetic powers of the medial woman suggests a relation to the ultimate which is different from the most common pattern in mainline Western religion. The experience of the Old Testament prophet is different from Martha's prophetic experience. The Old Testament prophet's experience may be characterized as the confrontation with an overpowering other. Jeremiah's famous line, "You have raped me, and I am raped" (Jer. 20:7), although an extreme version of this experience, represents the fundamental dynamic.[35] Martha's experience, on the other hand, does not involve a radical confrontation with an other. Her self is the center of an expanding horizon of experience. Whatever she initially experiences as alien to herself, is gradually understood to be as much internal as external, and conversely as much external as internal. For Martha, there is no radical duality between self and world, but there is also no denial of the boundaries between self and world. Martha experiences a kinship between an impersonal core of her self and the fundamental nature of being. Rosemary Ruether has said that feminism's challenging of sexual dualism has far-reaching epistemological consequences for "the psychic organization of consciousness, the dualistic view of self and world and the hierarchal concept of society, of man and nature, and God and creation, all these have been modeled on sexism." [36] Martha's experience of continuity between self and world without loss of personal integrity suggests a model for perceiving all the relations mentioned by Ruether in a nondualistic, nonhierarchial way.

Martha's confrontation with the self-hater likewise suggests a less dualistic understanding of the relation of the person to sin or the devil than many traditional understandings. While Martha is aware of the self-hater as a presence within her psyche, she never attempts to claim that the self-hater is an external demon or a devil. For a while, Martha struggles like a desert hermit to root the self-hater out of herself. But ultimately she realizes that she cannot do that; she comes to see the hater as an intrinsic part of herself. But she also recognizes that she need not be in the hater's power. I would call Martha's attitude toward the hater—toward sin, if you like—"realistic." A study of monastic psychology in Christianity would, I think, show that Martha took the wiser course in not attempting to *heroically* fight to the finish with her "devil." The disastrous history of the male projection of evil onto the female [37] is another indication that Martha's realism is less destructive than traditional, more dualistic, Western views of sin and evil.

Martha's experience is similar to that of other mystics East and West. Martha's mystical insight is clearly related to her initial experience of nothingness when she realized that she could not find an adequate image of self, either in literature or in life. In an earlier part of this paper, I suggested that the affinity between women and mysticism might be a legacy of women's cultural alienation. If this is the case, women moving out of the situation of cultural alienation through the new being of the women's movement will have to decide whether or not the mystical insight of a Martha ought to be transcended or affirmed in feminist religious consciousness.

Let me suggest a possible feminist appropriation of feminine mystical experience. Many feminists see a contradiction between the mysticism of a Martha and the new activism called for in the women's movement. Martha may be content to observe and to understand, but the new feminists demand action and change. This dissatisfaction with the mystical mode was expressed in the disappointment of a number of reviewers of Lessing's most recent novel, *The Summer Before the Dark.*

Many feminists had expected Lessing to provide them with a model of an active achieving competent woman. Instead Lessing explored again the darkness and chaos which underlay her protagonist's life.

It seems to me, however, to be wrong-headed to contrast the mystical insight of Lessing's heroines with the political activism sought by feminists. While Lessing does not make explicit the connections between mysticism and politics,[38] they can be shown. In fact I would suggest that an enduring politics must be built on mysticism—otherwise it will dissipate in disillusionment after a series of failures. Feminists would do well to meditate on the aphorism "Everything begins in mysticism and ends in politics only to begin again."[39] A feminism built on the experience of nothingness and deeply in touch with the currents of violence and chaos in our time will not expect dramatic overnight changes in personal or institutional lives. It will be prepared to face a long, hard struggle.

Moreover, Martha's understanding of her relation to the world in which she lives suggests an understanding of politics which is more like that of the wise man described in the *I Ching* than in traditional Western models. Like the wise man in the *I Ching,* Martha recognizes that political action can only be effective when the political actor is attuned with the currents of energy operating in her world. Keenly aware of her position within a larger field of action and interaction, she knows that the wise woman waits for the right time, that political action is as much a matter of knowing the forces and powers in the world in which one acts as it is having a program, a principle, or a vision.

Martha's quest confirms the intuition of Euripides' chorus. The feminine perception of the ultimate in one woman's story is fraught with potentially revolutionary implications for the human perception of the ultimate. Telling our stories may possibly begin a great revolution, unleashing the power to turn the world's great order around.

NOTES.

1. *Euripides,* 1, trans. Richard Lattimore (New York: Washington Square Press, 1970), p. 78, lines 410–420.
2. I use the term *feminine* advisedly; it does not refer here to the Jungian concept of the feminine, but to the set of stories and symbols which arise out of women's experience in modern Western culture.

3. See Michael Novak, *Ascent of the Mountain, Flight of the Dove* (New York: Harper & Row, 1971); and Stephen Crites, "The Narrative Quality of Experience," *Journal of the American Academy of Religion,* 39 (September 1971), pp. 291–311.

4. See Joseph Fichter, "Women in Charismatic Renewal," *The National Catholic Reporter,* September 28, 1973, pp. 11–13; Evelyn Underhill, *The Mystics of the Church* (New York: Schocken Books, 1964); Phyllis Chesler, *Women and Madness* (New York: Doubleday & Company, 1972).

5. Martin Heidegger, quoting Holderlin, in "Holderlin and the Essence of Poetry," *Existence and Being,* ed. by Werner Brock (Chicago: Henry Regnery Co., 1967), p. 270.

6. Mary Daly uses Tillich's "new being" in this sense; see *Beyond God the Father* (Boston: Beacon Press, 1973).

7. I do not deny that there are a few stories about women in the biblical tradition. It is not likely, however, that any of them were told by women. See Phyllis Bird, "Images of Women in the Old Testament" in Rosemary Ruether, ed., *Religion and Sexism* (New York: Simon & Schuster, 1974) pp. 41ff. "The Old Testament is a man's 'book', where women appear for the most part simply as adjuncts of men, significant only in the context of men's activities. . . . The Old Testament is a collection of writings by males from a society dominated by males."

8. See Annis Pratt, "The New Feminist Criticism," *College English,* May, 1971, pp. 872–889.

9. Doris Lessing, *Landlocked* (New York: The New American Library, 1970), p. 195.

10. Doris Lessing, *Martha Quest* (New York: The New American Library, 1970), p. 10.

11. Michael Novak, *The Experience of Nothingness* (New York: Harper & Row, 1970), p. 115.

12. The term is Ann Murphy's from a paper entitled "A Woman's Book," written at Wesleyan University.

13. Lessing, *The Four-Gated City* (New York: Bantam Books, 1970), p. 38.

14. *Ibid.,* p. 39.

15. *Ibid.,* p. 238.

16. *Ibid.,* p. 38.

17. *Ibid.,* p. 352.

18. *Ibid.,* p. 40.

19. *Ibid.,* p. 324.

20. *Ibid.,* p. 554.

21. *Ibid.,* p. 453.

22. *Ibid.,* p. 494.

23. *Ibid.,* p. 491.

24. *Ibid.,* p. 495.

25. *Ibid.,* p. 499.

26. *Ibid.,* p. 512.

27. *Ibid.,* p. 588.

28. *Ibid.,* p. 591.

29. Toni Wolff, "Structural Forms of the Feminine Psyche," privately printed for the C.G. Jung Institute, Zurich, July 1956, quoted in Ann Belford Ulanov, *The*

Feminine in Jungian Psychology and Christian Theology (Evanston: Northwestern University Press, 1971), pp. 207-210.

30. *Ibid.,* p. 208.
31. *Idem.*
32. The phrase is Judith Plaskow's.
33. "The Coming of Lilith," in Rosemary Ruether, ed., *Religion and Sexism* (New York: Simon & Schuster, 1974), and reprinted here in "The Coming of Lilith: Toward a Feminist Theology."
34. See Louis Ginsberg, *Legends of the Jews* (Philadelphia: The Jewish Publication Society, 1956), pp. 26-54.
35. This sense of God's total otherness is dramatically reflected in the Protestant interpretation of the divine freedom. See especially Barth's doctrine of God as Wholly Other.
36. "The Intimate Enmity: Sexism and Liberation," prepared for the American Theological Society, April 1974, p. 1.
37. See Daly, chapter 2.
38. Lessing appears to have abandoned traditional politics for the Sufi belief that the race will develop the new organs it needs to insure its survival. The "miraculous" appearance of the "new children" in *The Four-Gated City* is an example.
39. Michael Novak, *A Theology for Radical Politics* (New York: Herder and Herder, 1969), p. 125. Novak adapts Charles Peguy's "everything begins in mysticism and ends in politics." See *Basic Verities,* trans. Anne and Julian Green (Chicago: Henry Regnery Co., 1965).

Becoming Woman: Menstruation as Spiritual Challenge

PENELOPE WASHBOURN

My conviction is that religious questions and reflections about the meaning of what is holy or ultimate arise at times of crisis in the life of the individual and of the community. These crises may be historical or personal events, but because of them we are forced to respond to a new situation. The question of the meaning of our identity and our attitude toward life is challenged. A crisis is a time of change, anxiety, and possibility. Something new happens, and we summon resources from the past, as well as discover new strengths, to deal with the implications of our changed situation.

Psychologists since the time of Sigmund Freud have described human development in terms of *life crises* or stages of personal growth. From the viewpoint of psychology, one must more or less "successfully" negotiate each stage in order to advance to the next. Erik Erikson views these crises, particularly those from adolescence onward, as

Penelope Washbourn received her Ph.D. from Union Theological Seminary in New York and currently teaches at the University of Manitoba in Canada. An active lecturer in women's studies, her articles have appeared in *Male and Female, The Christian Century,* and *Women and Religion.* This essay is abridged from pp. 1–19 of her book *Becoming Woman* © 1977 by Penelope Washbourn, and is reprinted by permission of Harper and Row, Publishers, Inc.

involving questions of a religious nature, for the individual's identity must be renegotiated in terms of a new understanding of the meaning and purpose of the whole.[1]

For a woman, the most significant life crises are associated with having a female body. Most psychological literature writes of the "stages of man" or "man's search for meaning" and to a large extent ignores the distinctive aspect of the female life crises. I propose that a woman's search for psychological and spiritual wholeness goes through the particular life crises of being a female body. These stages are not just psychological phases to be negotiated but turning points that raise fundamentally religious questions. At each juncture, a woman must redefine her self-identity in relation to her perception of the purpose of life and in relation to her understanding of her own identity in relation to that ultimate value.

Traditional religious rituals in many societies are associated with these life crises. In primitive societies as well as in industrialized cultures, we humans have needed to construct rituals around the significant events in the life of a woman and her relation to the community. The birth of a child, the advent of puberty, growth into adulthood, marriage rites, and funeral rites exemplify our need to signify or make meaning out of the major events that mark our lives. Even in our secular society we have versions of religious rituals to symbolize our passage through life: graduation from high school, the stag party before the wedding, the retirement dinner, the golden anniversary, and the funeral service. These events are personal and communal. They mark significant changes in the life of the individual and the community. Richard Rubenstein, in his book *After Auschwitz,* suggested that ritual arises out of the need of the individual in community to give meaning to the questions of personal or social identity. Ritual expresses our search for a new identity in relation to the past and to the future and thus emerges from the life crises—events that force us to deal with questions of self-identity in relation to ultimate value.[2]

Building upon Erikson's understanding of the life crises and Rubenstein's view of the necessity for "rites of passage" to mark those events, I propose to explore the life crises of being a woman and the personal and spiritual questions implicit within those crises. The image of the new woman that is emerging from the contemporary discussion on the role of women in society has yet to deal significantly with the search for personal wholeness that includes the implications of being a female body. Women's new search for self-understanding implies an integration of the unique female body structure into a continuing personal quest. I believe that in and through the life crises the questions of personal meaning are most radically presented to woman today. They force her to choose what she will become, what type of identity she will have, and how she will interpret her femaleness in relation to the whole. The crisis opens an option for personal growth and also offers the possibility for a most destructive form of self-interpretation of femaleness and its relation to others. I call these options the *graceful* and the *demonic* possibilities. At each stage of life, it is possible for a woman to understand and interpret the dimensions of her identity as graceful or demonic. To perceive female sexuality gracefully involves seeing it within the process of becoming more fully human and with an understanding of the purpose of life. To interpret female sexuality demonically means to find a false sense of identity in the female role— to romanticize it, to manipulate it, or to see it as an end in itself. The ability to perceive the graceful dimensions of female sexuality will depend largely upon a woman's ability to express the questions of meaning raised by her life crises within a community context. Women *need* "rites of passage" that symbolize the hopes, fears, and questions of ultimate meaning in their search for personal and social identity in contemporary society. . . .

MENSTRUATION

One day I woke up and my bed was a sea of blood. I felt so ashamed and told my mother. She took me to the bathroom and I was shown the belt and pads and how to use them. My mother told me to keep myself clean, change the pads often, and wash out my pants if they got stained. I was told that now I was a woman and could get pregnant. I wasn't too sure I enjoyed the status of being a woman, but rather hated the restrictions that having my period placed on going swimming with the boys and doing Phys. Ed. at school. All of a sudden, I was different. I hated the odor that came with wearing the pads, their bulkiness, and fearing that they might show or leak through. I was so embarrassed at home when I had to dispose of the pads in case anyone should notice. Then there was the discomfort: it was real and the blood used to flow and flow, for days on end it seemed. I suppose I felt proud I had finally started since mother had told me about it some years before. (I remember how embarrassed she was!) and then other girls at school had started. We used to call it the "curse" in our house and so it was for me. It was several years before a friend told me you could have a bath during your period. In later years, one of the best side effects of being on the pill was that it lessened the flow dramatically.

The first major crisis in the life of a woman is the onset of menstruation. It shocks her radically. One day she is a child; the next she is a new reality, part of an ongoing process of life that inevitably conditions her self-understanding but whose purpose and nature she is as yet unable to comprehend. Menstruation creates anxiety, not only or particularly because of the physical discomfort or the lack of information about it, but because it implies the need for a new self-understanding based on a new body experience. Simone de Beauvoir wrote forcibly of the reactions of a girl to menstruation in terms of being trapped. "The set fate that up to now weighed upon her indistinctly and from without is crouching in her belly; there is no escape; she feels she is caught."[3]

It appears that for women in our own society the experience of menstruation is still ambiguous, not merely because of lack of information or old-fashioned methods of absorbing the blood. Our method of handling menstruation today is to approach it primarily on the physiological level. We give girls information about the reproductive organs and the names and the functions of the ova, the endometrium, the uterus, and the pituitary gland. We also give them pamphlets printed in pink entitled *The Miracle of You: What It Means to Be a Girl,*[4] which not only relay technical information but also present a thoroughly enthusiastic view of the changes inherent in menstruation. . . .

The problem with this approach is that it tends to ignore that anxiety created by menstruation is not only caused by a lack of knowledge concerning the processes or function of the female body structure but by the fact that menstruation is a crisis in self-identity. It is a dramatic event in the life of a girl who is full of hopes and real fears. It signifies the end of one life and the beginning of another whose character is as yet undisclosed. In menstruation, a female's body is taken over by what is experienced as a sudden force, determining, controlling, and affecting life from now on. The psychologist Judith Bardwick suggested that our culture's very denial of the crisis character of menstruation *increases* a woman's anxiety about it.[5] . . .

The experience of menstruation for the young girl as associated with shame, guilt, and fear is perceived by many psychologists as part of a learned response affected by parental and cultural conditioning and the persistence of traditional religious taboos. Germaine Greer suggested that "what we ought to see in the agonies of puberty is the result of the conditioning that maims the female personality in creating the feminine."[6] However, I feel that menstruation is experienced as anxiety by the young girl, not only because of cultural attitudes toward the female body or because of the personality type of the girl involved,[7] but because menstruation is essentially a dramatic physical and emotional event. It is physically dramatic because it involves a flow of blood that must be dealt with, not just in terms of sanitary procedures, but in terms of psychological implications. It is emotionally dramatic because one day it begins and will continue until menopause. Though the body has been preparing for that day for many years, for the young girl *that* day marks the end of childhood and the beginning of adulthood. . . .

The ambiguity of menstruation is also due to the fact that it involves a bloodlike discharge. Karen Paige's studies suggested that the anxiety associated with menstruation varies with the amount of blood, not with the hormone levels of the woman.[8] In most cultures blood is regarded as "life blood," to be preserved and not spilled. To give blood is to give someone else life. In menstruation, nature sheds blood in a manner contradictory to all usual understandings of the loss of blood. Here bleeding is a cleansing, the very opposite of other kinds of bleeding. While we may understand this rationally, on the emotional level this blood flow appears to violate our sense of what is normal. Perhaps our modern culture's failure to appreciate the ambiguity of menstruation causes many young girls to experience it in loneliness and with anxiety. We fail to see that it raises some fundamental and troubling questions about the meaning of a girl's identity. She is linked with the processes of nature in a manner that may be glorious in its outcome but initially is at best a nuisance. In our culture, where marriage and childbirth are so delayed, perhaps ten or fifteen years beyond the onset of menstruation, it is hard for the ten-year-old girl to appreciate that she is now a biologically mature female. With menstruation comes the possibility of pregnancy; yet that too is seen immediately as a liability rather than a potential joy. In North American society, fertility is devalued, and we prescribe for it certain limited means of expression. The young girl knows that she is now a sexual being, but the reality of her body and her emotional and social being are out of joint. She is a woman in body and still a child in spirit or in social standing. Her family and the community regard the potential of her body with suspicion, since the fertility of young girls is a cause for anxiety rather than celebration. It is hard for us in this society to find a way of celebrating. In our rational framework, we tend to ignore the experience of menstruation for the young girl as a major crisis which demands the formulation of a new identity and self-image.

Primitive cultures understand that the onset of menstruation is a special event that needs a ritual to mark it, a "rite of passage." This perception is not necessarily caused by a lack of understanding the female physiology but emerges from a wiser sense that the beginning of menstruation involves a qualitative change in a girl's being.[9] This change offers a possibility, both for the individual and for the community, of being a blessing or a curse. Menstruation symbolizes the advent of a new power that is *mana* or "sacred." A sacred power has life-giving and life-destroying possibilities, and in no case is *mana* to be taken lightly. A *taboo* expresses this feeling that something special, some holy power, is involved, and our response to it must be very careful. Even those societies which appear to have only negative attitudes toward menstruation—that is, place many restrictive taboos on the menstruating female and the community—are expressing a deep understanding of the essential sacredness of the event and of the need to ensure the beneficial effects of this sacred power.

In primitive cultures, the onset of menstruation is an ambiguous experience to be celebrated as well as feared. This explains why the rituals appear to fall into two categories, a cause for dancing and a cause for seclusion of the girl. In either case, the ritual marks an understanding that the girl needs a symbolic, interpretive framework as she negotiates her first life crisis and redefines herself as a mature female. These rituals also express an understanding that discovering our identity as women is not to be a solitary struggle but is to be worked out within the context of the community. In each primitive ritual a form of self-transformation is expressed through trials, symbolic acts, and words which promote healing and integrate the forces at play. The girls and the community move into a new identity *through* the crisis.

White Painted Woman spoke to the people and said: "When the girls first menstruate you shall have a feast. Let there be songs and dancing for the girls for four nights. Let the Gahe dance in the east in front of the ceremony."

Today masked dancers personify the Gahe in the rite. The girl herself must not
sleep for the four days and nights; on the fifth morning she must make four
runs around the ritual baskets, while the woman who has care of her during
the rite chants the shrill praisecall and prays for her. The songs are sacred
prayer songs, among them homeopathic songs to White Painted Woman.

> White Painted Woman carries this girl,
> She carries her through long life,
> . . . to good fortune,
> . . . to old age,
> She bears her to peaceful sleep.

On the morning of the fifth day, while the girl runs into the sunrise, the last
song is sung beginning with the moving words: "You have started out on the
good earth." [10]

Even in those cultures where rituals appear most cruel and restrictive,
there is an understanding that the sacred power involved is an
enormous potential for good or for evil and that a form of initiation or
integration of this new reality is necessary. At the end of the seclusion,
a new being emerges. . . .

Another element of menstruation taboos that is frequently ignored is
the real need of the girl to withdraw psychologically and physically
into solitude or into the presence of other women. This dramatic event
brings a need for introspection, aloneness, and recontacting inner
depths.[11] A girl must wrestle with the meaning of her female identity,
and withdrawal may have a positive function. Erich Neumann goes so
far as to suggest that all taboos originated in the menstruation taboos
which were *imposed by* women on themselves and on men. Monthly
segregation was a movement of women into a sacred female precinct
which focused around the life-giving power of the woman.[12]

The idea that ritual and taboos involve a positive as well as a
negative element corresponds to my suggestion that the onset of
menstruation is a time of danger, a *crisis*. The resolution is unclear at
the outset; it may be creative or destructive. Our culture has ignored
the crisis character of menstruation and so is unable to provide young
women with a framework within which the mystery—that is, the
joyful and fearful elements—may be expressed and integrated into a
new form of self-understanding. . . .

For the woman today menstruation involves danger in terms of the
choices she must make concerning her new self-understanding as a

sexually mature female. She may be overwhelmed by the frightening and fearful elements of the experience and internalize an understanding of her body as something to be mistrusted and to be ashamed of. Unfortunately, it is particularly hard for a woman in this culture to avoid two contradictory and finally psychologically limiting possibilities: she either identifies her new self with her body in its negative or positive aspects, or she tries to ignore the body completely by adopting a business-as-usual attitude toward it.

In this first life crisis, the young woman makes decisions, usually on an unconscious level, about an attitude toward her female identity as a sexual body and its relation to her self-image and her sense of purpose in life and the relation of her body to the world at large, particularly to men. The danger involved is that she may be unable to integrate the crisis into the formation of her continuing personal maturation which proceeds in and through the experiences of her female body but which is not identical with any one of them. This is a *spiritual* crisis because the issue at stake is not just a personal question but involves redefining the self in context of the purpose of nature, understanding one's physicality in relation to the procreativity of nature, and deciding about one's goal and purpose in life in human community. To answer the questions, "Who am I? What does this mean for my life?" one must come to terms with several other questions: "What does it all mean? What relation does my female sexuality have to that purpose of the whole? Is that purpose creative or destructive? Is there any point to it, or is my particular physiology irrelevant to questions of ultimate meaning?"

The ability of a young woman to "successfully" negotiate the life crisis of menstruation depends first on a recognition of it as a crisis by the girl and by the community. Ignoring its importance leaves the individual to struggle alone with her feelings and fears and provides no means for their expression. *Recognizing* does not necessarily imply *discussing* or providing information, although facts about menstruation are important as a preparation for the actual onset. *Recognizing* means marking the occasion so that the girl is supplied a symbolic framework within which to find resources for her questions of meaning. To ignore the event means that the girl's new framework will be casually formed by fears and rumors and by what the culture of school and society teach her about the nature of her identity as a woman. . . .

The resolution of the crisis of menstruation may be called *demonic* when it is not only destructive for the ongoing life of the woman but actively produces ill effects in the lives of others. A demonic resolution fails to understand the relation between the quest for personal identity and having a female body with its sexual structure; female sexuality is a positive part of that quest rather than outside it or restricting it. The first most common destructive solution to the crisis of menstruation is being overcome by fear, shame, and guilt and internalizing any negative parental or social attitudes. When this happens, a girl learns to experience her body primarily as dirty and disgusting. . . .

To experience the onset of menstruation as predominantly frightening rather than positive is, in my experience, fairly common for women in this society. This is partly because of the necessary ambiguity of the phenomenon, but it is also because the positive element is so difficult to articulate or locate in our framework. Menstruation is messy and inconvenient with emotional and physical discomforts, even in these days of tampons and pain remedies. We do not like to be inconvenienced. The image of humanness that predominates our industrialized society is based on the mind controlling the body. To be limited by our bodies, whether in sickness or death, or particularly by the female body processes, is considered weakness and threatens our "normal" forms of mastery and self-control. We try to overcome fatigue or pain with drugs and stimulants and fail to accept our bodies as part of an ongoing life process which has its own rhythms. To regard menstruation primarily as an unfortunate nuisance that now can be handled largely through better sanitary products is to treat female sexuality as an unfortunate burden or weakness which can to a large extent be overcome and thus ignored. This solution is very prevalent in our society, and it implies an inability to integrate the female body structure into the process of identity formation. This lack of self-acceptance and trust of the body stems from being unable to experience any value in female sexuality.

Another limiting interpretation of sexuality may be to identify oneself with it entirely. The traditional identification of the female with the role of mother may have provided previous generations with a sense of purpose and an identity in relation to the whole. Even in primitive societies the quest for personal wholeness is linked with an understanding of the ongoing procreative life process. In that sense, the onset of menstruation as the symbol of one's role within the ultimate purpose of the universe was not *demonic* but *graceful*. Fertility is seen, not as a woman's personal power, but as the power of the fertility Goddess in whose power all humans and animals participated and in relation to whom women can perceive their sexuality as a gift and a medium whereby the transcendent life-giving power of nature expresses itself.

This option is no longer open to women, for many years stretch between puberty and marriage, and women's life span extends beyond childbearing years. Also neither men nor women see their whole identity bound up with imitating the procreative power of nature. Our understanding of the creative purpose of life does include procreativity, but it is not identified with it or limited by it. Our understanding of fertility is also very different. We do not value persons *because* of their procreative potential; indeed, unrestricted numbers of children are now seen as destructive of the whole rather than creative.

The solution to the crisis of menstruation for a young woman in our society is not *gracefully* answered by the sole response, motherhood. . . . To answer "motherhood" is demonic, for it demands that a young girl find her identity in one biological role which restricts the integration of her sexuality into a mature relationship with a male. The problems caused for the woman by resolving this early life crisis in this manner are evident in our society, not only in the restrictive and possessive attitudes evident in mothers toward their children but also in the destructive effects for potential resolution of future life crises in the individual woman. To glorify, sentimentalize, and totally identify personal meaning with the fertile potential of the female body structure is a delusion, for it fails to recognize the ambiguity implicit within the experience of menstruation.

Another negative solution to the onset of menstruation would be to fail to take it seriously. This response can lead to an attitude that fails to integrate what is happening to the body with personal selfhood. . . . To ignore it does not mean that the young girl has succeeded in integrating the experience into her self-understanding. It can lead to later attitudes toward her body and its expression in relation to others that lack responsibility and are unconsciously manipulative. The impersonality of menstruation needs to be integrated into *personal* self-understanding in order for the next life crisis, a girl's expression of sexuality in relation to others, to be defined creatively.

The *graceful* experience of menstruation would be to accept it as a symbol of the potential of one's body for the enrichment of self and others. To emphasize that the life power and process made evident in your body every month is pleasure giving does not mean to underestimate the negativity and anxiety associated with the onset of menstruation. Menstruation is an ending as well as a beginning, and the ability to experience the new potential opened up by it depends on being able to wrestle with the fears associated with being biologically female. We must express the fears of our "being determined," the divisions between women and men made evident by it, and the anxieties concerned with our potential fertility. The graceful acceptance of menstruation is possible only through recognizing its ambiguous quality; it does not imply a simplistic attitude toward the body. Nature is cruel as well as kind, and life proceeds through loss. Our creative potential as individuals depends at all levels on giving up something, letting go some aspects of ourselves. At menstruation, childhood is no more; that freedom, innocence, and simplicity is gone forever.

To emerge gracefully from the life crisis of menstruation would imply in our society that we are able to celebrate the value of our female body structure as potentially childbearing without identifying ourselves with it. As young girls, we need to be able to participate imaginatively in that possibility offered by being female and to know that it is a good that we may be able, if we are fortunate and if we choose, to experience. The onset of menstruation can symbolize the power of our bodies to give us joy, deepen and enrich our experience of life, and increase the totality of our self-expression. The potential procreativity of our bodies is not a personal power but the linking of ourselves to the creative power of nature and to the creative aspect of all human relationships. . . .

To emerge enriched from the life crisis of menstruation implies finally trusting and liking one's body. Trusting it means being peaceful with it, knowing its potential, relaxing with the new experience of menstruation, understanding the possible good offered by the female body structure. Trusting in one's body includes comprehending physiologically what happens to the body of a woman each month. Knowing also includes understanding the fertility of the female body and how to use contraceptives to enable the use of that power to be expressed creatively and not destructively. Today's woman can celebrate the mystery, not from ignorance and obscurantism, but from the knowledge of exactly what happens and how potential fertility may be best used in the ongoing quest for self-identity. . . .

To emerge enhanced from the crisis of menstruation is to receive an increased sense of value as an individual and the goodness of one's body structure. It heightens rather than diminishes personhood. It gives pride and status rather than shame and mistrust. For a young woman to emerge gracefully from this crisis implies her ability to understand her body in relation to her personal maturation, its value to herself and to the community, and the use of its potential so that it can be creative for herself and the community. Her trust of her body depends on her seeing it in context of the whole. In that sense, it is part of the very goodness of life and of the creative structures of all living organisms. Her identity as an individual, trusting in her own body and able to experience its grace, means being able to integrate its negative and positive aspects into her personality.

Experiencing menstruation creatively is of immense importance, for it lays the foundation for resolving the next life crises which have to do with personal selfhood and expressing sexuality to others. A woman will be unable to experience menstruation gracefully unless the family and community provide a context within which the graceful and demonic elements of the life crisis may be expressed and her new identity as a woman celebrated. Perhaps in a time of a secular culture it is the role of the immediate family and friends to provide that context in a ritual and symbolic form, since it is from them that a woman learns her sense of what is ultimately valuable in the first place.

NOTES

1. Erik Erikson, *Childhood and Society,* 2d ed. (New York: W. W. Norton, 1963). Erikson's theory of the psychosocial stages of development was first proposed in this book and explicated further in his studies on adolescence and the identity crisis.
2. Richard Rubenstein, *After Auschwitz* (Indianapolis: Bobbs Merrill, 1966.)
3. Simone de Beauvoir, *The Second Sex,* trans. and ed. H. M. Parshley (New York: Alfred A. Knopf, 1952), p. 295.
4. *The Miracle of You* (Toronto: The Life Cycle Centre, Kimberly-Clark of Canada, Ltd.).
5. Judith M. Bardwick, *Psychology of Women: A Study of Bio-Cultural Conflicts* (New York: Harper & Row, 1971), p. 48.
6. Germaine Greer, *The Female Eunuch* (St. Albans: Granada Publishing Ltd., 1971), p. 89.
7. See W. Gifford-Jones, *On Being a Woman: The Modern Woman's Guide to Gynecology* (Toronto: McClelland and Stewart, 1969), pp. 28–31, 34.

8. Karen E. Paige, "Women Learn to Sing the Menstrual Blues," *Psychology Today,* September, 1973, p. 43.

9. Margaret Mead, *Male and Female: A Study of the Sexes in a Changing World* (New York: Dell Publishing Co., 1949), pp. 183–186.

10. Maria Leach, ed., *Funk and Wagnall's Standard Dictionary of Folklore Mythology and Legend,* vol. 2 (New York: Funk and Wagnall's, 1950), p. 707.

11. M. Esther Harding, *Women's Mysteries: Ancient and Modern* (New York: G. P. Putnam's Sons, 1971), p. 90.

12. Erich Neumann, *Great Mother,* trans. Frank Manheim (Princeton: Princeton University Press, 1963), p. 290.

Witchcraft and Women's Culture

STARHAWK

The unhewn stones are newly risen. Within their circle, an old woman raises a flint knife and points it toward the bright full moon. She cries out, a wail echoed by her clan folk as they begin the dance. They circle wildly around the central fire, feeling the power rise within them until they unite in ecstatic frenzy. The priestess cries again, and all drop to the earth, exhausted but filled with a deep sense of peace. A cup of ale is poured into the fire, and the flames leap up high. "Blessed be the mother of all life," the priestess says, "May She be generous to Her children."

The birth is a difficult one, but the midwife has brought many women through worse. Still, she is worried. She has herbs to open the womb and stop the blood, herbs to bring sleep, and others to bring forgetfulness of pain. But now her baskets are almost empty. This year she could not go gathering at the proper times of the moon and sun. The new priest and his spies are everywhere—if she were to be caught digging simples in the moonlight it would be sure proof of witchcraft,

Starhawk (Miriam Simos) is an author, freelance screenwriter, and priestess who has taught through open universities in the San Francisco Bay area. Active in feminist and pagan groups, she was the first national president of the Covenant of the Goddess (a church). Author of two unpublished novels, she is currently writing *The Spiral Dance,* a book on magic and earth religion. Her articles will appear in *The Holy Book of Women's Mysteries* and elsewhere. This essay was discussed at the 1977 meetings of the American Academy of Religion.

not just against herself but against her daughters and sisters and her daughter's daughters. As she pours out the last of her broth for the laboring woman, the midwife sighs. "Blessed Tana, Mother of mothers," she breathes softly, "When will the old ways return?"

The child is in a state of shock. Her memories of the last three days are veiled in a haze of smoke and noise that seem to swirl toward this climax of acrid smells and hoarse shouting. The priest's grip is clawlike as he forces her to watch the cruel drama in the center of the square. The girl's eyes are open, but her mind has flown far away, and what she sees is not the scene before her: her mother, the stake, the flames. She is running through the open field behind their cottage, smelling only clean wind, seeing only clear sky. The priest looks down at her blank face and crosses himself in fear. "Devil's spawn!" he spits on the ground. "If I had my way, we'd hold to custom and burn you too!"

It is the night of the full moon. Nine women stand in a circle, on a rocky hill above the city. The western sky is rosy with the setting sun; in the east the moon's face begins to peer above the horizon. Below, electric lights wink on the ground like fallen stars. A young woman raises a steel knife and cries out, a wail echoed by the others as they begin the dance. They circle wildly around a cauldron of smoldering herbs, feeling the power rise within them until they unite in ecstasy. The priestess cries again, and all drop to the earth, exhausted, but filled with an overwhelming sense of peace. The woman pours out a cup of wine onto the earth, refills it and raises it high. "Hail, Tana, Mother of mothers!" she cries. "Awaken from your long sleep, and return to your children again!"

From earliest times,[1] women have been witches, *wicce*, "wise ones"—priestesses, diviners, midwives, poets, healers, and singers of songs of power. Woman-centered culture, based on the worship of the Great Goddess, underlies the beginnings of all civilization. Mother Goddess was carved on the walls of paleolithic caves, and painted in the shrines of the earliest cities, those of the Anatolian plateau. For her were raised the giant stone circles, the henges of the British Isles, the dolmens and cromlechs of the later Celtic countries, and for her the great passage graves of Ireland were dug. In her honor, sacred dancers leaped the bulls in Crete and composed lyric hymns within the colleges of the holy isles of the Mediterranean. Her mysteries were celebrated in secret rites at Eleusis, and her initiates included some of the finest minds of Greece. Her priestesses discovered and tested the healing herbs and learned the secrets of the human mind and body that allowed them to ease the pain of childbirth, to heal wounds and cure diseases, and to explore the realm of dreams and the unconscious. Their knowledge of nature enabled them to tame sheep and cattle, to breed wheat and corn from grasses and weeds, to forge ceramics from mud and metal from rock, and to track the movements of moon, stars, and sun.

Witchcraft, "the craft of the wise," is the last remnant in the west of the time of women's strength and power. Through the dark ages of persecution, the covens of Europe preserved what is left of the mythology, rituals, and knowledge of the ancient matricentric (mother-centered) times. The great centers of worship in Anatolia, Malta, Iberia, Brittany, and Sumeria are now only silent stones and works of art we can but dimly understand. Of the mysteries of Eleusis, we have literary hints; the poems of Sappho survive only in fragments. The great collections of early literature and science were destroyed by patriarchal forces—the library of Alexandria burnt by Caesar, Charlemagne's collection of lore burnt by his son Louis "the Pious," who was offended at its "paganism." But the craft remains, in spite of all efforts to stamp it out, as a living tradition of Goddess-centered worship that traces its roots back to the time before the triumph of patriarchy.

The old religion of witchcraft before the advent of Christianity, was an earth-centered, nature-oriented worship that venerated the Goddess, the source of life, as well as her son-lover-consort, who was seen as the Horned God of the hunt and animal life. Earth, air, water, fire, streams, seas, wells, beasts, trees, grain, the planets, sun, and most of all, the moon, were seen as aspects of deity. On the great seasonal festivals—the solstices and equinoxes, and the eves of May, August, November, and February,—all the countryside would gather to light huge bonfires, feast, dance, sing, and perform the rituals that assured abundance throughout the year.

When Christianity first began to spread, the country people held to the old ways, and for hundreds of years the two faiths coexisted quite peacefully. Many people followed both religions, and country priests in the twelfth and thirteenth centuries were frequently upbraided by church authorities for dressing in skins and leading the dance at the pagan festivals.

But in the thirteenth and fourteenth centuries, the church began persecution of witches, as well as Jews and "heretical" thinkers. Pope Innocent the VIII, with his Bull of 1484, intensified a campaign of torture and death that would take the lives of an estimated 9 million people, perhaps 80 percent of whom were women.

The vast majority of victims were not coven members or even necessarily witches. They were old widows whose property was coveted by someone else, young children with "witch blood," midwives who furnished the major competition to the male-dominated medical profession, free-thinkers who asked the wrong questions.

An enormous campaign of propaganda accompanied the witch trials as well. Witches were said to have sold their souls to the devil, to practice obscene and disgusting rites, to blight crops and murder children. In many areas, the witches did worship a Horned God as the spirit of the hunt, of animal life and vitality, a concept far from the power of evil that was the Christian devil. Witches were free and open about sexuality—but their rites were "obscene" only to those who viewed the human body itself as filthy and evil. Questioning or disbelieving any of the slander was itself considered proof of witchcraft or heresy, and the falsehoods that for hundreds of years could not be openly challenged had their effect. Even today, the word *witch* is often automatically associated with "evil."

With the age of reason in the eighteenth century, belief in witches, as in all things psychic and supernatural, began to fade. The craft as a religion was forgotten; all that remained were the wild stories of broomstick flights, magic potions, and the summoning of spectral beings.

Memory of the true craft faded everywhere except within the hidden covens. With it, went the memory of women's heritage and history, of our ancient roles as leaders, teachers, healers, seers. Lost, also, was the conception of the Great Spirit, as manifest in nature, in life, in woman. Mother Goddess slept, leaving the world to the less than gentle rule of the God-Father.

The Goddess has at last stirred from sleep, and women are reawakening to our ancient power. The feminist movement, which began as a political, economic, and social struggle, is opening to a spiritual dimension. In the process, many women are discovering the old religion, reclaiming the word *witch* and, with it, some of our lost culture.

Witchcraft, today, is a kaleidoscope of diverse traditions, rituals, theologies, and structures. But underneath the varying forms is a basic orientation common to all the craft. The outer forms of religion—the particular words said, the signs made, the names used—are less important to us than the inner forms, which cannot be defined or described but must be felt and intuited.

The craft is earth religion, and our basic orientation is to the earth, to life, to nature. There is no dichotomy between spirit and flesh, no split between Godhead and the world. The Goddess is manifest in the world; she brings life into being, *is* nature, *is* flesh. Union is not sought outside the world in some heavenly sphere or through dissolution of the self into the void beyond the senses. Spiritual union is found in life, within nature, passion, sensuality—through being fully human, fully one's self.

Our great symbol for the Goddess is the moon, whose three aspects reflect the three stages in women's lives and whose cycles of waxing and waning coincide with women's menstrual cycles. As the new moon or crescent, she is the Maiden, the Virgin—not chaste, but belonging to herself alone, not bound to any man. She is the wild child, lady of the woods, the huntress, free and untamed—Artemis, Kore, Aradia, Nimue. White is her color. As the full moon, she is the mature woman, the sexual being, the mother and nurturer, giver of life, fertility, grain, offspring, potency, joy—Tana, Demeter, Diana, Ceres, Mari. Her colors are the red of blood and the green of growth. As waning or dark moon, she is the old woman, past menopause, the hag or crone that is ripe with wisdom, patroness of secrets, prophecy, divination, inspiration, power—Hecate, Ceridwen, Kali, Anna. Her color is the black of night.

The Goddess is also earth—Mother Earth, who sustains all growing things, who is the body, our bones and cells. She is air—the winds that move in the trees and over the waves, breath. She is the fire of the hearth, of the blazing bonfire and the fuming volcano; the power of transformation and change. And she is water—the sea, original source of life; the rivers, streams, lakes and wells; the blood that flows in the rivers of our veins. She is mare, cow, cat, owl, crane, flower, tree, apple, seed, lion, sow, stone, woman. She is found in the world around us, in the cycles and seasons of nature, and in mind, body, spirit, and emotions within each of us. Thou art Goddess. I am Goddess. All that lives (and all that is, lives), all that serves life, is Goddess.

Because witches are oriented to earth and to life, we value spiritual qualities that I feel are especially important to women, who have for so long been conditioned to be passive, submissive and weak. The craft values independence, personal strength, *self*—not petty selfishness but that deep core of strength within that makes us each a unique child of the Goddess. The craft has no dogma to stifle thought, no set of doctrines that have to be believed. Where authority exists, within covens, it is always coupled with the freedom every covener has, to leave at any time. When self is valued—in ourselves—we can see that self is everywhere.

Passion and emotion—that give depth and color and meaning to human life—are also valued. Witches strive to be in touch with feelings, even if they are sometimes painful, because the joy and pleasure and ecstasy available to a fully alive person make it worth occasional suffering. So-called negative emotion—anger—is valued as well, as a sign that something is wrong and that action needs to be taken. Witches prefer to handle anger by taking action and making changes rather than by detaching ourselves from our feelings in order to reach some nebulous, "higher" state.

Most of all, the craft values love. The Goddess' only law is "Love unto all beings." But the love we value is not the airy flower power of the hippies or the formless, abstracted *agape* of the early Christians. It is passionate, sensual, personal love, *eros*, falling in love, mother-child love, the love of one unique human being for other individuals, with all their personal traits and idiosyncrasies. Love is not something that can be radiated out in solitary meditation—it manifests itself in relationships and interractions with other people. It is often said "You cannot be a witch alone"—because to be a witch is to be a lover, a lover of the Goddess, and a lover of other human beings.

The coven is still the basic structure of the craft, and generally covens meet at the times of full moons and the major festivals, although some meet also on new moons and a few meet once a week. A coven is a small group, at most of thirteen members—for the thirteen full moons of the year. Its small size is important. Within the coven, a union, a merging of selves in a close bond of love and trust, takes place. A coven becomes an energy pool each member can draw on. But, because the group remains small, there is never the loss of identity and individuality that can happen in a mass. In a coven, each person's individuality is extremely important. Each personality colors and helps create the group identity, and each member's energy is vital to the working of the group.

Covens are separate and autonomous, and no one outside the coven has any authority over its functioning. Some covens may be linked in the same tradition—meaning they share the same rituals and symbology—but there is no hierarchy of rule. Elder witches can and do give advice, but only those within the coven may actually make decisions.

Covens are extremely diverse. There are covens of hereditary witches who have practiced rites unchanged for hundreds of years, and covens who prefer to make up their own rituals and may never do the same thing twice. There are covens of "perfect couples"—an even number of women and men permanently paired, and covens of lesbian feminists or of women who simply prefer to explore women's spirituality in a space removed from men. There are covens of gay men and covens that just don't worry about sexual polarities. A few covens are authoritarian—with a high priestess or high priest who makes most of the decisions. (Coveners, of course, always have the option of leaving.) Most are democratic, if not anarchic, but usually older or more experienced members—"elders"—assume leadership and responsibility. Actual roles in rituals are often rotated among qualified coveners.

Rituals also vary widely. A craft ritual might involve wild shouting and frenzied dancing, or silent meditation, or both. A carefully rehearsed drama might be enacted, or a spontaneous poetic chant carried on for an hour. Everyone may enter a deep trance and scry in a crystal ball—or they may pass around a bottle of wine and laugh uproariously at awful puns. The best rituals combine moments of intense ecstasy and spiritual union, with moments of raucous humor and occasional silliness. The craft is serious without being dry or solemn.

Whether formal or informal, every craft ritual takes place within a circle—a space considered to be "between the worlds," the human world and the realm of the Goddess. A circle can be cast, or created, in any physical space, from a moonlit hillside to the living room of a modern apartment. It may be outlined in stones, drawn in chalk or paint, or drawn invisibly with the point of a sword or ceremonial wand. It may be consecrated with incense, salt water, and a formal invocation to each of the four quarters of the universe, or created simply by having everyone join hands. The casting of the circle begins the ritual and serves as a transition into an expanded state of consciousness. The power raised by the ritual is contained within the circle so that it can reach a higher peak instead of dissipating.

The Goddess, and if desired, the Horned God (not all traditions of the craft relate to the male force) can be invoked once the circle is cast. An invocation may be set beforehand, written out and memorized, but in our coven we find the most effective invocations are those that come to us spontaneously, out of the inspiration of the season, the phase of the moon, and the particular mood and energy of the moment. Often we invoke the Goddess by chanting together a line or phrase repeated over and over: "Moon mother bright light of all earth sky, we call you" is an example. As we chant, we find rhythms, notes, melodies, and words seem to flow through us and burst out in complex and beautiful patterns.

Chanting, dancing, breathing, and concentrated will, all contribute to the raising of power, which is the essential part of a craft ritual. Witches conceive of psychic energy as having form and substance that can be perceived and directed by those with a trained awareness. The power generated within the circle is built into a cone form, and at its peak is released—to the Goddess, to reenergize the members of the coven, or to do a specific work such as a healing.

When the cone is released, any scattered energy that is left is grounded, put back into the earth, by falling to the ground, breathing deeply, and relaxing. High-energy states cannot be maintained indefinitely without becoming a physical and emotional drain—any more than you could stay high on methedrine forever without destroying your body. After the peak of the cone, it is vital to let go of the power and return to a calm, relaxed state. Silent meditation, trance, or psychic work are often done in this part of the ritual.

Energy is also shared in tangible form—wine, cakes, fruit, cheesecake, brownies, or whatever people enjoy eating. The Goddess is invited to share with everyone, and a libation is poured to her first. This part of the ritual is relaxed and informally social, devoted to laughing, talking, sharing of news and any business that must be done.

At the end, the Goddess is thanked and bid farewell, and the circle is formally opened. Ending serves as a transition back into ordinary space and time. Rituals finish with a kiss and a greeting of "Merry meet, merry part, and merry meet again."

The underlying forms of craft rituals evolved out of thousands of years of experience and understanding of human needs and the potentials of human consciousness. That understanding, which is part of women's lost heritage, is invaluable, not just in the context of rituals and spiritual growth, but also for those working toward political and social change, because human needs and human energies behave the same in any context.

Witches understand that energy, whether it is psychic, emotional, or physical, always flows in cycles. It rises and falls, peaks and drops, and neither end of the cycle can be sustained indefinitely, any more than you could run forever without stopping. Intense levels of energy must be released and then brought down and grounded; otherwise the energy dissipates or even turns destructive. If, in a ritual, you tried to maintain a peak of frenzy for hours and hours, you would find that after a while the energy loses its joyful quality, and instead of feeling union and ecstasy, you begin to feel irritated and exhausted. Political groups that try to maintain an unremitting level of anger—a high-energy state— also run out of steam in precisely the same way. Releasing the energy and grounding out allows the power itself to work freely. It clears channels and allows you to rest and recharge and become ready for the next swing into an up cycle. Releasing energy does not mean losing momentum; rather, real movement, real change, happens in a rhythmic pattern of many beats, not in one unbroken blast of static.

Craft rituals also add an element of drama and fantasy to one's life. They allow us to act out myths and directly experience archetypes of symbolic transformation. They allow us, as adults, to recapture the joy of childhood make-believe, of dressing up, of pretending, of play. Magic, by Dion Fortune's definition, "the art of changing consciousness at will," is not so far removed from the creative fantasy states we enter so easily as children, when our dolls become alive, our bicycles become wild horses, ourselves arctic explorers or queens. Allowing ourselves, as adults, to play and fantasize with others, puts us in touch with the creative child within, with a deep and rich source of inspiration.

The craft also helps us open our intuitive and psychic abilities. Although witchcraft is commonly associated with magic and the use of extrasensory powers, not all covens put a great deal of stress on psychic training. Worship is more often the main focus of activity. However, any craft ritual involves some level of psychic awareness just in sensing the energy that is raised.

Ordinarily, the way into the craft is through initiation into an already established coven. However, because covens are limited in size and depend on some degree of harmony between personalities, it is often difficult to find one that is open to new members and that fits your preferences. In San Francisco, Los Angeles, and New York, covens often run open study groups and can be found through publications and open universities. In other areas of the country, it may be difficult to locate a practicing coven at all.

However, there is nothing to stop you from starting a coven or a *circle*—a term I use for a group whose members meet for rituals but are not formally initiated—on your own. Women, especially, are more and more joining together to explore a Goddess-oriented spirituality and to create rituals and symbols that are meaningful to us today. Starting your own circle requires imagination, creativity, and experimentation, but it is a tremendously exciting process. You will miss formal psychic training—but you may discover on your own more than anyone else could teach you. Much of what is written on the craft is biased in one way or another, so weed out what is useful to you and ignore the rest.

I see the next few years as being crucial in the transformation of our culture away from the patriarchal death cults and toward the love of life, of nature, of the female principle. The craft is only one path among the many opening up for women, and many of us will blaze new trails as we explore the uncharted country of our own interiors. The heritage, the culture, the knowledge of the ancient priestesses, healers, poets, singers, and seers were nearly lost, but a seed survived the flames that will blossom in a new age into thousands of flowers. The long sleep of Mother Goddess is ended. May She awaken in each of our hearts—Merry meet, merry part, and blessed be.

NOTE

1. This article is limited to the history of traditions that come from northern Europe. Southern and eastern Europe, Asia, India, Africa, and the Americas all have rich traditions of Goddess religions and matricentric cultures, but to even touch on them all would be impossible in a short essay. The history presented here is the "inner" or "mythic" history that provides a touchstone for modern witches. Like the histories of all peoples, its truth is intuited in the meaning it gives to life, even though it may be recognized that scholars might dispute some facets of the story.

Self-Blessing Ritual

ZSUZSANNA E. BUDAPEST

There is a ritual in the craft, called the *self-blessing ritual,* that comes to us from oral tradition. It has not been written down for a long time. We really don't know how old it is, but, because of all the elements involved, it feels very ancient. It is a woman's own blessing on herself; her own divinity is honored in a ritual with herself. It is a self-affirmation, a very private, and a very powerful ritual.

To do it, first take a shower or a bath to purify yourself. Have assembled on your altar some salt, in a nice container, and some wine and water. The altar is an important part of women's rituals, and a very female part of dwellings. Every house used to have an altar, for the house spirits, for the ancestors. Every woman would do well to have one of her own. On it, you represent the Goddess in some symbolic manner—by a rose, for instance, or any flower, because all that is green, all that grows above the earth, is sacred to Persephone. Arrange your altar in a creative manner, for example, with a white cloth, two white candles on the two sides, and a rose in the middle. Put your chalice in front and fill it half with water and half with wine. Take the salt and put it down in front of your altar on the floor and stamp on it. The salt here symbolizes the salt of the earth—wisdom—

Zsuzsanna E. Budapest, a Hungarian–born genetic witch, is founder of the Sisterhood of the Wicca and the Susan B. Anthony Coven #1. She is author of *The Feminist Book of Lights and Shadows* and *The Holy Book of Women's Mysteries* (forthcoming). Her articles have appeared in *Moon, Moon* and *WomanSpirit.* This selection is revised from the transcript of an interview in *Women, Ritual, and Religion,* © 1977 by Gloria Kaufman, and is reprinted by permission of Ms. Kaufman and the author.

so you are standing on your wisdom. And the water represents Aphrodite; there is no organic life without water, it is the life force. The wine gets you into ecstasy and is sacred to the Goddess because it represents joy and stimulation. By mixing them half and half, you are also representing temperance, which is important in women's wisdom.

After preparing yourself, step to your altar, and light your two candles, and say, "Blessed be, thou creature of fire." Then light your incense. You can make your own incense with flower petals you have around your house; something you make is always more powerful than anything else.

Next, dip your fingers in your chalice and, touching your forehead, say, "Bless me, Mother, for I am your child." This is an acknowledgement of where your life comes from, of how you got here. It also makes a connection with the spirit you are addressing in yourself.

Then dip your fingers again, touch your nose, and say, "Bless my nose to smell your essence." Smell is the most neglected sense we have. Most of the brain cells can be stimulated with a certain scent, which in turn stimulates the deep mind. Actually, while your conscious mind is tending to modern life, your deep mind can work for you and straighten out your problems. To smell the Goddess' essence is also to be close to nature, to remember the smell of roses, or the smell of a clear evening.

Again dip your fingers, and touch your lips and say, "Bless my lips to speak of you." The lips are an important symbol in the craft. They stand for the word, for utterance, for ordinance, for Themis, Goddess of social consciousness. Indeed, words are revolution. Mouth is revolution. The conscious manifestation of a thought is a word, and, once uttered, the vibration never stops, it just keeps going around. Sound never stops. We have a responsibility to be conscious of what we say, because what we say is magic, it is a ritual. Words have power. It is estimated that most of a culture's energy is expended on speaking. Speech is how we touch each other's minds. We influence each other with words. We organize with words. We have to articulate in order to achieve changes. So when you bless your lips, you think of all that. Each time you touch a part of yourself, linger on it; allow it to carry you and teach you. A candlelight flickering is a good reminder of the need for psychic thinking, psychic meditation.

Then dip your fingers again, and touch your breasts, and say, "Bless my breasts, formed in strength and beauty." In matriarchies, the beauty standard was strength and beauty combined. Weakness was not rewarded. Weakness was not considered beautiful.

And then again, dip your fingers, touch your genitals, and say, "Bless my genitals that bring forth life as you have brought forth the universe." Touching genitals and speaking of bringing forth life does not mean that all women must give birth to children. It is simply a recognition of our connection with all that is female. The biological destiny that was used against us actually is the basis of our divinity. People come to me and say, "Z., how can you allow biology to become destiny again? You know what they did with that before." "I'm sorry," I reply, "we do give birth, we do issue forth people, just as the Goddess issues forth the universe. That is a biological connection and manifestation of the Goddess. It is not something I'm going to keep quiet about. It is what women do, we make people."

And then, last, dip your fingers, and touch your feet, and say, "Bless my feet, to walk in your paths." Whatever your mind thinks, your feet will soon follow. So you want to create a life orientation toward yourself, toward your world, toward your people, toward everything around you. And the responsibility you accept is that you are divine, and that you have power. You are not powerless. You are powerless only if you allow a structure to exist that makes you powerless. Once you realize that you don't want to be a slave, and you speak of it, the Goddess of freedom is evoked. Social consciousness, Themis, is also evoked, and influences for change are working around you.

When you finish the spell, stay on your salt, and feel the power flowing through you. Then extinguish your candles, and say, "Thank you, spirits, for being with me." And that's the end of that.

In self-blessing, you affirm the divine you. Self-blessing is very important for women, because too many of us have internalized our own oppression. It is important for us to change the influences working in our deep minds. Religion controls inner space; inner space controls outer space. If a woman internalizes her oppression and thinks she is inferior, or unclean when she menstruates, she internalizes a policeman. She will then act accordingly. She will not need to be policed by the actual oppressors because she will have assimilated their values, and she will police herself. The easiest and most efficient way for small numbers to oppress large numbers of people is to sell them a religion. If that religion is embraced by the majority of people, they will police themselves and act according to a value system that actually oppresses them. But they have internalized it, so they have lost. This is what so many women have done in patriarchy. Self-blessing rituals are a way of exorcising the patriarchal policeman, cleansing the deep mind, and filling it with positive images of the strength and beauty of women. This is what the Goddess symbolizes—the divine within women and all that is female in the universe.

Why Women Need the Goddess: Phenomenological, Psychological, and Political Reflections

CAROL P. CHRIST

At the close of Ntosake Shange's stupendously successful Broadway play "For Colored Girls Who Have Considered Suicide When the Rainbow Is Enuf," a tall beautiful black woman rises from despair to cry out, "I found God in myself and I loved her fiercely."[1] Her discovery is echoed by women around the country who meet spontaneously in small groups on full moons, solstices, and equinoxes to celebrate the Goddess as symbol of life and death powers and waxing and waning energies in the universe and in themselves.[2]

It is the night of the full moon. Nine women stand in a circle, on a rocky hill above the city. The western sky is rosy with the setting sun; in the east the

This essay, which was the keynote address at the University of California at Santa Cruz Extension conference "The Great Goddess Re-Emerging," in the spring of 1978 appeared in slightly different form in *Heresies,* Spring, 1978, and is reprinted with permission of *Heresies.*

moon's face begins to peer above the horizon. . . . The woman pours out a cup of wine onto the earth, refills it and raises it high. "Hail, Tana, Mother of mothers!" she cries. "Awaken from your long sleep, and return to your children again!"[3]

What are the political and psychological effects of this fierce new love of the divine in themselves for women whose spiritual experience has been focused by the male God of Judaism and Christianity? Is the spiritual dimension of feminism a passing diversion, an escape from difficult but necessary political work? Or does the emergence of the symbol of Goddess among women have significant political and psychological ramifications for the feminist movement?

To answer this question, we must first understand the importance of religious symbols and rituals in human life and consider the effect of male symbolism of God on women. According to anthropologist Clifford Geertz, religious symbols shape a cultural ethos, defining the deepest values of a society and the persons in it. "Religion," Geertz writes "is a system of symbols which act to produce powerful, pervasive, and long-lasting moods and motivations"[4] in the people of a given culture. A "mood" for Geertz is a psychological attitude such as awe, trust, and respect, while a "motivation" is the *social* and *political* trajectory created by a mood that transforms mythos into ethos, symbol system into social and political reality. Symbols have both psychological and political effects, because they create the inner conditions (deep-seated attitudes and feelings) that lead people to feel comfortable with or to accept social and political arrangements that correspond to the symbol system.

Because religion has such a compelling hold on the deep psyches of so many people, feminists cannot afford to leave it in the hands of the fathers. Even people who no longer "believe in God" or participate in the institutional structure of patriarchal religion still may not be free of the power of the symbolism of God the Father. A symbol's effect does not depend on rational assent, for a symbol also functions on levels of the psyche other than the rational. Religion fulfills deep psychic needs by providing symbols and rituals that enable people to cope with limit situations[5] in human life (death, evil, suffering) and to pass through life's important transitions (birth, sexuality, death). Even people who consider themselves completely secularized will often find themselves sitting in a church or synagogue when a friend or relative gets married, or when a parent or friend has died. The symbols associated with these important rituals cannot fail to affect the deep or unconscious structures of the mind of even a person who has rejected these symbolisms on a conscious level—especially if the person is under stress. The reason for the continuing effect of religious symbols is that the mind abhors a vacuum. Symbol systems cannot simply be rejected, they must be replaced. Where there is not any replacement, the mind will revert to familiar structures at times of crisis, bafflement, or defeat.

Religions centered on the worship of a male God create "moods" and "motivations" that keep women in a state of psychological dependence on men and male authority, while at the same legitimating the *political* and *social* authority of fathers and sons in the institutions of society.

Religious symbol systems focused around exclusively male images of divinity create the impression that female power can never be fully legitimate or wholly beneficent. This message need never be explicitly stated (as, for example, it is in the story of Eve) for its effect to be felt. A woman completely ignorant of the myths of female evil in biblical religion nonetheless acknowledges the anomaly of female power when she prays exclusively to a male God. She may see herself as like God (created in the image of God) only by denying her own sexual identity and affirming God's transcendence of sexual identity. But she can never have the experience that is freely available to every man and boy in her culture, of having her full sexual identity affirmed as being in the image and likeness of God. In Geertz' terms, her "mood" is one of trust in male power as salvific and distrust of female power in herself and other women as inferior or dangerous. Such a powerful, pervasive, and longlasting "mood" cannot fail to become a "motivation" that translates into social and political reality.

In *Beyond God the Father,* feminist theologian Mary Daly detailed the psychological and political ramifications of father religion for women. "If God in 'his' heaven is a father ruling his people," she wrote, "then it is the 'nature' of things and according to divine plan and the order of the universe that society be male dominated. Within this context, a *mystification of roles* takes place: The husband dominating his wife represents God 'himself.' The images and values of a given society have been projected into the realm of dogmas and 'Articles of Faith,' and these in turn justify the social structures which have given rise to them and which sustain their plausibility."[6]

Philosopher Simone de Beauvoir was well aware of the function of patriarchal religion as legitimater of male power. As she wrote, "Man enjoys the great advantage of having a god endorse the code he writes; and since man exercises a sovereign authority over women it is especially fortunate that this authority has been vested in him by the Supreme Being. For the Jew, Mohammedans, and Christians, among others, man is Master by divine right; the fear of God will therefore repress any impulse to revolt in the downtrodden female."[7]

This brief discussion of the psychological and political effects of God religion puts us in an excellent position to begin to understand the significance of the symbol of Goddess for women. In discussing the meaning of the Goddess, my method will first be phenomenological. I will isolate a meaning of the symbol of the Goddess as it has emerged in the lives of contemporary women. I will then discuss its psychological and political significance by contrasting the "moods" and "motivations" engendered by Goddess symbols with those engendered by Christian symbolism. I will also correlate Goddess symbolism with themes that have emerged in the women's movement, in order to show how Goddess symbolism undergirds and legitimates the concerns of the women's movement, much as God symbolism in Christianity undergirded the interests of men in patriarchy. I will discuss four aspects of Goddess symbolism here: the Goddess as affirmation of female power, the female body, the female will, and women's bonds and heritage. There are, of course, many other meanings of the Goddess that I will not discuss here.

The sources for the symbol of the Goddess in contemporary spirituality are traditions of Goddess worship and modern women's experience. The ancient Mediterranean, pre-Christian European, native American, Mesoamerican, Hindu, African, and other traditions are rich sources for Goddess symbolism. But these traditions are filtered through modern women's experiences. Traditions of Goddesses, subordination to Gods, for example, are ignored. Ancient traditions are tapped selectively and eclecticly, but they are not considered authoritative for modern consciousness. The Goddess symbol has emerged spontaneously in the dreams, fantasies, and thoughts of many women around the country in the past several years. Kirsten Grimstad and Susan Rennie reported that they were surprised to discover widespread interest in spirituality, including the Goddess, among feminists around the country in the summer of 1974.[8] *WomanSpirit* magazine, which published its first issue in 1974 and has contributors from across the

United States, has expressed the grass roots nature of the women's spirituality movement. In 1976, a journal, *Lady Unique,* devoted to the Goddess emerged. In 1975, the first women's spirituality conference was held in Boston and attended by 1,800 women. In 1978, a University of Santa Cruz course on the Goddess drew over 500 people. Sources for this essay are these manifestations of the Goddess in modern women's experiences as reported in *WomanSpirit, Lady Unique,* and elsewhere, and as expressed in conversations I have had with women who have been thinking about the Goddess and women's spirituality.

The simplest and most basic meaning of the symbol of Goddess is the acknowledgement of the legitimacy of female power as a beneficient and independent power. A woman who echoes Ntosake Shange's dramatic statement, "I found God in myself and I loved her fiercely," is saying "Female power is strong and creative." She is saying that the divine principle, the saving and sustaining power, is in herself, that she will no longer look to men or male figures as saviors. The strength and independence of female power can be intuited by contemplating ancient and modern images of the Goddess. This meaning of the symbol of Goddess is simple and obvious, and yet it is difficult for many to comprehend. It stands in sharp contrast to the paradigms of female dependence on males that have been predominant in Western religion and culture. The internationally acclaimed novelist Monique Wittig captured the novelty and flavor of the affirmation of female power when she wrote, in her mythic work *Les Guerilleres,*

There was a time when you were not a slave, remember that. You walked alone, full of laughter, you bathed bare-bellied. You say you have lost all recollection of it, remember . . . you say there are no words to describe it, you say it does not exist. But remember. Make an effort to remember. Or, failing that, invent.[9]

While Wittig does not speak directly of the Goddess here, she captures the "mood" of joyous celebration of female freedom and independence that is created in women who define their identities through the symbol of Goddess. Artist Mary Beth Edelson expressed the political "motivations" inspired by the Goddess when she wrote,

The ascending archetypal symbols of the feminine unfold today in the psyche of modern Every woman. They encompass the multiple forms of the Great Goddess. Reaching across the centuries we take the hands of our Ancient

Sisters. The Great Goddess alive and well is rising to announce to the patriarchs that their 5,000 years are up—Hallelujah! Here we come.[10]

The affirmation of female power contained in the Goddess symbol has both psychological and political consequences. Psychologically, it means the defeat of the view engendered by patriarchy that women's power is inferior and dangerous. This new "mood" of affirmation of female power also leads to new "motivations"; it supports and under-girds women's trust in their own power and the power of other women in family and society.

If the simplest meaning of the Goddess symbol is an affirmation of the legitimacy and beneficience of female power, then a question immediately arises, "Is the Goddess simply female power writ large, and if so, why bother with the symbol of Goddess at all? Or does the symbol refer to a Goddess 'out there' who is not reducible to a human potential?" The many women who have rediscovered the power of Goddess would give three answers to this question: (1) The Goddess is divine female, a personification who can be invoked in prayer and ritual; (2) the Goddess is symbol of the life, death, and rebirth energy in nature and culture, in personal and communal life and (3) the Goddess is symbol of the affirmation of the legitimacy and beauty of female power (made possible by the new becoming of women in the women's liberation movement). If one were to ask these women which answer is the "correct" one, different responses would be given. Some would assert that the Goddess definitely is *not* "out there," that the symbol of a divinity "out there" is part of the legacy of patriarchal oppression, which brings with it the authoritarianism, hierarchicalism, and dogmatic rigidity associated with biblical monotheistic religions. They might assert that the Goddess symbol reflects the sacred power within women and nature, suggesting the connectedness between women's cycles of menstruation, birth, and menopause, and the life and death cycles of the universe. Others seem quite comfortable with the notion of Goddess as a divine female protector and creator and would find their experience of Goddess limited by the assertion that she is not *also* out there as well as within themselves and in all natural processes. When asked what the symbol of Goddess means, feminist priestess Starhawk replied, "It all depends on how I feel. When I feel weak, she is someone who can help and protect me. When I feel strong, she is the symbol of my own power. At other times I feel her as the natural energy in my body and the world."[11] How are we to evaluate such a statement? Theologians might call these the words of a sloppy thinker. But my deepest intuition tells me they contain a wisdom that Western theological thought has lost.

To theologians, these differing views of the "meaning" of the symbol of Goddess might seem to threaten a replay of the trinitarian controversies. Is there, perhaps, a way of doing theology, which would not lead immediately into dogmatic controversy, which would not require theologians to say definitively that one understanding is true and the others are false? Could people's relation to a common symbol be made primary and varying interpretations be acknowledged? The diversity of explications of the meaning of the Goddess symbol suggests that symbols have a richer significance than any explications of their meaning can express, a point literary critics have long insisted on. This phenomenological fact suggests that theologians may need to give more than lip service to a theory of symbol in which the symbol is viewed as the primary fact and the meanings are viewed as secondary. It also suggests that a *thea*logy[12] of the Goddess would be very different from the *theo*logy we have known in the West. But to spell out this notion of the primacy of *symbol* in thealogy in contrast to the primacy of the *explanation* in theology would be the topic of another paper. Let me simply state that women, who have been deprived of a female religious symbol system for centuries, are therefore in an excellent position to recognize the power and primacy of symbols. I believe women must develop a theory of symbol and thealogy congruent with their experience at the same time as they "remember and invent" new symbol systems.

A second important implication of the Goddess symbol for women is the affirmation of the female body and the life cycle expressed in it. Because of women's unique position as menstruants, birthgivers, and those who have traditionally cared for the young and the dying, women's connection to the body, nature, and this world has been obvious. Women were denigrated because they seemed more carnal, fleshy, and earthy than the culture-creating males.[13] The misogynist anti*body* tradition in Western thought is symbolized in the myth of Eve who is traditionally viewed as a sexual temptress, the epitome of women's carnal nature. This tradition reaches its nadir in the *Malleus Maleficarum (The Hammer of Evil-Doing Women)*, which states, "All witchcraft stems from carnal lust, which in women is insatiable."[14] The Virgin Mary, the positive female image in Christianity does not contradict Christian denigration of the female body and its powers. The Virgin Mary is revered because she, in her perpetual virginity, transcends the carnal sexuality attributed to most women.

The denigration of the female body is expressed in cultural and religious taboos surrounding menstruation, childbirth, and menopause in women. While menstruation taboos may have originated in a perception of the awesome powers of the female body,[15] they degenerated into a simple perception that there is something "wrong" with female bodily functions. Menstruating women were forbidden to enter the sanctuary in ancient Hebrew and premodern Christian communities. Although only Orthodox Jews still enforce religious taboos against menstruant women, few women in our culture grow up affirming their menstruation as a connection to sacred power. Most women learn that menstruation is a curse and grow up believing that the bloody facts of menstruation are best hidden away. Feminists challenge this attitude to the female body. Judy Chicago's art piece "Menstruation Bathroom" broke these menstrual taboos. In a sterile white bathroom, she exhibited boxes of Tampax and Kotex on an open shelf, and the wastepaper basket was overflowing with bloody tampons and sanitary napkins.[16] Many women who viewed the piece felt relieved to have their "dirty secret" out in the open.

The denigration of the female body and its powers is further expressed in Western culture's attitudes toward childbirth.[17] Religious iconography does not celebrate the birthgiver, and there is no theology or ritual that enables a woman to celebrate the process of birth as a spiritual experience. Indeed, Jewish and Christian traditions also had blood taboos concerning the woman who had recently given birth. While these religious taboos are rarely enforced today (again, only by Orthodox Jews), they have secular equivalents. Giving birth is treated as a disease requiring hospitalization, and the woman is viewed as a passive object, anesthetized to ensure her acquiescence to the will of the doctor. The women's liberation movement has challenged these cultural attitudes, and many feminists have joined with advocates of natural childbirth and home birth in emphasizing the need for women to control and take pride in their bodies, including the birth process.

Western culture also gives little dignity to the postmenopausal or aging woman. It is no secret that our culture is based on a denial of aging and death, and that women suffer more severely from this denial than men. Women are placed on a pedestal and considered powerful when they are young and beautiful, but they are said to lose this power as they age. As feminists have pointed out, the "power" of the young woman is illusory, since beauty standards are defined by men, and since few women are considered (or consider themselves) beautiful for more than a few years of their lives. Some men are viewed as wise and authoritative in age, but old women are pitied and shunned. Religious iconography supports this cultural attitude towards aging women. The purity and virginity of Mary and the female saints is often expressed in the iconographic convention of perpetual youth. Moreover, religious mythology associates aging women with evil in the symbol of the wicked old witch. Feminists have challenged cultural myths of aging women and have urged women to reject patriarchal beauty standards and to celebrate the distinctive beauty of women of all ages.

The symbol of Goddess aids the process of naming and reclaiming the female body and its cycles and processes. In the ancient world and among modern women, the Goddess symbol represents the birth, death, and rebirth processes of the natural and human worlds. The female body is viewed as the direct incarnation of waxing and waning, life and death, cycles in the universe. This is sometimes expressed through the symbolic connection between the twenty-eight-day cycles of menstruation and the twenty-eight-day cycles of the moon. Moreover, the Goddess is celebrated in the triple aspect of youth, maturity, and age, or maiden, mother, and crone. The potentiality of the young girl is celebrated in the nymph or maiden aspect of the Goddess. The Goddess as mother is sometimes depicted giving birth, and giving birth is viewed as a symbol for all the creative, life-giving powers of the universe.[18] The life-giving powers of the Goddess in her creative aspect are not limited to physical birth, for the Goddess is also seen as the creator of all the arts of civilization, including healing, writing, and the giving of just law. Women in the middle of life who are not physical mothers may give birth to poems, songs, and books, or nurture other women, men, and children. They too are incarnations of the Goddess in her creative, life-giving aspect. At the end of life, women incarnate the crone aspect of the Goddess. The wise old woman, the woman who knows from experience what life is about, the woman whose closeness to her own death gives her a distance and perspective on the problems of life, is celebrated as the third aspect of the Goddess. Thus, women learn to value youth, creativity, and wisdom in themselves and other women.

The possibilities of reclaiming the female body and its cycles have been expressed in a number of Goddess-centered rituals. Hallie Mountainwing and Barby My Own created a summer solstice ritual to celebrate menstruation and birth. The women simulated a birth canal and birthed each other into their circle. They raised power by placing their hands on each other's bellies and chanting together. Finally they marked each other's faces with rich, dark menstrual blood saying, "This is the blood that promises renewal. This is the blood that promises sustenance. This is the blood that promises life." [19] From hidden dirty secret to symbol of the life power of the Goddess, women's blood has come full circle. Other women have created rituals that celebrate the crone aspect of the Goddess. Z. Budapest believes that the crone aspect of the Goddess is predominant in the fall, especially at Halloween, an ancient holiday. On this day, the wisdom of the old woman is celebrated, and it is also recognized that the old must die so that the new can be born.

The "mood" created by the symbol of the Goddess in triple aspect is one of positive, joyful affirmation of the female body and its cycles and acceptance of aging and death as well as life. The "motivations" are to overcome menstrual taboos, to return the birth process to the hands of women, and to change cultural attitudes about age and death. Changing cultural attitudes toward the female body could go a long way toward overcoming the spirit-flesh, mind-body dualisms of Western culture, since, as Ruether has pointed out, the denigration of the female body is at the heart of these dualisms. The Goddess as symbol of the revaluation of the body and nature thus also undergirds the human potential and ecology movements. The "mood" is one of affirmation, awe, and respect for the body and nature, and the "motivation" is to respect the teachings of the body and the rights of all living beings.

A third important implication of the Goddess symbol for women is the positive valuation of will in a Goddess-centered ritual, especially in Goddess-centered ritual magic and spellcasting in womanspirit and feminist witchcraft circles. The basic notion behind ritual magic and spellcasting is energy as power. Here the Goddess is a center or focus of power and energy; she is the personification of the energy that flows between beings in the natural and human worlds. In Goddess circles, energy is raised by chanting or dancing. According to Starhawk, "Witches conceive of psychic energy as having form and substance that can be perceived and directed by those with a trained awareness. The power generated within the circle is built into a cone form, and at its peak is released—to the Goddess, to reenergize the members of the coven, or to do a specific work such as healing."[20] In ritual magic, the energy raised is directed by willpower. Women who celebrate in Goddess circles believe they can achieve their wills in the world.

The emphasis on the will is important for women, because women traditionally have been taught to devalue their wills, to believe that they cannot achieve their will through their own power, and even to suspect that the assertion of will is evil. Faith Wildung's poem "Waiting," from which I will quote only a short segment, sums up women's sense that their lives are defined not by their own will, but by waiting for others to take the initiative.

> Waiting for my breasts to develop
> Waiting to wear a bra
> Waiting to menstruate
>
> . . .
>
> Waiting for life to begin, Waiting—
> Waiting to be somebody
>
> . . .
>
> Waiting to get married
> Waiting for my wedding day
> Waiting for my wedding night
>
> . . .
>
> Waiting for the end of the day
> Waiting for sleep. Waiting . . . [21]

Patriarchal religion has enforced the view that female initiative and will are evil through the juxtaposition of Eve and Mary. Eve caused the fall by asserting her will against the command of God, while Mary began the new age with her response to God's initiative, "Let it be done to me according to thy word" (Luke 1:38). Even for men, patriarchal religion values the passive will subordinate to divine initiative. The classical doctrines of sin and grace view sin as the prideful assertion of will and grace as the obedient subordination of the human will to the divine initiative or order. While this view of will might be questioned from a human perspective, Valerie Saiving has argued that it has particularly deleterious consequences for women in Western culture. According to Saiving, Western culture encourages males in the assertion of will, and thus it may make some sense to view the male form of sin as an excess of will. But since culture discourages females in the assertion of will, the traditional doctrines of sin and grace encourage women to remain in their form of sin, which is self-negation or insufficient assertion of will.[22] One possible reason the will is denigrated in a patriarchal religious framework is that both human and divine will are often pictured as arbitrary, self-initiated, and exercised without regard for other wills.

In a Goddess-centered context, in contrast, the will is valued. *A woman is encouraged to know her will, to believe that her will is valid, and to believe that her will can be achieved in the world,* three powers traditionally denied to her in patriarchy. In a Goddess-centered framework, a woman's will is not subordinated to the Lord God as king and ruler, nor to men as his representatives. Thus a woman is not reduced to waiting and acquiescing in the wills of others as she is in patriarchy. But neither does she adopt the egocentric form of will that pursues self-interest without regard for the interests of others.

The Goddess-centered context provides a different understanding of the will than that available in the traditional patriarchal religious framework. In the Goddess framework, will can be achieved only when it is exercised in harmony with the energies and wills of other beings. Wise women, for example, raise a cone of healing energy at the full moon or solstice when the lunar or solar energies are at their high points with respect to the earth. This discipline encourages them to recognize that not all times are propitious for the achieving of every will. Similarly, they know that spring is a time for new beginnings in work and love, summer a time for producing external manifestations of inner potentialities, and fall or winter times for stripping down to the inner core and extending roots. Such awareness of waxing and waning processes in the universe discourages arbitrary ego-centered assertion of will, while at the same time encouraging the assertion of individual will in cooperation with natural energies and the energies created by the wills of others. Wise women also have a tradition that whatever is sent out will be returned and this reminds them to assert their wills in cooperative and healing rather than egocentric and destructive ways. This view of will allows women to begin to recognize, claim, and assert their wills without adopting the worst characteristics of the patriarchal understanding and use of will. In the Goddess-centered framework, the "mood" is one of positive affirmation of personal will in the context of the energies of other wills or beings. The "motivation" is for women to know and assert their wills in cooperation with other wills and energies. This of course does not mean that women always assert their wills in positive and life-affirming ways. Women's capacity for evil is, of course, as great as men's. My purpose is simply to contrast the differing attitudes toward the exercise of will *per se,* and the female will in particular, in Goddess-centered religion and in the Christian God-centered religion.

The fourth and final aspect of Goddess symbolism that I will discuss here is the significance of the Goddess for a revaluation of woman's bonds and heritage. As Virginia Woolf has said, "Chloe liked Olivia," a statement about a woman's relation to another woman, is a sentence that rarely occurs in fiction. Men have written the stories, and they have written about women almost exclusively in their relations to men.[23] The celebrations of women's bonds to each other, as mothers and daughters, as colleagues and coworkers, as sisters, friends, and lovers, is beginning to occur in the new literature and culture created by women in the women's movement. While I believe that the revaluing of each of these bonds is important, I will focus on the mother-daughter bond, in part because I believe it may be the key to the others.

Adrienne Rich has pointed out that the mother-daughter bond, perhaps the most important of woman's bonds, "resonant with charges . . . the flow of energy between two biologically alike bodies, one of which has lain in amniotic bliss inside the other, one of which has labored to give birth to the other,"[24] is rarely celebrated in patriarchal religion and culture. Christianity celebrates the father's relation to the son and the mother's relation to the son, but the story of mother and daughter is missing. So, too, in patriarchal literature and psychology the mothers and the daughters rarely exist. Volumes have been written about the oedipal complex, but little has been written about the girl's relation to her mother. Moreover, as de Beauvoir has noted, the mother-daughter relation is distorted in patriarchy because the mother must give her daughter over to men in a male-defined culture in which women are viewed as inferior. The mother must socialize her daughter to become subordinate to men, and if her daughter challenges patriarchal norms, the mother is likely to defend the patriarchal structures against her own daughter.[25]

These patterns are changing in the new culture created by women in which the bonds of women to women are beginning to be celebrated. Holly Near has written several songs that celebrate women's bonds and women's heritage. In one of her finest songs she writes of an "old-time woman" who is "waiting to die." A young woman feels for the life that has passed the old woman by and begins to cry, but the old woman looks her in the eye and says, "If I had not suffered, you wouldn't be wearing those jeans/Being an old-time woman ain't as bad as it seems."[26] This song, which Near has said was inspired by her grandmother, expresses and celebrates a bond and a heritage passed down from one woman to another. In another of Near's songs, she sings of a "a hiking-boot mother who's seeing the world/For the first time with her own little girl." In this song, the mother tells the drifter who has been traveling with her to pack up and travel alone if he thinks "traveling three is a drag" because "I've got a little one who loves me as much as you need me/And darling, that's loving enough."[27] This song is significant because the mother places her relationship to her daughter above her relationship to a man, something women rarely do in patriarchy.[28]

Almost the only story of mothers and daughters that has been transmitted in Western culture is the myth of Demeter and Persephone that was the basis of religious rites celebrated by women only, the Thesmophoria, and later formed the basis of the Eleusian mysteries, which were open to all who spoke Greek. In this story, the daughter, Persephone, is raped away from her mother, Demeter, by the God of the underworld. Unwilling to accept this state of affairs, Demeter rages and withholds fertility from the earth until her daughter is returned to her. What is important for women in this story is that a mother fights for her daughter and for her relation to her daughter. This is completely different from the mother's relation to her daughter in patriarchy. The "mood" created by the story of Demeter and Persephone is one of celebration of the mother-daughter bond, and the "motivation" is for mothers and daughters to affirm the heritage passed on from mother to daughter and to reject the patriarchal pattern where the primary loyalties of mother and daughter must be to men.

The symbol of Goddess has much to offer women who are struggling to be rid of the "powerful, pervasive, and long-lasting moods and motivations" of devaluation of female power, denigration of the female body, distrust of female will, and denial of the women's bonds and heritage that have been engendered by patriarchal religion. As women struggle to create a new culture in which women's power, bodies, will, and bonds are celebrated, it seems natural that the Goddess would reemerge as symbol of the newfound beauty, strength, and power of women.

NOTES

1. From the original cast album, Buddah Records, 1976.
2. See Susan Rennie and Kristen Grimstad, "Spiritual Explorations Cross-Country," *Quest,* 1975, *I* (4), 1975, 49–51; and *WomanSpirit* magazine.
3. See Starhawk, "Witchcraft and Women's Culture," in this volume.
4. "Religion as a Cultural System," in William L. Lessa and Evon V. Vogt, eds., *Reader in Comparative Religion,* 2nd ed. (New York: Harper & Row, 1972), p. 206.
5. Geertz, p. 210.
6. Boston: Beacon Press, 1974, p. 13, italics added.
7. *The Second Sex,* trans. H. M. Parshleys (New York: Alfred A. Knopf, 1953).
8. See Grimstad and Rennie.
9. *Les Guerilleres,* trans. David LeVay (New York: Avon Books, 1971), p. 89. Also quoted in Morgan MacFarland, "Witchcraft: The Art of Remembering," *Quest,* 1975, *I* (4), 41.
10. "Speaking for Myself," *Lady Unique,* 1976, *I,* 56.
11. Personal communication.
12. A term coined by Naomi Goldenberg to refer to reflection on the meaning of the symbol of Goddess.
13. This theory of the origins of the Western dualism is stated by Rosemary Ruether in *New Woman: New Earth* (New York: Seabury Press, 1975), and elsewhere.
14. Heinrich Kramer and Jacob Sprenger (New York: Dover, 1971), p. 47.
15. See Rita M. Gross, "Menstruation and Childbirth as Ritual and Religious Experience in the Religion of the Australian Aborigines," in *The Journal of the American Academy of Religion,* 1977, *45* (4), Supplement 1147–1181.
16. *Through the Flower* (New York: Doubleday & Company, 1975), plate 4, pp. 106–107.
17. See Adrienne Rich, *Of Woman Born* (New York: Bantam Books, 1977), chaps. 6 and 7.
18. See James Mellaart, *Earliest Civilizations of the Near East* (New York: McGraw-Hill, 1965), p. 92.
19. Barbry My Own, "Ursa Maior: Menstrual Moon Celebration," in Anne Kent Rush, ed., *Moon, Moon* (Berkeley, Calif., and New York: Moon Books and Random House, 1976), pp. 374–387.
20. Starhawk, in this volume.
21. In Judy Chicago, pp. 213–217.
22. "The Human Situation: A Feminine View," in *Journal of Religion,* 1960, *40,* 100–112, and reprinted in this volume.
23. *A Room of One's Own* (New York: Harcourt Brace Jovanovich, 1928), p. 86.
24. Rich, p. 226.
25. De Beauvoir, pp. 448–449.
26. "Old Time Woman," lyrics by Jeffrey Langley and Holly Near, from *Holly Near: A Live Album,* Redwood Records, 1974.
27. "Started Out Fine," by Holly Near from *Holly Near: A Live Album.*
28. Rich, p. 223.